Hanging Quotes

HANGING QUOTES

Talking Book Arts,
Poetry & Typography

Alastair M Johnston

CUNEIFORM PRESS / 2011

tout, au monde, existe pour aboutir à un livre

— Stéphane Mallarmé,
"Variations sur un sujet,"
La Revue blanche, 1 July 1895

talk is cheap, but Flair pens cost 69 cents

— Darrell Gray

CONTENTS

NICOLAS BARKER

Nicolas Barker was Deputy Keeper of the British Library until he retired in 1992. He is a prolific author, keen bicyclist, editor of The Book Collector *(since 1965) and the preëminent bookman in the world today. He has written a biography of Stanley Morison and edited several of his works, including* Early Italian Writing-Books. *Barker is the author of* Aldus Manutius and the Development of Greek Script & Type in the 15th Century, The Oxford University Press & the Spread of Learning, *books on calligraphy, forgery, and many others. He was in San Francisco in April 1987, to attend a conference at Stanford University. He agreed to an impromptu interview for* Ampersand *in the kitchen of Poltroon Press co-founder and artist Frances Butler.*

AMJ: Most people involved in the book world to the degree you are, are either book dealers making a killing with rare material, or in some way trading on their knowledge. You are in fact just a servant of the book in a very sort of altruistic, humanitarian way.

NB: If you get hooked on something, and I can't remember what it was like not to be hooked on books, how could you possibly make money out of it? I've never found out how you do it. It's like making money out of breathing. If we could make money out of breathing we'd all be a lot richer.

AMJ: But you don't have any opportunities for insider trading?

NB: [*laughs*] No.

FCB: As a matter of fact, I didn't really understand the point of those huge, fulsome thank-yous at the beginnings of university press books, but now that I've been involved in writing a little more I can see that anybody who actually helps you with information is somebody you surely do want to thank.

NB: Also, if you don't thank them then they absolutely know. But, of course, in the Middle Ages people were extremely secretive, and indeed the ownership of secrets is a very important part of art, architecture, warfare, everything. A marvellous case I found the other day: Jacquemart de Hesdin, who was the leading French illuminator of his age, was working on a big design project, involving a whole castle for the Duc de Berry, and one of the other painters involved, a man called John of Holland, accused him of having stolen his *patrons* — his specimen book as it were. The case was sent for mediation, and, at a meeting of the parties concerned, Jacquemart de Hesdin's assistant murdered John of Holland's brother. So obviously passions ran high when it came to trade secrets in the Middle Ages. I suppose that in a sense, you know, in the way people are at least prepared to scratch each other's backs —'You give me a ream of paper, I will print your visiting cards for you,' — there's at least a slightly cheery side about the future; it's not quite so cutthroat. And that's perhaps because printing is moving from an industry into a craft, from a money economy into a barter economy.

AMJ: Rapidly.

FCB: I've always had businesses, and I found I was sort of infiltrating the general culture at various levels.

NB: I printed books solidly from 1947 to 1961. I haven't had the time to print anything since then.

FCB: Was this part of your being at Oxford University Press?

NB: No, I was a schoolboy printer, and at college. It used to fill vacations very nicely.

FCB: What was your press called?

NB: It was called St Nicolas Press. I printed a total of six or seven books. And the last one was a demy octavo of ninety-six pages, handset, printed in seven colours in an edition of fifteen hundred copies. And once you've printed fifteen hundred copies by hand, seventy-three colour workings, ninety-six pages, you begin to get a bit skeptical about these fellows who go into ecstasies over their latest forty-eight page brochure printed in an edition of eighty-seven copies in one or two colours.

In a sense, one can see the private press movement of the twenties and thirties as part of the general sighing for a world lost before the First World War. And great though the Ashendene Press was, and admirable though the work of the Golden Cockerel Press was, there's a kind of artificiality about it which you do not feel in the work of William Morris and Thomas Cobden-Sanderson. It's rather hard to put one's finger on, because I mean, after all, what could be more artificial in some ways than the Kelmscott Press? Who the hell ever read a Kelmscott Press book?

But the interesting thing about the private press movement before the War was the Nonesuch Press and the demonstration that you could do marvellous things with machine-set type and machine printing. I think that the reason why the private press movement has taken off so in the last twenty years is directly related to the collapse of industrial printing. After all, in both America and England from the forties through to the mid-sixties the general run of books were very nicely printed and they aren't now. The bottom has fallen out of trade books.

Posterity is going to have a thing or two to say to us. I don't know what they're called in this country, but off-machine-coated paper, that is, an art paper which is not a true art paper, but a sheet of paper which is produced by mixing up China clay in the slurry or whatever you call it, in the beaters, and then precipitating this onto the Fourdrinier, and so what you've got, when it comes off — and then of course you scrape the thing fine with a doctor blade at the end of the Fourdrinier — and what have we got? Just an ill-made unshaped collection of paper fibers held together by some glue and China clay. The glue is not going to last forever and that paper's going to disintegrate. You know so much modern lithographic printing is done on it.

FCB: That's true. It's funny: on the one hand there has been an incredible improvement, it seems to me, in the quality of ink, and the quality of colour separations, just in the last fifteen years. I've watched it move into incredible luxuriousness, but still the substratum is inferior and it's all going to fall apart.

NB: You're absolutely right. The ups and down are extraordinary. I have one pet piece of mathematics on this: when I first started printing, a page of halftone cost four times a page of composed type. A page of halftone now costs probably one-tenth of a page of composed type. One can say that paper's gone down, the quality of composition's gone down in every sense. The quality of ink has gone up, because lithography being so much dodgier a process than letterpress, the ink chemists have really done some very fancy stuff in the last twenty years. And of course the quality of four-colour separation has become breathtakingly good. It just bothers me it's all going on this rotten paper.

FCB: The other thing that is interesting is the major shift towards high-quality illustration as something that's reflected in the general culture: the shift from reading to looking at visual imagery.

NB: You go into a bookstore now, and the bookstore used to have books on shelves, and the act of moving around a bookstore was to look at shelves and reach up, pull down a book and open it and look at it. Nowadays you go into a bookstore they don't have shelves anymore. They have tables with huge piles of books face up, and *face-upness* is the way that people look at books now. So many books that I see, so many books you look at, and it's like television, it is aimed at persuading people. The old message was, 'You've read the book now see the film,' now it says, 'You've seen the film, now buy the book.'

FCB: That's actually one of the reasons why I'm spending a lot of time looking at the way we read pictures. The legibility of pictures is decried. People don't actually consider that it might have some other information-bearing qualities than have been addressed in the past.

NB: It's terribly important, and you see it's a lost art. This is another hobbyhorse of mine. You see, before the invention of photography, people who made pictures were artisans as well as artists, and there is a letter that I once found in a frame hanging on the wall that I think reveals the whole situation of the place of the artist in society before the camera was invented. It's a letter from the Earl of Strafford, Charles I's minister, to Van Dyke, and it relates to one of the greatest of all Van Dyke's paintings. The painting is full-size. It's Strafford in black armour coming towards you on a black horse. The picture stands about twelve, fifteen feet high, and there are many versions of it, of which the best is, I think, at Petworth. At any rate, it's a popular Van Dyke image. And the letter reads: 'Mr Van Dyke, I am well pleased with my likeness, and I will have ten of it, whereof the one for my lady is to be from your own pencil.' Strafford is treating Van Dyke as a photographer. It's what we would say, 'I like the print and I'll have ten, and the one for my wife's dressing table is to be a specially good print.' The answer, and the extension of this, is that the detail in pictures is not there because, 'I, the great artist, thought that a stormy sky or a background of trees would become you.' All these details matter. This is terribly true in mediaeval pictures.

When my much-loved colleague Lotte Hellinga from the British Museum was over for a week in Los Angeles, giving a lecture in my Clark series of lectures, we went over to the Huntington to examine the unique Caxton which has the engraving of Caxton kneeling and presenting his book to Margaret of Burgundy — at any rate it's a donor giving it to a noblewoman — and there is a figure of a man coming in through a door, and he's halfway through the door in the left-hand corner. Lotte knew that this figure, which was probably Charles the Bold, is a Dutch proverb. And I said, "Look, there's a woman there with a lapdog," and I suddenly remembered that lapdogs represent fidelity. That dog is there to show the owner's loyalty to his patron. Then we went round the Getty Museum together and just started working through all the detail in the pictures. I mean we've lost the art of seeing the point of details in pictures.

FCB: We don't have that emblematic system anymore, like the famous Hieronymus Bosch. Or the other one is Pieter Breughel, the mad feast day. There are about three hundred folk maxims in that, and we don't know what they are.

AMJ: If you drink, don't drive, I think, is one of them.

FCB: [*laughs*] There still are some that are spatial systems (not much more than relative scale), that we read, but we don't have much, and a lot of it is because in Western culture realism has been somewhat downgraded for the last two hundred years.

NB: I wouldn't begin to pretend that you can look at a picture painted in the last hundred years and extract that kind of meaning from it; on the other hand, there is a basic kind of geometry about it, which was the artist's original geometry and which makes some appeal to a kind of geometric language on our part...

FCB: Shreds of Neoplatonism.

NB: Yeah, I know, but there's been a kind of basic conspiracy. There is a communicable something, but actually there has to be a basic language behind all this; otherwise, the vision wouldn't communicate itself.

FCB: That's true. You have to fill up the web of accepted conventions, but the range of individuality is so tiny. It's just like the difference between 1 and 1.2. We tend to say, 'Oh yes, a lapdog, that's just a woman holding a lapdog.' The details will then relate to the viewer's experience, and if they don't have those details and the shreds of emblems that we still understand — which is like a tiny layer of fat on this huge body of things that we used to know — if we don't have those extraneous details, we won't relate to the painting enough to understand its main meaning. It does seem to me that the level of understanding of visual imagery has shifted, and we have to begin to track what is left of the old emblematic system and then what kinds of things will appeal to people beyond that.

NB: I feel that all we've been saying about pictures and visual images could be said about the shape of letters and layout. I've just been at a conference called "Men and Machines" at Stanford which has been a very kind of highfalutin, interdisciplinary affair with social anthropologists, psychologists, artificial intelligence specialists, philosophers, and all sorts of people, you know, all homing in on this central issue which is, 'Can a machine think?' or the ultimate fallacy: 'Can a machine be taught to do something that a human being can't imagine being done?' At any rate, I fell to thinking about the shape of letterforms. There's a very, very good book by a man called Jack Goody, called *The Domestication of the Savage Mind*, in which he points out that letters are essential to logical thought. An oral culture can go so far, where basically the only trick that an oral culture has to preserve or build on its previous experience is memory, and memory as we all know is a very fallacious tool, whereas letters, however primitive they are, pictograms or syllabary or something like that, give you firm fixed storage: 'We know that was where we were when that was put down on a clay tablet or engraved on stone.'

FCB: Well, it gives you pretty much of a firm fixed story. I mean there is the shift in meaning of language. I think memory is supposed to last — back in those kinship charts — seven generations back, after which it falls away.

NB: No, it can go a lot further back. The Congolese kings' bards can recite their genealogy going back, way, way into the Middle Ages. What's more, you can certify their accuracy because from time to time they drop in astounding natural phenomena — like a total eclipse of the sun, so you can date these things. Although we may say that logic in the sense of brick-building thought is only possible with writing, this doesn't mean that non-writing possessors were incapable of intellectual processes. Of course they were, and indeed, their whole views on kinship were amazingly complex and subtle and very interesting. The only trouble about kinship is that it's basically just a chain, a recording of a series of details that are obviously important to you, but it's not like the logic for building.

Anyway, the possibility of using changes in the shapes of letters as a map of the human mind fascinated me. A letterform is the most instinctive of human arts: even if some letter designers from Francesco Griffo up to today say, 'That's my letter, that's me.' To some extent the *me*-ness of the letter has some meaning, but basically, on a large scale, letterform changes are much more instinctive and are impersonal and unstudied.

FCB: They're such minimal strokes.

NB: Tiny, minimal changes.

FCB: But they are exactly the right amount, so it's very sophisticated too.

NB: I have a belief, which one can't exactly chart: I think that the way in which the basic old style letter changed from the sum of forms popular in the sixteenth century, which maybe goes back to Griffo and includes Granjon, Garamond, and company — the way it changes in the seventeenth century in the hands of Van Dijck to Kis, as it were, is a reflection on superior presswork, that because the Blaeu family, who after all employed both Van Dijck and Kis, had put some new technology into the common press, instinctively the shape of letters changed.

AMJ: Better optics would have made punchcutting easier too.

NB: You know that marvellous engraving of jolly old Fleischman with his tools that appears as a frontispiece to the 1768 Enschedé specimen? His glass is the thing that is nearest to his hand. Obviously that had become part of a punchcutter's kit in a way which one has no right to assume a sixteenth-century punchcutter had.

AMJ: Or the most he would have had would have been a globe with a candle behind it.

NB: Exactly, like the lacemaker's lamp.

FCB: Don't you think the inclusion of the copperplate

Fleischman portrait from 1768
Enschedé specimen

engravings in the seventeenth century set up a preference for thinner lines?

NB: Well, the interaction of the calligrapher, the copperplate engraver, and the general mass of calligraphic letters in the seventeenth century is absolutely fascinating. I'm quite sure that copperplate engraving caught on in an amazing way in a very short period, I mean it's 1570, give or take ten years. Before 1560 there were copperplate books but there were very, very few. By 1570 it had absolutely swept the whole thing: everything was being illustrated with copperplates, and for the first time, indeed, appear copperplate writing manuals. Now the action of the burin on a copperplate tends to push the stress nearer the vertical. You may be imitating a pen, which naturally wants a twenty-degree off stress, but if you're actually operating a burin, you tend to get it upright. So the French calligraphers in the seventeenth century, faced with a desire and a need to produce letters that were different and grander than printed letters, produced this magnificent calligraphy, which is obviously slow stuff. If you're having, in fact, to produce letters with your pen holder held at a slightly unnatural angle, it will be slower, but that wasn't the point, the result was extreme grandeur, and those things that [Nicolas] Jarry produced for Louis XIV are absolutely breathtaking. And of course that was the letter that the *académiciens* converted into 2,304 squares and Grandjean — the other Grandjean, Philippe Grandjean — converted into typographic form.

And I was just thinking while I was talking to these people at Stanford, why did it take a century for the modern face to be born from that? The answer was that the *Imprimerie du Roi* actually had a monopoly, and an artist as inventive as Fournier, if there'd been the slightest possible chance of getting away with a *Romain du Roi*, would have done it.

AMJ: He was prosecuted for trying to do it!

NB: For trying to do it, exactly. And it's very significant that just at the very end of the *Ancien Régime*, that the Didots, obviously encouraged by court patronage and so forth, the whole situation was loosened up to the point where they actually put it over. Bodoni picks it up within the month, more or less, at Parma, and suddenly: *Bingo!* Neoclassic types had arrived.

AMJ: On the other hand you have John Pine engraving the text of his *Horace* back in 1730.

NB: That proves my point. The copperplate engraver has a natural tendency to switch toward the vertical. There's Sturt before Pine, and in fact if you look at the captions, the written part of pictorial prints, you'll see Bickham's *Universal Penman* has a tendency to tilt things upright.

FCB: I think it's even a broader culture preference for the upright. That's the period when buildings shifted, for example, from being accumulations to being symmetrical, and the ballet was invented at that time and kept people in order. And lettering can't be symmetrical, but they tried, they brought it into as much of a grid system as possible, so your idea that it's a pervasive cultural expression is true. The more you look out the wider you see the basic ideas that will shape the line form.

NB: Absolutely, and ballet is a very interesting idea, because, of course, it's at the end of the seventeenth century, the beginning of the eighteenth century that you get these geometric ballet instruction manuals, like an ice-skating manual, full of exquisite geometric shapes, but all geometrically organized. You might say there was Feliciano, and Pacioli, and Leonardo da Vinci, not to mention old Ruano, trying to construct geometric diagrams which would control lettering, but of course, again they were doing it the other way round. They were saying: 'A lovely letter looks like this — the Golden Section must be in there somewhere if only we can get it in.' I don't think anyone has pointed out that the *académiciens* were doing something quite different, constructing a geometric figure first (2,304 squares), and demanding that the letter conform to *it* — not the other way round.

AMJ: But don't you think Grandjean reinterpreted it for the exigencies of cutting punches?

NB: Oh sure, which comes back to what I was saying earlier, that there is always in every engraved letter the personality of the engraver. I'm very interested in the concept of "Metafont" — [Donald] Knuth's "Metafont" — that somewhere if you can define it by computer analysis, there is a platonic idea of a letter, out from which you can extrapolate any form you want — the difference between six point and seventy-two point, the difference between upright and sloped, the difference between light and bold, the difference between expanded and condensed — and retain the central character. This was a problem which Morison and Van Krimpen used to argue about like anything and never solved. Van Krimpen's attempt, the sloped Romulus, is a failure. It doesn't work, it bores you. But at any rate, I'm very interested to see if they can conceptually produce an ideal, a base character, could they reverse the procedure? And if I fed them, for example, visual images of all the types that Granjon was responsible for, all the types that Garamond was responsible for, that Sanlecque was responsible for, that the Le Bé family was responsible for, could they analyse out Granjon*ness*, and Sanlecque*ness*? And then could I turn them on to the great problem of the *Gros Romain Romains*, and the Garamond *De Premier taille* and *La Seconde taille,* and could they say, 'Yeah, that one's by Sanlecque.'

FCB: Because it has exactly this curve.

NB: Because it has this curve, or that special conformation of the top serif to the lowercase *p*.

FCB: Well, you know the problem is, for example, Postscript, which is the Adobe system, is not the same as Knuth's, but it's the same idea, of prescribed pathways. There's a great variety but you activate them one after another in building up letter-forms. And I remember reading an article years ago, talking about Metafont and the intellectual difficulty of assuming that you could take even an infinite series of mathematical curves and generate an infinite variety of letterforms, so that this issue is really critical to letterforms right now. And what I'm wondering about is this issue of the curves: the eight-eenth century (that's the period of the major development in Frakturs, too, and all those calligraphic scripts) was a period when those curves existed and they've been copied thereafter, like Dwiggins used eighteenth-century curves, but we haven't generated a new set of curves. The curves after that were like Futura, they're compass-drawn.

NB: Futura is a good example. I was reading something the other day and thinking about Futura, Kabel, Gill, and all that. It's actually an interesting and not wholly realised idea, because of the essential differentness of approach involved in Gill Sans, Kabel and Renner. There was a groping for a new style of curve there, and actually it was closed off after the war when so many people said, 'No, Gothic 215 and 216, Helvetica, and above all Univers,' which are actually stultifying, they go back to the late nineteenth century.

  Incidentally, I noticed that the word serif never appears except in the concept of its absence in the 1820s. It's spelt in any number of ways, *c-e-r-i-f*, *s-e-r-r-i-f*, or *s-e-r-r-i-f-f-e*.

AMJ: *S-u-r-r-y-p-h-s*.

NB: That's Thorowgood. Anyway, Harry Carter deduced from this, I'm sure correctly, that these people who needed to talk about letters without serifs, were actually using a word which was in oral tradition, which they had never seen written down. So from there Harry moved on to say, 'Where would there have been a need to talk about the terminations of letters without writing about it? Answer: Only in the type-founding trade.' And so, he who knew Dutch so well, said, 'I know exactly what the answer is. It is a Dutch word with that unpronounceable, except to Dutchmen, consonantal sound "ch" and the word in Dutch is *Schrief* meaning writing or stroke, like *scribere* or *Schrift*.

He said, given the way English anglicized foreign languages —
you know, firmly referring to places as Lyons and Milan and
that sort of thing — it was likely of them to reduce *Schrief* to
serif, convening this unpronounceable consonantal sound, and
I'm sure he's right.

FCB: Did you ever read that article by Hans Ed Meier on Syntax?
The white spaces in Syntax — it's not the shape of Futura or
Renner. I don't want to put Gill quite into the same…but let's
say Metro. They are all compass-drawn essentially. Helvetica is
a nineteenth-century face that essentially closes off the inte-
rior over and over again, whereas in Syntax the *s* is shaped
more like this, there's space coming in and out, the *e* is much
more open. It has that kind of inter-relation of white and black
that some of the faces like the Granjon faces, or some of the
eighteenth-century faces had, and that's why it's a more lively
and sparkling face.

NB: It's very interesting. Yes. The tendency of Victorian types to
enclose is a very marked characteristic. In fact one of the things
I say in my little piece about Wise and Foreman is that I had
this agonizing task of trying to identify all the types in all the
forgeries, and frankly, to sit down — I mean St Bride's has shelf
after shelf after shelf of Victorian type specimen books, deep
riches in there, and so the ability existed but my eye wasn't
trained. Now I can't remember what it was like not to be able
to tell one type from another. I can't remember when I couldn't
tell Fournier from Bembo. There was I in my forties, a lot of
experience behind me, my eyesight in reasonable nick, looking
at these Victorian types and simply unable to tell one from the
other, to identify this type in this book with any type I could see,
and I had to educate my eye or my eye (to be more modest about
it), had to educate itself — just like a Kurzweil optical scanner
will educate itself, in its mechanical way, to make less errors,
if you switch it from six point Ehrhardt to twelve point Times.
Victorian text types are immensely homogeneous, immensely
enclosed, and however spindly they are, they have these huge
serifs so that the feet of an *H* almost touch. Victorian display
types of course go off in a wild set of three-dimensional varie-
ties: open, shaded, every conceivable kind of visual distortion.
I always used to think it's rather like the difference between
men's clothes and women's clothes in the Victorian era. The
text types are like gentlemen: they get more boring, a black
and white straightjacket of respectability descends on them,
whereas ladies go off in bustles and frills and furbelows and

crinolines and so forth. I don't know that I'd press this picture too far, but there's certainly a constriction about it.

I was rather fascinated at this conference at Stanford by one aspect. A woman called Sherry Turkle, who is a psychologist whose subject is the impact of the computer on human society and the way we think and write, said that one of the factors in the way in which the computer has played a subsidiary but important part is that we have abandoned transparent for opaque machines.

Machines in the nineteenth century, their works were visible, were understandable, that's why we like Victorian locomotives so much. And she had a very good example of one of her students whom she had recorded who had fallen in love with the insides of an old radio at the age of five. [*laughter*] I could quite see this, how beautiful the complex of valves that glow and spin round, and how beautiful things made of blown glass and delicate wire, and spun copper, all are mounted on an elaborate chassis. I suddenly got an image of the chassis of a radio as a kind of beautiful modernistic city, and how boring the modern radio is, just how boring the modern aeroplane is, it's opaque: you can't see how it works. What's a chip, you know?

FCB: It really, I think, comes down to the fact that our public understanding of the way labor relates to product has not shifted out of the mechanical age. In effect, what has to happen is that we have to begin to think, the way one uses Postscript, that is you conceive mathematically of the letterform and you have to generate it, not by hand movements, not by calligraphic control and that body-mind relationship, but purely by projection. And we can't do that. There still is a mechanical relationship in computers, there still are electric things that move this way, but it's too small and we haven't shifted off to this purely non-body structure. We're still back there with 'Value is made out of human action,' with human impact on wood. You make a table and you know how long it's going to take to make, and to last. So I think it will take some time, a long long time.

NB: Yes. I can see dimly how this might operate. After all an oscilloscope pattern can be a beautiful and even compelling thing. One can watch the recording of a sine wave on an oscilloscope screen and see it varying and see some beauty in that and one can imagine perhaps translating the kind of visual/ mental appeal in it into a sequence of variations that would produce a letterform.

FCB: You see I have to deal with this very directly now in trying to get my students to switch from the frame of mind; the frame of imagining that has to do with muscular control, when they're going to draw what they see as either a person or letterform, into a halfway house.

There's still some muscular control in using a computer tablet, but the other problem is purely something that you generate. You put out a formula, and it gives you a certain curve, and the combination of the two of them — it's like any combined system in recent knowledge, the possibilities for freeing new letterforms on the one hand, but the possibility for major confusion because there's not a long support system.

NB: There's that marvellous passage in Harry Carter's *A View of Early Typography* in which he talks about the 'backward look,' this desire that the more novel the task the designer is setting himself, the further back in time he seeks security, because that which has lasted longest already may last best in the future. Translating, obviously, what is going to happen certainly initially until they're used to the kind of activity you're talking about, is a translation process; one is going to seek to perpetuate the curves one is used to until one gets used to floating off those curves.

FCB: More to the point. Your mentioning the eighteenth-century faces brings up the fact that in many fields there's a rerun of eighteenth-century conceptions: garden designs are now sort of downscale Baroque; PoMo architecture is downscale Baroque with lots of overlays. I see the Dwiggins enthusiasm, which is oozing out on all sides; I see all of this as now looking back to that period. First of all there was this great "Voyage into Substance," looking out into the world, and then also a tremendous effort to make all of that legible. There were letterforms seen in rocks. It was exactly the same kind of period that we have now: expansion and lack of control, and the desire to bring it into geometry and real control from the level of the king down to symmetrical buildings. And so I think that there is a pervasive sense that these two periods are parallel.

NB: I absolutely share your view about the importance of Dwiggins, but it isn't Dwiggins, it's Dwiggins plus Griffiths. Now Dwiggins plus Griffiths was a much closer partnership. I mean the Morison-Monotype-Pierpont axis was one of essential opposition. It was getting what Morison saw through the opposition of the machine works at Salfords. Dwiggins and Griffiths was a real meeting of minds. I know what the book I was talking about earlier is, of course: Walter Tracy's *Letters of Credit*. I think the chapter on Dwiggins is the best chapter, partly because Walter too spent his active life in Linotype and perhaps knew more about it and could identify with it more clearly. There are letters between Griffiths and Dwiggins quoted which bear out what you're saying, that this is the way we want to think about letters and not try and impose our own geometry on them. I promise you, *Letters of Credit* is a very good read.

AMJ: What other recent books have you found worthwhile?

NB: Nicolete Gray's *A History of Lettering*, which is a marvellous book, but is essentially about architectural lettering — viewed, as she says, the title is *A History of Lettering*, not *The History of Lettering*. The best part is that the book has three hundred pictures in it, but it is still an organized text. You know, it goes over the old "Politics and Script" ground again from ancient Greek to modern times, tending on the whole…well, she's really polite and understanding about Morison, but obviously she really feels that it's rare that you're seeing anything more than a tradition passed on from one engraver to another, or changes in public taste and materials — for example, the availability of cast iron made more exotic three-dimensional letterforms possible. But calligraphy as such — meaning "beautiful writing" as distinct from ordinary writing, that is, something which can only be defined in relation to ordinariness — only really started with the printing press, because up to that point everything was written. So there's not a lot about that. There's not a lot about printing type, it just comes in but no more. It's a very nice book.

The other books are a very nice picture book of Irene Wellington's calligraphy in four-colour, very cheap, I don't know how they brought it out; and the other is somebody who has reprinted all Bernard Newdigate's articles in the *London Mercury* on typography and type design. All four are out in the last year. A very rich crop.

AMJ: Do you find yourself being forced into a position of an apologist for Morison more and more?

NB: Well, in a sense, yes. I think with the collapse of the International Typeface Corporation one will probably hear a good deal less of this. Aaron Burns wrote a very funny letter to Morison, in fact it is a correspondence which reveals a total misunderstanding on both sides. Aaron Burns wrote to Morison and said, "Stand up and be counted." [*AMJ laughs*] "Type designers of the world unite, we have only our names to lose." And Morison wrote back a very reasoned account of his belief that the job of the lettering designer was to provide such lettering and to arrange it in such lines and such a format as to convey the message from the writer to the reader in the most appropriate and least fidgeting and disturbing form.

FCB: The "Crystal Goblet" argument.

NB: And I don't think Mr Burns began to understand what Morison was talking about. And in a sense of course, ITC in its short lifetime has stood for the personality of the letter designer, and of course, as a great many useful letter designers are unfortunately without a name, various people with names have made a fortune out of redesigning old letters and putting their names to them.

And I mean, Morison's big enough to look after himself, frankly. About ten years before Morison died, somebody made a programme, a radio portrait of Eric Gill. He was a person who didn't know very much about the subject, and he'd come to the conclusion that the influence of Morison at Monotype Corporation had been wholly bad [*laughter*], that the brutal financiers had forced a wretched Gill, with too much family and not enough money, to debase his talents by forcing him to fit into this commercial mould of letter design. Morison was immensely polite to this man, but did let off some absolutely splendid remarks about Gill's real quality. And there is a recording of this interview in which Morison says there was no indirectness or fudging with Gill: he was an engraver. You can't do anything with an engraved line. You can't get a piece of process white and some India ink and touch it back in again. And he said, that was Gill all the way through. The implication was there was no power on earth which would persuade Gill to do that which he did not believe in.

FCB: Mmhmm. It's funny that every aspect of Gill's life was that he said what he wanted to, he did what he wanted.

NB: He wore what he wanted to wear, and no damned nonsense about it.

FCB: And he made all of his types more or less exactly alike…

AMJ: No he didn't. Not like Fred Goudy did.

FCB: No, but essentially there's that Gill curve.

All: The Gill curve!

NB: That's what I was saying, I think the Gill curve, or perhaps one should truthfully say, the Johnston-Gill curve, because it does go back to Edward Johnston, is, or if it wasn't so original and important and basic, why the hell would we worry about Edward Johnston, a man who hardly ever finished a job in his life? It's the same, of course, with Arrighi, because Arrighi was not a perfect calligrapher. There were other calligraphers who could produce a surer line, who could write the letter *a* three times in a row that you couldn't tell apart: Arrighi couldn't. But it's just this variety, and the inability to repeat themselves, with the underlying geometry of it, which appeals to us.

FCB: I think one of the things that we are reinvestigating now is that quality of the peculiar curve, a curve that's not part of our late-industrial mechanical system. For example think about Kris Holmes' Rhapsody, and there have been some new attempts at italic and swash capitals. Because we have reduced our understanding of the visual world to rather simple spatial relationships, there's going to be more effort at broadening those out, not in a symbolic sense, but just in a very detailed visual understanding of curves and their qualities, or straight lines and their length. Essentially we shifted from Modernism and the Modernist systems of proportions and spaces, and the Swedish curve which is a graceful curve, into a whole series of curves, into the Baroque and fairly ghastly curves in PostModern architecture and design.

NB: PostModernism, God help us, is the backest of all backwaters!

FCB: It's exactly the fifties. Ettore Sotsass working then did what he's doing now. All those things that are fashions are really ways of asking questions about form. And designers, the act of picking up, looking at, even in their own subintelligent manner, the shapes of earlier letterforms is certainly looking at a different spatial relationship within the world.

When there were instinctive conventions it's because the assumptions about spatial relationships carried across the culture, through letterforms, into buildings and gardens, and now we have accumulated so many records of past efforts, we've got such an eclectic display all around us, that there isn't this convention or standard, so that's why I wanted to get back to your original point. Your feeling that letterforms were like pictures, and that you could talk about letterforms the way you talk about spatial relations in pictures, because that seems to me...

NB: Accepting your point, which I do very much, about the problems created by a sheer plethora of letterforms and the ability that one now has to do anything one likes with them, of course, is slightly analogous to the problems of works of art nowadays. You can call almost anything you like a work of art in some form or another, and what is lacking is a valid grammar to interpret them by. We've now got to build up the conventions that we have thrown away. The reasons they've been thrown away may be good or bad reasons but that they have been thrown away is undeniable. If there's going to be progress, in some form or another, it's only going to be with the aid of some kind of grammar.

Have I ever told you the story of the instructor on the Ludlow caster? There's poetic truth in this. The man who taught the Ludlow caster at the London College of Printing was an absolutely humourless man, a pedant of the old school, and he would explain while teaching the Ludlow caster that its great advantage and facility was the gift it gave you to, as it were, detach the face from the body so that you could cast any size of face on any size of body. And, he would say, you can even cast a 48 point face on a 6 point body. And at this point, some evil-minded wag at the back of the class said, "Can it cast a six point sort on a 48 point body?" There was a long, long pause, and then he said, "You could do, but you don't." Which I've always thought a nice universal truth. [*laughter*]

FCB: We could make that a motto for a development of new spatial conventions in typography.

AMJ: You mentioned the grand book about the history of printing in Texas which used a 48 point swash *J* for an *F*.

NB: *Jine Printing in Texas.*

AMJ: Yes. There's a new book out called *The Ludlow Anthology*, a lavishly overproduced $250 book, and throughout they discuss the same thing: 'Jine Printing.'

NB: Yes, things are just jine!

MATTHEW CARTER

Matthew Carter has ridden the crest of the technological revolution in typography, creating typefaces for each stage from metal to photo to digital type. He learned punchcutting at Enschedé in Holland, worked on identifying the Plantin-Moretus collection of type punches, was a designer at Linotype in the dark days of Phototype, and is a star in the galaxy of digital type design. Chances are you read one of his typefaces every day. At the time of this interview, he was a designer with the Boston firm of Bitstream, which he left in 1999 to co-found Carter & Cone Type Incorporated in Cambridge, Massachusetts. His typefaces include Verdana, Georgia, Bell Centennial, Sophia, Miller, Galliard, and Yale. In 2010, Carter was named a MacArthur Fellow.

In the upper reaches of the San Francisco Hilton is a lounge reserved for guests special enough to be lodged on the topmost floors. It was here, by bluff rather than by right, that Frances Butler and I installed ourselves to tape the following interview with Carter on 31 May 1989.

AMJ: Obviously, being the son of Harry Carter didn't give you too many options for careers.

MC: You'd be surprised. In a polite sort of way, my father tried to dissuade me from following him. In our occasional 'what are you going to do in life?' chats he pushed me away from typography towards working in a museum or a library, some situation where I could advance as people at the top died off. Knowing him, he probably thought one typographer in the family was plenty; my doing something different would make for more interesting conversation at the dinner table.

Meanwhile I had been accepted to go up to Oxford to read English. Those were still the days of National Service — the draft — in England, but declining days, and I wasn't accepted. Oxford colleges were used to people coming up after two years in the army and hadn't yet figured out what to do with anyone fresh out of school. They said, 'At least go away for a year so that you're not completely out of step.' Faced with this, my dad packed me off to Enschedé's, the Dutch printers, where Jan van Krimpen was a great friend of his, and where they had an internship scheme for trainees from overseas, one at a time, unpaid, for a year. This was in 1956; Alan Dodson and John Miles had done it before me, and Carl Dair and others after.

The idea was that you would work in different departments and, as you know, Enschedé is a fascinating place, doing security work — they print stamps and bank notes as well as doing high-class colour — a lot of their own design, their own house museum, and of course they're one of the last printing companies to have their own typefoundry. I started there and in fact spent the whole year working with Paul Rädisch their punchcutter.

Rädisch was approaching retirement by then and had mellowed, slightly. For most of his long career he had refused any pupils, but by the time I got there he had trained Henk Drost (who's still there) as his assistant and would tolerate amateurs. I was amused to find he also tolerated a pantographic engraving machine. It was used to cut complicated display faces like Molé. Rumour had it that when the management had previously installed a machine, Rädisch had dismantled it surreptitiously and dropped the pieces in the canal on his way home in the evenings, until the machine had completely dematerialized! Anyway, it turned out that Rädisch had a soft spot for me because my dad was the first to recognise his contribution to Van Krimpen's types, so we got on alright, and, in practice, Henk did most of the instructing.

So by the time I'd had that experience I really couldn't face going up to Oxford to do Anglo-Saxon. I expected my dad to insist — he being very academically inclined — but after a slightly *mauvais quart d'heure* when I confessed an interest in type, he came around. I even worked for him for a time at the University Press at Oxford, helping organize a small museum there, and cutting a few punches to replace lost sorts in the Fell types. Once I moved to London and tried to make a living he was very helpful with introductions.

AMJ: As a young man you must have been surrounded by people like Morison.

MC: By some more than others. And by the way, it's hard to imagine anyone like Morison: there was Morison, and there was everyone else. My dad and Morison had known each other for ages, but I don't think that they were ever close personal friends. For example, I never remember Morison coming to the house. Of course he disapproved of families as a frivolous distraction from the real business of life — work, and good food. I did once hear him say he'd been to an Oxford don's home for a meal and had been served *blancmange* [*a sort of milk jello*]. He said *blancmange* with such withering contempt — he probably avoided all Oxford households after that.

Once when I called on him at his office at Printing House Square to ask a technical question about typefounding he said it must be in Legros & Grant. When I murmured that I hadn't read Legros & Grant, he thumped the desk, fuming that one must read Legros & Grant once a year!

The printing people I remember as close to my parents were the Simons, Oliver and Bobbie, particularly Bobbie, Noel Carrington, and Francis Meynell who my dad had worked for at the Nonesuch Press and remained a good friend. Francis considered himself my godfather and would give me a half-crown once in a while and a pat on the head. I did meet a lot of people like Morison and Beatrice Warde, but they weren't really familiar figures when I was a kid.

AMJ: Were you able to glean any typographical knowledge incidentally from being around them?

MC: I did once hear Francis say 'blue is not a printer's colour,' but that's so obvious it hardly counts. What I did learn from Francis was how to use a two-person cross-cut saw; how to make a mill pond deep enough to swim in by damming with bags of cement; and how to play tishy-toshy.

AMJ: Huh?

MC: Tishy-toshy is played with a tennis ball and a large table. A player stands at each end of the table, taking turns to throw the ball (throwing hard is not cricket — this is a game of finesse); the receiver must catch it; the ball must bounce at least once on the table and must come off the end, not the sides. The trick is to bounce the ball so your opponent can't judge whether it will just miss the edge of the table or just hit it. If you stand close in order to catch the ball that just misses, it will hit you in the chest if in fact it bounces. If you back off in order to catch the ball that bounces it will fall at your feet if in fact it does not hit the edge. An elderly gent and a ten-year-old make a perfect match (I have competed as both): low down cunning versus lightning reactions.

AMJ: You and your father worked at the Plantin-Moretus Museum. How did that come about?

MC: My father spent a lot of time there; I only visited a couple of times. The City of Antwerp organized a conference in 1955 to commemorate the four hundredth anniversary of Plantin's first printing in Antwerp. My dad was asked to talk on the typographic collection at the Museum and spent time there beforehand sorting punches and casting type in ancient matrices in order to indentify the surviving material. Part of what was there was known from Max Rooses' book, published fifty years before, but most of the punches and matrices and moulds were stored away in a pretty muddled condition and had never been studied. The curator Leon Voet, and Dis Vervliet, his second in command, were not type experts (although Dis certainly made himself into one later), so my dad was really the first to realize what an incredible treasure-trove was there. He gave an overview at the "Plantin Days" conference in 1955 and went back there afterwards to continue the job of cleaning and cataloguing. I went to help on a couple of occasions. I was lucky to have been there at that time because exciting discoveries were still being made. It was a heady experience to sort through a pile of punches, cleaning them with a toothbrush, scrubbing at matrices so you could see what the faces were and sorting out the sets, beginning the work of identifying them and looking at the punches and trying to identify them from the faces and the style of cutting.

AMJ: Or from the shape of the punches.

MC: Yes, exactly, the shape of the punches, and it was very useful to be able to 'read' the workmanship of different cutters because not all the faces were known from printed specimens.

Mike Parker, who continued the work at the Museum, became the expert at this and could distinguish changes of workmanship over time from the same cutter. In any case, the Plantin Museum in my experience is quite the most numinous place that I know. If I'd still had any hesitations about going into the type business, these epiphanies certainly made up my mind for me.

AMJ: Did you cut any punches after leaving Enschedé?

MC: The few Fell replacements I mentioned, and several binders' brasses of flowers for Oxford.

AMJ: Didn't you work on Dante?

MC: I must have, since John Dreyfus reminded me about it recently — his memory is much better than mine. Yes, I cut some trial characters for a heavier weight of Monotype Dante, but I must admit I had forgotten that. I remember cutting a couple of punches for Mardersteig. He had second thoughts about the *A* and *T* in the titling size of Dante and, this being after Charles Malin's death, turned to me, *faute de mieux*. I also cut a strange letter for a cap sigma in archaic Greek for his edition of Felice Feliciano's *Alphabetum Romanum*. It didn't turn out very well — I mean my punch didn't — the book was gorgeous.

My favourite punchcutting project was done for Rowley Atterbury at the Westerham Press who really became a sort of guru of mine and still remains a very good friend. He had an ambivalent relation with Monotype; he was dependent on their typesetting equipment, as any British printer was at that time, but failed to treat them with the pious deference they were used to. In fact, he enjoyed baiting them, and being generally provocative. He had observed that Monotype Van Dijck, which was a very favourite typeface of his, and indeed of mine, had substituted figures. In other words it used the Bembo numerals. I never discovered why. You know that was the face that Van Krimpen was supposed to be involved in advising on, but he afterwards disavowed the whole thing.

Anyway, Rowley said, Why don't you cut some punches for appropriate figures and an ampersand for Van Dijck? And I did that. He took these to Monotype as though to say, 'look at the trouble a poor printer has to go to to get a decent typeface out of you guys. I have to have punches cut at my own expense.' Well, he probably paid me all of five pounds, but at any rate, he did this to tease Monotype and insisted that Monotype should make alternative figures. Anyway, those were made by Monotype and you can still get them as alternatives with the face. The whole story enhanced Rowley's reputation as an

*Flyer for Mantinia & ITC
Galliard (FontHaus) 1993*

irritant (all the more irritating for being right), but I guess the establishment got the last laugh because I heard the punches had gone on display at the Cambridge University Press, the ultimate temple of orthodoxy.

But really, as you can imagine, cutting punches and binders' brasses was hardly a commercial proposition. I soon got into the business of drawing letters rather than engraving.

M A N T I N I A
&
ITC Galliard Roman

A	B	C	D	E	F	G	H	I
J	K	L	M	N	O	P	Q	R
S	T	U	V	W	X	Y	Z	&
a	b	c	d	e	f	g	h	i
j	k	l	m	n	o	p	q	r
s	t	u	v	w	x	y	z	&
1	2	3	4	5	6	7	8	9
I	2	3	4	5	6	7	8	9
0	fi	fl	?	¢	$	£	ß	@
A	B	C	D	E	F	G	H	I
J	K	L	M	N	O	P	Q	R

A	B	C	D	E	F	G	H	I
J	K	L	M	N	O	P	Q	R
S	T	U	V	W	X	Y	Z	&
a	b	c	d	e	f	g	h	i
j	k	l	m	n	o	p	q	r
s	t	u	v	w	x	y	z	&
1	2	3	4	5	6	7	8	9
I	2	3	4	5	6	7	8	9
0	fi	fl	?	¢	$	£	ß	@
À	É	Î	Ö	F	G	H	I	J
K	L	M	Ñ	P	Q	R	S	U

Both MANTINIA and ITC Galliard Roman are new releases from Matthew Carter's new foundry: Carter & Cone Type, Inc. MANTINIA is a new design and ITC Galliard is a newly digitized release of the Roman; complete with a full set of Italics, Old Style, Expert, Alternates, Numeric Fractions and Ornaments. All together, Carter & Cone's ITC Galliard Roman contains 11 fonts! This brochure illustrates only a sampling of all the characters in these fonts. FontHaus is pleased to announce that we have packaged MANTINIA and ITC Galliard Roman at a special "New Release" price of $199. Fonts are also available individually.

AMJ: Was that a relief in a certain sense?

MC: From starvation, yes.

AMJ: Easier on your eyes?

MC: Not necessarily, drawing in black and white is often more tiring. The problem with punchcutting was that it was not so much the technique that interested me — fascinating though that is — but the letters themselves.

Rädisch's job was to follow designs provided to him, with some degree of interpretation that his great experience and skill brought to the task. The result was a beautifully finished punch. But punchcutting is not a designer's medium — presuming alternative ways of making letters — because it's so costly to change your mind or correct mistakes. I mean if you've made one serif of a capital *H* a little bit too light, you've got to grind down the whole face of the punch and recut all of it. I'd come to an instinctive realization that the way you design letters is to change the ones you don't like. Really it's an iterative process. So it's immensely longwinded when you reckon that in those days I was probably able to cut one punch a day, and if at the end of the day you decided it was wrong, then you started the next day from scratch. This was frustrating to a designer although I enjoyed the skill of making punches and of course I had to make all of my own gauges and tools, and that side of it I liked very much: the craft angle. But I wasn't at all reluctant to find myself drawing letters instead of cutting punches and obviously it made economic sense.

Big Figgins & Big Caslon
(Carter & Cone) 1992 & 1994

FCB: This leads into the heart of the question I wanted to ask you, which is that it seems to me that your Snell Roundhand or Galliard, or types you say you like, such as Fournier's or Baskerville's, are ones in which structure is clearly defined. In Charter too you can see the skeleton. I'm wondering how you would describe your own preferences in type?

MC: Robert Norton once paid me a compliment — all the more
appreciated since our friendship is otherwise based on a lifetime's insults. He said I drew letters with backbones and if I had to choose an epitaph I'd be very happy to settle for that. Indeed I do like letterforms where you can see the underlying bone structure. I like to see how they work. Come to that, I like that in other things as well — buildings, furniture. I need to sense how the lines of force go, how the loads are carried, how the joints are made.

But having said that, my taste in type is fairly catholic and there are very few faces I out and out hate. Perhaps I'm too close to the whole thing for that. I often find things that interest me in faces I otherwise dislike. Take Souvenir — not a face with the kind of structural qualities I warm to. But for all its softness, it succeeds in using some very eccentric letterforms. On a sort of insider professional level I find that intriguing and rather admirable. It must be like a painter seeing another painter use very unexpected imagery, or a writer using bizarre figures of speech — and get away with it. Hats off! But I wouldn't want to do it that way myself.

at twelve, to walk 60 pt.
safely home under
a full moon. This
picture of Caslon's
comfortable and
cultured domestic
life is reflected in
his types, or rather
in the harmonious
smaller sizes it is.

Arnold Bank, wise man, told me that in his idealistic youth he would look at a letter and say 'no man that drew an *o* like that could ever be my friend.' Later in life he found himself saying 'I like old so-and-so, and as far as I'm concerned he can make an *o* any way he damn well pleases.' It's hard to maintain a rigorous critical attitude. It's hard to dislike Souvenir if you know Ed Benguiat.

Mike Parker describes poorly designed boldfaces as looking 'dipped in chocolate.' I suppose if there is a class of types I detest it's boldfaces — or worse yet, those miserable things called semibolds — that got heavier by oozing. A chocolate coating is fine if it's good and thick and rich, like in Cooper Bold where it's the whole point of the design, but as a way of adding weight to a Bembo or a Baskerville, it's atrocious. 'Bold' should connote 'fearless' or 'brazen,' not 'bloated.'

FCB: Your preference for letters with spines and for tables with visible structure reminds me of a wonderful article I read years ago, called "Tables, a Pin, and Works of Art," discussing how in tables we know how things are put together, we know what wood is and how long it will last: it has a certain value therefore. Pins, on the other hand, are essentially invisible and valueless, like nails. But at one time they used to burn down houses in America to get the nails out and reuse them. I wonder if your preference for structural types might be because you were brought up in the machine age, whereas people brought up in the computer age seem to produce spineless types across the board. Do you think, one, that my wild-eyed speculation has any bearing on the truth and, two, are there any computer-designed types that are not spineless?

MC: A sense of values is conditioned by time: it has to be. And yes, I'm a product of the machine age. Computers would make much more sense to me if I could take the lid off and see cogs and pulleys and flywheels whirring inside. Anything post-Babbage is a mystery to me as far as understanding how it works. The fact that micro-circuitry has no moving parts makes it a religion, not a technology — something you just have to believe in as an act of blind faith. But I don't agree with your general speculation that equates computer design with spinelessness in letterforms. For example, Stone is a computer-designed typeface that is far from spineless, particularly in the sanserif version, and I could think of others.

The wild-eyed speculation that I think is valid equates computer design with lack of historical reverence, which is a different matter. I remember in your interview with Nic Barker in *The Ampersand*, he talked about the 'backward look,' the cautious advance of type design by small steps, always looking back over the shoulder at the historical past and reluctant to risk a stride big enough to put the past out of sight. This gradual Darwinian process has occurred because it has been difficult for people to get close enough to type to design it without the habit of the 'backward look.' But computers are changing that. It is now possible to design type with nothing more than about one day's experience with the Macintosh. I envy this freshness. After looking closely at letters for some thirty-odd years, it's now difficult for me to see them without a whole baggage of associations and cross-references, historical, aesthetic, technical — through a glass darkly, in other words. It takes a conscious effort to see them face to face. Computers help with this: they encourage the 'forward look.' Even so, it's hard to be an Arcadian at heart and a Utopian at will.

People expect a type designer to have a mandarin mentality, to say that everything done with a computer is bad, that you can't design type without knowing the whole history of typography, readability, legibility, blah blah blah. Screw that.

FCB: In the nineteenth century there were things that affected type like three-dimensional signs on building façades. I'm wondering what sort of metaphoric transformations will affect type in the computer age. You saw my students, what did they bring? Art Deco reruns and Art Nouveau reruns: things from the typographic culture, not from the larger culture. I wonder if you see anything in the larger computer culture that will be absorbed.

MC: Hard to say because we don't really know what a computer culture is yet. Alan Kay says we are not using computers properly as long as we are conscious of using them, and the computer still has the very conscious fascination of a brand new toy. We are playing at science, using the jargon, often claiming hunch as logic, and so on. What we really have is a computer ideology, particularly in typography. A lot of people believe that technical and economic ideas have influenced typography profoundly in the past. I don't. But I must admit there's one thing that's unprecedented in history about the present effect of technology on typography: democratization. What Wendy Richmond calls 'erasing the boundaries.' The fact that there's now a typographic laity as well as a typographic clergy — thanks to desktop publishing, thanks to personal computers — must have some effect. But even so, and even allowing for

MILLER

CARDBOARD
DISPLAY ROMAN

Boxes in strange dimensions
DISPLAY ITALIC

63 Cubits
DISPLAY ROMAN

ROLLS OF CLEAR PACKING TAPE
DISPLAY ROMAN

POINTED KNIVES
DISPLAY ITALIC

Little Styrofoam Peanuts Were So Adorable
DISPLAY ITALIC SMALL CAPS

New Acquaintances
DISPLAY ROMAN SMALL CAPS

They became my most trusted confidantes
DISPLAY ROMAN

Late Practice
DISPLAY ITALIC

I taught them some dance routines
DISPLAY ITALIC

Let me tell you, getting them to listen carefully was difficult
DISPLAY ROMAN

SYNCHRONIZE
DISPLAY ROMAN

Packing Material on Ice Opens on Broadway
DISPLAY ROMAN & ITALIC SMALL CAPS

Ecstatic Review
DISPLAY ROMAN

Miller (Carter & Cone) 1997

Miller, designed by Matthew Carter with Tobias Frere-Jones, is a "Scotch Roman", a class of sturdy general-purpose types of Scottish origin, widely used in America in the second half of the last century, but neglected since and overdue for revival. Miller is faithful to the Scotch style – though not to any one historical example of it – and authentic in having both Roman and Italic Small Capitals, a feature of the originals. cc & FB, 1997.

Text Roman, Text Italic, Text Roman Small Caps, Text Italic Small Caps, Text Bold,

the atmosphere of innovation that goes with the whole computer ethos, there's an important practical difference between innovation and change. What is traditional and intuitive about typography is very old and very, very stubborn.

The whole question of metaphoric influences on type needs more consideration. On the one hand is Barthes' idea that anything designed has to connote something on top of denoting something, because 'every use becomes the sign of that use.' This has to apply to type. On the other hand, you cannot design type in the way that Mallarmé said he wrote poetry: to depict not the thing itself but the effect it produces. Eric Gill wrote that you can't design an *a* that's not a real *a* but gives the effect of one, because 'letters are things, not pictures of things.' Either it's an *a* or it isn't. An *a* is so busy denoting, it has very little room for connoting.

There's something awfully literal about letters. If the larger computer culture, when and if it happens, allows letters to connote more without denoting less, then it will have transformed type. I don't see a true digital style in type; the question is will there be a silicon style?

FCB: I recently have been thinking about layout as punctuation and the disintegration of the Swiss grid, and certainly the LA "Slash and Spritz" style of leaping text ties into the breakdown of placement, place as a framing for value. To some extent, some of the types invented with digital typography are also doing that, they are sort of deconstructed type. Think of the latest Zuzana Ličko type, it's like all the parts got shaken around and put back together [*gestures frantically*], and it seems to me that type is reflecting a lot of the fashion for reshuffling.

MC: Yes, and it's a paradox because what you normally associate with computers is putting things into order. That's what they're good at; they are very orderly machines. The fact, as you say, that they have now come to be associated with deconstructed typography is odd, but it's interesting. Perhaps it's the creeping connotation — or perhaps the epochal metaphor is not the computer, but the computer crash!

One problem with predicting the effects of technology in our industry is that when they do occur they are often unexpected and certainly unplanned. A couple of examples: Linotype's VIP typesetter was predicated mechanically on something called a stepping motor — some gizmo spun off by the space programme. The Linofilm, predecessor to the VIP, had a writing lens that shuttled constantly back and forth across the film. Because of the stepping motor, the writing lens of the VIP moved in a succession of saccadic jumps and could be also be left stationary for multiple exposures. Now I don't believe that the engineers who designed the VIP realized the typographic implications of this — a fabulous machine for building composite characters, like heavily accented Greek. Suddenly you're in the Greek typesetting market — as a by-product of space engineering.

Another example: In order to have characters of different point size base-align in the Linofilm, the baseline ran through the middle of the lenses in the optical system. In practice, normal characters used only the small central part of the lens. There was a lot of good glass left over. For what? Yippee! Colossal kerns [*waves arms*]. Snell Roundhand was an unexpected bonus from the technology. Free kerns with every baseline alignment!

FCB: Have you got that all stuff on the technological evolution recorded somewhere?

MC: No. There are people older than me who remember much more, who go back much further. It would be very well worthwhile getting them in front of a tape recorder or a video camera and getting it all down. And not just out of historical curiosity: there's interest now in reviving the idea of non-linear scale of type, varying the proportions of letterforms and their spacing as a function of output size, and the last people who knew how to do that operated Benton pantographic punchcutting machines. And they are now in retirement, or, more likely, dead.

AMJ: Like Victor Lardent and John Tarr who did so much work on Times New Roman and got no credit at all.

MC: Credit is another matter. There are a lot of unsung heros. I think of George Ostrochulski, who spent his whole life in the letter-drawing department at Mergenthaler, most of it in charge. Not a very lovable man, but I learnt a lot from him about the mechanics of making type, and now I wish I had talked to him more — and to Harry Smith at British Linotype, and M Mouchel at Deberny-Peignot, and several others.

FCB: What kind of type are you going to do next?

MC: Most faces I have worked on in the past have been for text. Making type readable is more intriguing to me than making it eye-catching. This is not a value question, nor a moral issue…

FCB: Oh yes it is.

MC: Well, for me it's not. Not that I don't like display typefaces, I'm just not very good at them. I'm not really a very inventive designer; I don't get bolts from the blue. If I sit down in front of a blank sheet of paper it stays blank. I have to have a starting point. I'm comfortable working with the tension that exists between the functional need for legibility and the aesthetic need to be slightly different. But perhaps as a result of doing rather utilitarian designs, I'm interested now in doing faces that are a bit more differentiated, in pushing the pact with the reader a bit, taking a few liberties with the strict canon. But not as far as real display types.

AMJ: Hermann Zapf said he felt it was time to stop rerunning historical types and to get on with new designs. Do you think that's valid?

MC: Not entirely. We were talking earlier about the 'backward look,' and it's difficult for me to escape completely from that, even if I wanted to. I've done historical reinterpretations — Snell, Galliard — and I don't feel guilty about them. I see myself as a continuator, not as a plagiarist. Even in designs that are relatively original, like Charter, good critics like John Lane and Max Caflisch have seen the influence of Fournier on the italic, and I wouldn't quarrel with that. I would do more revivals if I could find things to revive, but there are few historical styles worthy of revival that don't already have decent contemporary versions (although Gerard Unger and I are playing with one idea). Reviving old faces is not a soft option; there's no saying that because a face was once successful there is necessarily new life in it. The revivals I've done have absolutely nothing to do with nostalgia — I have no interest in that whatever — but with the opposite: looking for qualities that are undatable and have no period associations.

What is difficult is to force oneself to try something new and risk failure, rather than to stay within the security of reworking proven ideas. I see the choice not as between historical and new, *pace* Hermann, but between reworked and new, and you can easily rework yourself as rework Bodoni or Garamond.

AMJ: Galliard strikes me as a really great synthesis of a lot of Granjon's ideas. Just as Granjon cut different styles at different sizes and at different times, it would be possible to do another companion type, another italic or weight of roman.

MC: To enlarge the Galliard family? You certainly could do that, yes. The method of doing Galliard, Mike and I marinated ourselves in Granjon and when it came time to start drawing, what came out came out. One could do that to other versions.

I like the idea of enlarging type families in other directions, as Sumner did with Stone. While I was working on Charter I remembered that Luce and Fournier made rather lazy script types by substituting cursive caps and looser ascenders and descenders in an italic. I did try that in Charter and I still like that idea. I haven't released that yet, but perhaps I will. I hadn't thought of doing anything like that to Galliard, I did make a set of titling caps to work with Galliard and maybe I'll talk to ITC about them.

ROBERT CREELEY

Robert Creeley (1926–2005) was arguably the most important American poet of the second half of the twentieth century, and one of the most influential. In the early fifties he lived in Mallorca with his family, where he ran Divers Press.

  During his hectic visit to the Bay Area in November 1986, I was able to talk to Creeley about this publishing venture, as I drove him from Berkeley to San Rafael.

AMJ: What motivated you to become a publisher, was it like your prospectus says, because "Printing is Cheap in Mallorca"?

RC: Well, partly that. We came to Mallorca thanks to a dear pen pal met through classic letters. I'd seen John Sankey's magazine *The Window*, one of the curious literary magazines of the period. There was a poem by Martin Seymour-Smith called "All Devils Fading," and I was struck by this Coleridge-like tone to the poem, a kind of spooky…interesting spookiness of it and I wrote to say how much I liked it, care of the magazine. Not long after comes back this letter from Martin. Turns out he's living in Mallorca with his wife Janet. They had a holiday so they decided to come up and see us. That was great. We were living in Lambesc, above Aix-en-Provence. I described meeting them in the novel, *The Island*. The couple Artie and Marge are Martin and Janet. It describes the meeting in Marseilles. We go then to Mallorca thanks to Martin.

AMJ: Were you inspired by Seizin Press?

RC: I think partly inspired by Seizin Press, started by Graves and Riding. Apparently Tómas Graves is starting it up again — the youngest son. In any case this was that tradition. I think Martin's real impulse initially was to print his mother's poems — Elena Fearn — that was her *nom de plume*. Her husband was a great bookman, a really brilliant bibliographer, Frank Seymour-Smith, and this was a really powerful woman dissatisfied with her workaday-world husband. She was a curious *femme fatale*. Martin seemed determined to publish the poems. I was interested in the possibilities of publishing and Martin seemed to know his way around. So we had a little money thanks to Ann's trust fund; we decided to do some books. First we tried a collaboration: we published his mother's poems. Actually it was called the Roebuck Press and at that point I realized, as much as I loved Martin, that this was not going to work. He was a classic Englishman in obvious ways and his pleasures were not, finally, mine. So we managed to back off quite nicely. Then Ann and I began to publish in our own interests.

AMJ: Dealing with Mossèn Alcover?

RC: Louis Ripoll is the actual name, a sweet man, ran Mossèn Alcover's as shop foreman. Just incredible, in those days it was actually cheaper to handset than it was to use Linotype because the machinery was such an awful expense initially. He was a job printer who did newspapers and any kind of work that came along. Again, they were incredibly careful with their type fonts and literally picked through and kept reusing every single piece of type. The books I remember most vividly are Katue Kitasono's *Black Rain*, Olson's *Mayan Letters*, for which Ann copied the glyphs freehand…

AMJ: The first book you did was Paul Blackburn's *Proensa*, following Olson's *In Cold Hell, In Thicket* (*Origin* VIII).

RC: That's right. That was a dear pleasure. I remember the printers were fascinated with it because they could read the Provençal: the Majorquin was very close. There were some old-timers in there. Guasp, for example, I think was possibly the most continuous printing establishment in Europe, since the Renaissance. That part of it became delicious. It seems to me we could produce a book for… *Proensa* cost between 300 and 400 dollars, which was something then. The same book today would cost fifteen hundred dollars. So then we really got into it.

AMJ: Later on you published Blackburn's own poems, in *The Dissolving Fabric*.

RC: This was a book fraught with many painful dilemmas for Paul and me, I would say now, thanks to the antagonism of our wives who had got into an oblique argument. Let's see, there are letters of Paul's published in an issue of Bertholf's magazine and Paul at that point thought I was absolutely insane and so flooded with impotent egocentricity that I was completely — "forget it!" Anyhow the problem was it was such a curious emotional contest between Ann, my wife then, and Freddie, his wife, who were somehow fighting. Then he left and went on to Toulouse and, thankfully, we went ahead with the book.

[*Oncoming car honks as we make a U-turn*]

RC: Drive, you sonofabitch!

AMJ: You were receiving manuscripts in the mail, through correspondence with Duncan, Larry Eigner…

RC: I remember Douglas Woolf's *The Hypocritic Days* came out of the blue: that was great. I thought it was terrific. Also, we'd been wanting to publish some prose. I published my volume *The Gold Diggers* after I'd stupidly mistaken Alex Trocchi's — and the Merlin people's — real interest in the book, and I thought they were just being nice to me so I refused their generous offer of publication and we published it ourselves.

René Laubies was a friend we met through Pound. He was a translator and did covers. We improvised some from Kitasono. He was also a well-established painter who showed at Fachette's in Paris along with the Americans Sam Francis and Lawrence Calcagno. It's where I first saw Pollock's work. I went to Black Mountain and returned. I met John Altoon while in New York

City, he was a friend of Julie Eastman who had come from El Paso. Arthur [Okamura] and John had known each other from LA, I think. Arthur got this prize, some money, and heard from John about this good place to live. So Arthur and John both showed up. Liz and Arthur had just got married.

AMJ: What kind of editorial control did you exercise on the manuscripts, apart from editing Olson's *Mayan Letters*?

RC: None, really.

AMJ: What about design?

RC: We did the design. That was what was so terrific about these printers, they were so articulate in translating our...neither one of us were really artists, so we would mock up or improvise what we wanted it to look like.

AMJ: You managed to get a nice balance between the classical Spanish types for the text...

RC: I love that.

AMJ: ...and then modern Bauhaus-style layout on the title-page of Futura sans serif.

Paul Blackburn, The Dissolving Fabric, *Mallorca, Spain: Divers Press, 1955*

RC: You would know, for example, the absolute horror of the classical European printer when you mix fonts.

AMJ: Mmhmn.

RC: That really got to them. Our heads were in Futura and the body in…

AMJ: Mercedes. A weird Spanish type.

RC: Well-rounded, good-natured.

AMJ: Right.

RC: So the thing — they were terrific with us, being a small shop. I remember trying to reproduce the drawing for the cover of *The Gold Diggers*, which has the drawing of Laubies'. There's a red background, the red kept bleeding through, but they overprinted at least twice. They went through these incredible efforts and they charged us virtually nothing. Extremely sweet. Their shop was down from the central plaza, going along the sea wall. There was a beautiful prospect. They used to keep the back door of the shop open to get this lovely breeze. Extremely good-natured. They were extraordinarily patient.

AMJ: Did you run into Graves at all?

RC: Yeah. We met him when we first arrived thanks to Martin and Janet. Palma was already a very desirable place to live so suggestions of various other places included Banalbufar, which was the end of the road. In those days it dead-ended. I remember when the first washing-machine arrived. It had a sort of fan…

Robert Creeley, A Snarling Garland of Xmas Verses, Mallorca, Spain: Divers Press, 1954

A Snarling Garland

Of Xmas Verses

by Anonymous

AMJ: You were the Ur-colonists.

RC: Dig it. On the buses, for example, my wife wouldn't understand Spanish and the Spanish ladies therefore assumed she was deaf.

AMJ: At your reading the other night you expressed malcontent with the idea of a "Table of Contents."

RC: I had the imagination that a book would be an entire process or thing, more accurately, that almost — not simply like one's mother saying, "eat all your food," but the idea of, I like the sense of, someone's beginning and reading through the whole continuity. So that I had this rather simple sense that if one didn't provide a table of contents that more or less committed people to reading the whole thing, but obviously a contents page is a very useful thing to include.

AMJ: For access and retrieval.

RC: Right.

AMJ: To your own ideas on book design: I remember when your *Collected Poems* came out you were very pleased with the way Marilyn [Perry] had laid out the running headings so that you knew exactly where you were in the book.

RC: Extremely good. We were thinking of that yesterday. I was back in the same company and Bill McClung was sitting with that book under his hand. That book has such a physical clarity for me, not just its size, but it's extraordinarily comfortable with those poems: the shifting lengths and line patterns, it just holds them with such good-natured clarity. I think Marilyn did a great job. The only typo in the book is a bleak one. When the stuff was together for the final printing of the jacket, someone either brushed or disturbed it so that her credit went. On the paper it's returned, but on the hardback she got brushed.

AMJ: A designer is the most invisible part of a successful book.

RC: Yet the most crucial.

AMJ: In an unsuccessful book their name is usually on the cover in big letters.

RC: Her rapport with what the poems are is impeccable.

AMJ: Coming from a press like UC it helps to have a designer who's at least familiar with the terrain.

RC: A classic alternative therefore of what else can happen is the design of *Selected Poems* with Scribner's. That was an absolute mess. The print, the layout is pedestrian. The order gets shifted in order to accommodate some imagination of spacing, which has nothing to do with the text. The cover is grotesque, with that weird type and the curlicues. No rapport with the text whatsoever. In that case, sadly, it was the eldest editor, who'd been the book's authority, got ill and it was handed to two younger persons and they were new in the business and they didn't know what to do. And the Art Department was always negligible, you know, and it just fell apart.

Therefore back to that sense of the Divers Press and having this extraordinarily small local printing shop to work with, all of the work being handset. Their patience and ability to stay with us through our own sort of inchoate attempts to resolve design work were terrific. And they had such a physically clear sense of what a page could look like and so — their sense of spacing was so graceful — they could do any kind of text and give it that very comfortable feel of words progressing. Just delicious.

AMJ: Was the format determined by what paper supply was available?

RC: To some extent. But we would at times, probably, not wastefully, but add to expense. We had basic folds. I remember *The Snarling Garland* is printed on stock that Paul retrieved from his work in the printshop that Larry Bronfman's uncle runs. So there'd be waste and Paul would pack it up and send it over to us. Again they were the kind of printers that would work with that and not feel that we were putting some awful burden on them. This was fun to them. This was fooling around in ways that were out of the regular run.

Louis Ripoll, the owner of the business, used to come out to the house at times and I think we were all variously intrigued with each other and so it was sort of playful. It wasn't a big job, but they got very involved with it. The relation must have lasted at least three years.

AMJ: You had a great pool of artistic talent on your doorstep too. With Dan Rice, Arthur Okamura, John Altoon, Katue Kitasono...

RC: He was in Japan. This is the Pound connection. He'd been immensely responsive and helpful. He publishes several of my poems in an edition of his own as curious American haiku he translates and publishes. He also publishes parts of "Notes for a New Prose" in his magazine *Vou*. Finally he and I parted ways in a very old-time human confusion. He was an old friend through correspondence with Kenneth Rexroth and when he sadly learned of Kenneth's and my dilemma he felt that he, in honor of his old friend — the precedent friend — must stay loyal to Kenneth. I remember he wrote this very sad letter, in no way accusing, but just saying, "My commitments are sadly necessarily with Kenneth and I'm afraid that must end our relationship."

I didn't, obviously, enjoy it, but I could dig what he was saying.

AMJ: Did you have any dealings with Jonathan Williams back then when he was just starting his own press?

RC: I met Jonathan in Mallorca. There are some photographs of Jonathan's of Ann and myself at the place we then lived, the first place we had there, before I went to Black Mountain. He had been a student at Black Mountain and now in the Army in Stuttgart and came, as I recall, on vacation to visit us in Mallorca. And I think it was he who gave me an extraordinary classic book of typefaces, which I still have. I can't recall the name of it — it was lovely — a German book. It gave all the range of historic types and was a very useful book. He was using a printer in Stuttgart.

AMJ: You used whatever types your printer had?

RC: Alcover had also a Bodoni that we used for Paul Blackburn's *Proensa*. The type that we used for the magazine, the basic working type, the one he had the most of, was the Mercedes.

We used a printer who was a little more expensive, I don't know why we were persuaded to use him, to publish the book of Irving Layton's *In the Midst of My Fever*. It was okay but it wasn't nearly the fun of working with Louis. He wasn't just the cheapest. His work permitted ways for books to get in, you dig. He was one of the smallest printers on the island.

AMJ: Next to Graves.

RC: He knew of Graves — Señor Grah-ways — everyone knew him. Graves wasn't hostile to our attempts but he certainly wasn't remarkably impressed, because of the contents mainly. He felt them negligent.

I was just determined to publish Americans of my own interests. I was far more idealistic than Martin. I haven't seen Martin now for twenty-two years though I've had occasional correspondence. I thought it was deliciously ironic he should write the official biography of Graves. He left under a cloud, as they say.

PAUL HAYDEN DUENSING

Paul Hayden Duensing (1929–2006), the typography editor of Fine Print, *was a type-founder who also cut type. This interview was conducted at Moscone Center, San Francisco, on the occasion of the American Psychiatric Association convention in May 1989.*

Before the interview, he told me of his first visit to Oxford University Press. The director of the press wrote to say that the archivist, Harry Carter, would show him around. To Duensing, this was like being shown around the Vatican by the Pope. However, in his naïve enthusiasm, he inquired, on being shown the famous Fell types, whether he might have a couple of each character to take home, not as a souvenir, but in order to make electrotype duplicates. "Not only is that impossible," replied Mr Carter, "it's unthinkable." Then, calling over one of the employees, Carter muttered, "Watch him!"

AMJ: First of all, I want to ask you about the American Typecasting Fellowship, of which you are a stalwart member. How long has that been going?

PHD: This is now approaching the twelfth year. We held the first meeting ten years ago in Terra Alta, West Virginia, and Rich Hopkins invited people to come there. He thought he might have eight or nine people come to this ski resort in summer time. Much to his surprise, thirty-three people showed up and they had a wonderful time. They elected to meet again every two years since then. They have met in New York City near American Type Founders; we had a meeting in Oxford; in Washington, DC; then in Indianapolis; again in Terra Alta; and in 1990 we will meet in Nevada City, California, at the foundry of Harold Berliner. Attendance has grown, with the high point at Oxford: a little over one hundred people attended. Generally, it runs from thirty to fifty people, depending on where it is. We have a general meeting for about three days, then an intensive workshop devoted to technical aspects of casting, metallurgy, etcetera. We usually have someone there who is an imported expert, like Harry Wearn from English Monotype who is very adept at running workshops.

AMJ: Is the increased interest in typecasting related to the closing of available sources for type?

PHD: It's partly related to that and partly to the availability of machinery on the market. People get some idea that these things are going and they should do something to save them. Interestingly enough, at our English meeting people there said they did not have a sense of urgency because they could simply call up the Monotype works and have someone sent out to solve their problems. Because of this long tradition of availability they did not feel a sense of panic that this would disappear.

AMJ: And it has, in fact, all come down in the last year or so.

PHD: Yes, it has. There are only, I think, about four or five active typecasters in a non-commercial way in England and perhaps five on the Continent, and all the rest are in the United States. In the US we have Dan Carr in New Hampshire, Pat Taylor in New York, Stan Nelson in Washington, and Roy Rice in Atlanta, myself in Michigan, Les Feller and Ed Leibhart in Chicago, Bob Halbert in Texas, Dave Churchman and David Peat in Indianapolis, then it jumps to the West Coast; there's Pat Reagh in Los Angeles and the people in the Bay Area.

AMJ: There's someone in Vancouver, too?

PHD: Gerald Giampa and Jim Rimmer.

AMJ: Did they buy things from Mackenzie-Harris recently?

PHD: They bought the American Monotype matrix punching equipment and the punches and matrix inventory, I believe.

AMJ: How many of these people are going to be in a position to make type commercially? Or are they mainly interested in preserving matrices for posterity?

PHD: The people in the American Typecasting Fellowship are largely committed to making type for others and for themselves. They continue to do this as a service to the craft and to keep the traditions alive. I think there are a few others that I don't really count among the typecasters who are collectors of equipment and machinery and so on, but who never bought it to be operable. I really consider them to be museums of dead equipment, not of any consequence in producing type.

AMJ: There was a move at the Smithsonian a few years ago to start making type available from ATF mats, or rather mats that ATF had acquired from older American foundries. They offered some William Morris Satanick. Do you know the status of that programme?

PHD: The prime mover in this was Pat Taylor, in conjunction with Stan Nelson and Elizabeth Harris at the Smithsonian, but they had a few problems. Number one, the mats are of all different depths of drive so they have to keep re-engineering moulds to accommodate them, and secondly there's the question of liability. What happens if a mat burns out or if they lose a font of mats? Who's responsible? How are they going to divide the royalties or whatever monies accrue from this? Who will decide what mats are going to be done and which mats simply cannot be lent out on account of scarcity? And who decides who will be allowed to cast them?

AMJ: Isn't it possible to make electrotypes or duplicates of mats?

PHD: It is, but there again, the number of people who are providing this service has shrunk greatly, and now in the US probably only two or three will do it. Stan Nelson has told me that he has made preliminary experiments to duplicate mats by electrodeposition, but I don't think he has that on stream.

AMJ: One of the really tragic events of recent years has been the gradual closing of, first of all, the small English foundries like Stevens Shanks, Riscatype, and Mouldtype, and now the big European foundries like Stempel. The only hope in all this is Walter Wilkes' typefounding museum in Darmstadt if it is going to fulfil a role for people who want to get metal type. Bauer, I think, is functioning in Spain to a small extent.

PHD: The former Bauer foundry has been transferred to Barcelona.

AMJ: To Richard Gans?

PHD: No, Neufville, and that's owned by the same management that owned the Bauer foundry. Wolfgang Hartmann runs the foundry and produces a large number of faces. Some of them are cast on American height and American point body; others are on the Didot system but could be milled down to American height. He does a fairly roaring business with Third World countries in things like Arabic, and he has done several fonts of mats in what's called "the Africa script," which is basically the Latin letterform with a number of additions so they can then produce most of the languages of Africa.

Richard Gans is a separate foundry in Barcelona. They are very, very low key and it's almost impossible to get a catalog, but if you know what you want, they have some lovely faces and will indeed sell them to you. Haas is now closed, I understand, in Switzerland; Typefoundry Amsterdam in Holland closed; the Enschedé foundry still functions in a way but there is really only one man who is responsible for running all of the Monotype composition and all of the foundry work — but he's also expected to make plastic signs in whatever time he has available.

In Germany, Reiner Gerstenberg, who was formerly the foundry superintendent at Stempel, still runs the Letterservice Gerstenberg out of Darmstadt and will continue to do so when the museum is operating there. The idea is that he will continue to provide a few of the most popular faces from stock and he will cast on special order anything that Klingspor or Stempel had previously available. The program at Gerstenberg's is recasting some of the finer types. Two years ago they recast the Original Janson and we may soon see types such as Michelangelo, Smaragd and Diotima. One of the problems is getting the word out when the faces become available. My contacts are efficacious in getting the word to me and I put it in *Fine Print* and other publications, but I suspect that we're still missing a number of people. There's just not a good mailing list for all of the people interested in metal type, yet those who are interested are vitally interested and feel they need it.

AMJ: But at great price presumably?

PHD: At great price — about $25 to $30 a pound. That's about what ATF charges now.

AMJ: Their prices just went up. Does that include the whole library of Klingspor or Stempel?

PHD: Yes, but you must consider that they will not do a single font for you; you must order sorts lines. You will wind up getting a lot more *q*'s and *x*'s than are needed. ATF continues to do this. Schumacher-Gebler has a very large collection of Monotype fonts. He has just brought his foundry casting equipment on line. He has four and a half tons of mats from the Bauer foundry plus he has four or five tons of mats from the Reichsdruckerei — the former German National printing office — and from other foundries as well. As a matter of fact, he has some very interesting mats, which were apparently done originally by Fournier, by Luther, by Ploos van Amstel brothers, Rosart, and others. So if he is really successful in casting those, it will be a boon to those who would like to use historic faces.

XVI Century Roman QUADRATA

𝔄 and 𝔨 were re-cut for 12, 24, 36 and 48 pt of Wilhelm-Klingspor Schrift by Rudolf Koch

RUSTICA·WAS·THE·FIR
ST·FACE·TO·BE·CUT·AT·
THE·PRIVATE·PRESS·A
ND·TYPEFOUNDRY·AND
IT·HAS·AROUSED·SOME
CRITICISM·BY·ITS·LACK
OF·A·CROSSBAR·IN·THE

AMJ: So, although things look bad now, we're no longer in the position of mats just being melted down wholesale for brass, and there is the possibility that the next generation may have a great variety of types going back to the sixteenth and seventeenth centuries.

PHD: Yes, it always depends, of course, on whether there is enough interest to make it economically feasible. If you try to do just one font you'd best do it for yourself because you can't make one font economically for someone and get your costs out of it. If you can get several people to go in together, say fifteen or twenty people, and they each order a font, then it becomes economically feasible to make those fonts. I suspect the subscription casting is the way of the future.

AMJ: In your own private press and typefoundry you've cut sorts for a number of types, how did you learn how to do that?

PHD: Just dogged determination I think, and some lucky correspondents who taught me a great deal. Early on I struck up a friendship with John Carroll who was a sort of autodidact and engineer. He and I corresponded frequently over a period of five or six years and he finally sold me his pantograph for cutting mats. It was a learning process: I thought about it a great deal, I dreamt about it. I formed all kinds of theories and so on; some of them actually worked and I did succeed eventually in cutting fonts and individual sorts. Andy Dunker, who was the other great source of information, was a tool and die maker who was extremely careful and methodical in his work, just a model of good workmanship, good craftsmanship. He made a number of electrolytic mats for me, also taught me a number of things about how to grind cutting tools. Bob Middleton, the former type director of the Ludlow Company, was another source. He was a great inspiration for me and indeed finally got me a cutter-grinder and a pantograph that was used by Ludlow to make punches. The rest was just experimentation. I made a lot of bad mats but eventually the law of averages was on my side. The other thing that was really important was that the technology of the times provided Dycril and then Nyloprint plates, which I could make in my basement. They make excellent engraved patterns for mats. There have been occasions when I've come home, made a film positive, developed and printed it, made the plate and let it dry, and after dinner engraved the mat while the caster was heating. I cast the type and can look at the character. It's not a standard thing but I have been able to do that.

Since we're here at the American Psychiatric Association, I think we could submit an agenda item. Several people, including my wife, have indicated that most fine printers and private press people, and certainly all private typefounders, are mad. I had once offered the suggestion that typefounders were really frustrated fathers and that they found a certain Freudian symbolism in typecasting, because they could insert the matrix and then cast in their own image as many progeny as they wished. This became a surrogate family for them whom they did not have to support and could sell to whatever high bidder, so they had all the fun of creation without the burden of support. My wife then looked at me in her best Elaine May manner, and said, "You are really cuckoo!"

AMJ: Where did you get the Wilhelm Klingspor Schrift that you have?

PHD: The Klingspor and the Jessen I had coveted for a long time. I was able to conclude a deal with a commercial printer friend in Germany that he would give me five percent of the

Rustica, Quadrata, 16th-century Roman, Wilhelm Klingspor Schrift, four of the types issued by Paul Hayden Duensing through his private typefoundry

font, he and I would split the cost and I had just enough to make electrolytic copies. I have the entire run of sizes in Klingspor Schrift and 8, 10, 12 and 14 in the Jessen-Schrift. Although I made a number of electrolytic mats, I did not feel as though I was pirating money away from the Stempel foundry since they had virtually discontinued these faces from their active catalogue. It was, however, necessary in the case of the Klingspor types to recut a few characters and make electro mats for them: the capital *A* because it looks to American eyes like a cap *U* and the lowercase *k* which looks like a *t* that needs a haircut. The Fraktur letterform is not easily recognised in this country.

AMJ: Did you use Koch drawings or did you redraw them?

PHD: I redrew them. At that time they had a very affable, pleasant and cooperative art director at the Stempel foundry. I sent him my drawings, and he suggested changes that enhanced their appearance. Then I cut the characters and made electrolytic mats from them so they would fit very tightly. Fortunately they match the rest of the font very well.

AMJ: The faces that you have in your foundry are a very odd collection: Rustica, Uncial, a peculiar sixteenth century type. Did you acquire these by chance or did you want unusual faces?

PHD: The original premise of my foundry was not to provide another source for Bookman and Cheltenham and Caslon. I saw the mission of my foundry as providing letterforms that had not been cut in type before, in order to extend the spectrum of choice to the printer. A case in point is the Rustica and Quadrata, both of which are manuscript letterforms, but had never been cut in type before, at least not accurate reproductions of them. I felt they were useful letterforms, so why not cut them in type? In the case of the uncials, some of them are by Victor Hammer. One of them, Andromaque, is a very interesting amalgamation of Roman and Greek letterforms in an uncial environment. I thought it was a startling and ingenious thing to do, so I made replica mats. I have hopes of doing a couple of more original designs before I finally hang it up, one of which might be a calligraphic script: something along the lines of Zapf Chancery, but perhaps in a large size for imprinting certificates, diplomas and awards. The sixteenth century punches were acquired during a trip to Italy many years ago. They were extremely rusted and I was only able to get them because the owner and his wife could not agree whether they were valuable. Someone, I think it was Roderick Cave in his review of the Sixteenth Century Roman, said it looked like seventeenth-century English printing at its very nastiest. But there have been a number of people who really rejoice in the face and like to use it.

AMJ: It's an effect that's easy to attain and hard to avoid for some people.

PHD: Well, the one overriding virtue of it is you can't tell when it's worn out. I think the bite of the type in letterpress is an indigenous quality and type does a great job of it. But some things in letterpress hit a mark very close to perfection but never really brought it off totally. Unless there are things like connected copperplate scripts, they used expedients, and this is where digital types will outperform them. One of the few things that letterpress still can do is the one-off, imprinting a name on a certificate. As our society increasingly tends to give awards in place of pay raises, that becomes a large market.

AMJ: Never mind the overinking, feel the impression!

PHD: Right. I'm very much impressed by the young generation of printers that are coming along now with a devotion to the field and who are willing to forego high monetary rewards to keep the craft alive. It's strange when you'd expect the young to be most enamored with high tech, digitization, electronics and so on, that there's still this hard core of those who are basically humanistically oriented, and want to do things by hand. Apparently for some they feel that they have an abundance of time at their disposal and that they can use this to offset the high speed of other media and they are willing to do that to maintain this edge of uniqueness. I'm also encouraged by the number of women and girls who are interested in the craft of printing. I think in the future we'll see a great deal of gender-free printing, and the world will be much richer for it.

ROBERT GRENIER

Born in Minnesota in 1941, poet Robert Grenier received his BA from Harvard and MFA from the Iowa Writers' Workshop. He has taught at Berkeley, Tufts, Franconia, Mills, and Sonoma State. He has lived in the Bay Area since the late seventies, and for a period of time took care of poet Larry Eigner, who had cerebal palsy. Many of his books of poetry and essays are printed from his typescript. I thought this was an expedient he would gladly relinquish for a book printed from type. However, when I asked him for his next manuscript to publish he gracefully refused, generating an extensive exchange about the real differences between a typed page and a typeset version of it. This interview was conducted in the parking lot of Scandinavian Massage in Berkeley, on 21 February 1986 and appeared in Ampersand *under the heading "Typewriter vs Typeface."*

poet: The thing that came up for me the other day was, that you don't think about this stuff until you have to speak to it, and it's very private after all, what forms one works in. Especially in this society, where you have to find them and then declare them to yourself, and maybe they have some currency. It's best not to concentrate on these kinds of intimate workings, in many senses, except as I was saying, the typewriter fetish seems to have passed. I would use "fetish" in the sense of some object that gains access to the other world which then shows itself as the way daily life is actually represented. So through the fetish, daily life is seen to be what it is, and it has always been that, so we need it. It has the negative connotation of a crutch and also the positive connotation of spiritual access. So the typewriter showed me how letters occurred in the word, and that was essential to me. Nobody else told me that words were made out of letters, and except when I did set type in seventh grade, if I didn't pie what was in the stick, the activity was insistent enough, but I didn't associate that with language because I was taught that that was just this mechanical skill that you did in shop and English was a traditional classroom number where you studied something academically. But in fact as a writer what you do, whatever instrument you use, you make this mark, then that mark and that mark. In handwriting they seem to flow together so that in fact you may not notice that you're writing each letter and you may be convinced that you're making words out of meanings. The thing that struck me about what I was speaking to the other night is that you're given a condition of formal possibility by the culture that you're raised in. This includes your mother tongue and it includes the physical access to print that you have at the time. An image I have of you is struggling away, almost as if you were Bach at the organ, with your Linotype machine, it throwing out pieces of hot lead and you banging away at the keyboard like a pump organ. What you do is not something I would want to, or be able, necessarily, to learn.

It just so happens that I started to print in junior high school. From that time I could no longer write. I could write only by printing quickly and painfully, but it wasn't actually script. There was some decision that I made before I began to think about it, and it had to do with writing these comic operas and little scripts at that time and mock radio dramas. It's like an agrarian base of local composition given certain breaks and holes, etcetera, and whatever the IBM — irrespective of the fucking despicable political focus that that brings — the machines are churned up, and the machines are your actual possibility, and you work with them. The hand is a machine and all that stuff, like bending the muscles, and the mind lives in these materials, and they depend on a time and place and a local focus, and so the thing is to use them and acknowledge them because that's what you have. And not think that this can be altered by flying it around the room five times or by introducing some other look to it. It's more important to live the life that you're given to live and stretch its boundaries through these puny little extensions than to....

printer: Yes, but it is essentially crude mechanical access...

poet: Very crude, agrarian. But it's grand and noble to enact the mechanical access of the time, like if you have a hoe and the hoe is just invented. I'm like the Selectric typewriter was just invented.

printer: So you're comfortable at that level?

poet: It isn't that I'm comfortable, it's that, that's it, you know? I saw that and I had the energy and life to see it, and used it, and it used me and we made this, and everybody does that in their time and place. I think it's glorious to be stuck with it. The actual possibilities in life are very small and limited. You can only go from the Mississippi River west some little distance and then you confront the ocean, and at that time, maybe you have your hand to write with, and you happen to print from this unconscious determination of yours, and from that time on you think of the words in conformance with the conditions of the time and place in which you find them. That's the way it goes, and then you die, basically. It's not tragic, it's just you. It's like a person taking a few steps in a certain direction, they count the steps and they jump over a puddle and that's the next word, and land on the ground and make a few more gestures and strides and perhaps they're also hunting or running away from home. Whatever they're doing, it doesn't matter. So the form is absolutely interknit with the materials that are available at the time.

printer: So that's why you don't want to let it go beyond that stage, because that's the point of transmission?

poet: No, it's already gone beyond that. But that was the idea at the time. But subsequently, it's much more interesting just to let the mind wander and the hand ramble so that I don't count the letters to speak of any more, or if I do it's only training, like ABCs. When you learn A - B - C, then you can think and function and you don't have to be so stupid.

printer: Well, let's see what Michael St John has to say about this. [*Turns on car radio to KRE 1400 AM*].

Michael St John: Don't come to me talking about your feelings!

poet: [*laughs*] I'll try to stay on the track a bit more. That was just like a statement of the whole condition of the material at that point.

printer: And you like to retain that level of control over the appearance of your material. In the case of publishing, when you publish your books as typewritten rather than typeset pages, you're making a specific decision not to go beyond the level at which you type it.

poet: It isn't that I like to. That would imply I had a choice.

printer: Well, you're mistrusting sophistication.

poet: No, it's just the result given to people should be what it is. The thing should be presented in as intimate an accommodation of the home condition of the poet or artist as possible.

printer: And so it's interesting because it represents your real voice.

poet: Actually it's a prosodic invention. I think about Zukofsky counting the number of words in a line over against the Anglo-Saxon accentual and later Latinate syllabics making Elizabethan accentual-syllabic blank verse as a measure. To count five words, as Zukofsky did, then you have a different line, and you can count the number of letters in words, which are so related that you have another prosody based on the number of letters in the words. It's just an invention.

printer: Have you ever thought of an invention like using the typewriter abstractly? Rotating the platen to all the possible areas of the surface in typing.

poet: Well that's what I was thinking Larry Eigner has done. He does it free-floating; sometimes he doesn't get the measure right and letters do sort of wander around the page and you have to think of the whole page as the measure. I would side with that sense of things. One could say Larry Eigner was deprived of these various possibilities because all he could do was type, and he had difficulty managing the page and he had to use that sheet that he'd got in the typewriter and his ability to turn the platen. But that's what it's like for everybody. He's not in a primitive circumstance there, he has mechanical access and it's glorious too! It's just a question of scale. Supposing someone had a terrific megalomania and a marvellous kind of world verbal aptitude and could learn all languages and by studying, training could — and access to different kinds of presses — do anything and everything, that person would be the most boring individual that I could ever meet. That person would be an idiot. Because that person would be so busy shifting the apparently possible shapes that they would never get down to it, and they would never see the shape growing out of the fundamentally limited human condition that we're all born into. We're just like dogs or trapped lizards: you have a range of access. Now it seems — that's the garbage we're fed — my political experience is that Americans think they could do anything they wanted to and it's just a question of following their skill and intelligence and their ingenuity and nothing would stop them...

printer: But instead they worship nothing. They're totally nihilistic.

poet: They don't have time to think about it. I don't think there's any worship. Somehow the idea of infinite possibility was plugged in, and that was the way people proceeded, like the space thing: that's an absolute symbol of the world condition. When the thing blows up, people ask what went wrong as if it were an isolated incident.

  What went wrong was the incredible pride and presumption in thinking that it was just a question of inventing anything and everything can be done. I guess I'm, in part, in reaction against that. Even though I could do perhaps 'more' than I've wanted to do, it's not a question of learning how to do more with the shapes that you're given, but of enacting the perception of the world that we have, given your limited equipment. I like the idea of big jumps made in the human condition by single inventions like the wheel. Though that's a hypothetical possibility: someone began to roll over in a cartwheel? It probably came from gymnastics.

printer: What about the appearance that the typewriter imparts to the text?

poet: The vision of the way the work looks is activated by the equivalence, which gives them a magical letter value as number, which motivates their replication as ones. Instead of syllables, each word, in a democratic society, is seen to be made up of individual letters. It's true of handwriting in an ideological sense that each time you make a word you make it out of letters and not syllables, so why not give each letter its significant potential place in the word? Also because it frees up different pronunciation and different understandings, like s-a-i-d, also r-o-a-m is like that: it's a one-word poem.

printer: aram saroyan / my arm is warm / where e'er I roam…

poet: They group together in these funny ways and it controls the pronunciation.

printer: Of course, however you look at the word dictates how something can be said, like s-a-i-d as sa-yeed.

poet: It gives you a sense of the words as being equal to speech, or hand printing, so you don't look at a page as secondary or even a third remove from reality. There's an insistence on units. Each one is one. The lovely differences among the characters are reduced to this patently false insistence upon their equivalence. The difference in width in letterpress: are the narrow ones more narrow to save space?

printer: No, to have a more natural approximation to handwriting proportions. Our fixed notion of print evolved through copying the scribal tradition. Typewriter is a more primitive means of recording with these symbols. It doesn't have the fluidity of personal communication that typeface could suggest. It's arranged in rows because of the limitations of the machine. I understand your sense of the page when you're typing your works, but if you were to put them in print they don't lose the letter-to-letter or word-to-word relationships that you are worried about.

poet: You do, though. The up/down relationship is distorted.

printer: No, it's more insidious, but the grids you are worried about are just modified in a way that makes them more fluid and legible. Any harmonious typeface is going to make the words look better, more integrated than the typewriter where it's all spread out, hunched in the page. You just can't be too obsessed with the numerology of your lines.

poet: It's how the actual beasts exist in the landscape. It's like changing the relationship among the elements in the page, you don't see it. It's a problem of translation.

printer: How do you envisage someone dealing with your box of cards, *Sentences*?

poet: That's an interesting problem. More of a problem than flipping a page. It's kind of ugly and monumental, you know, and has this tiny little, well, an infinity of possible ways. You can pick it up, look at it, flip it over. Many things don't mean anything and don't appeal to you. Sometimes you can pull out different cards and set them together in different relations, that's one thing I've done with it, to make a wall of different relations among them, and, then you make another one. Each should be complete in itself but have almost intellectually available mechanical access to the others. By putting one next to the other you can make an extended sentence that would be part of a storyline. Actually it's an investigation of narrative. What you can break it down into, then what the units could make, what the building blocks could tell by being either sequenced or just sort of piled up together in a page. Then you remember them.

printer: Do you know about Raymond Queneau's experiments in France in the fifties along those lines of die-cut books and strips of words? Famous books: one's called *Cent Mille Milliards de Poemes*, which means hundreds of thousands of thousands of poems, because there's so many possible little books you can make up out of one book.

*Robert Grenier, Sentences,
Cambridge, Mass: Whale
Cloth Press, 1978*

poet: I don't know what the possibilities are? 500 x 1 x 2 x 3 x 4…I wish I were a mathematician so I could have figured it out.

Look at this, little blossoms coming out… It seems to me you have a prejudice in terms of your political and social associations with the typewriter, its correlation of number and what one of the structures might be. The number patterns are based on the visual and intellectual balance of the ones. You get a lot of different effects from that.

Type is like a window. The shape of the world is contributed to by the language forms we have made. I'm like a mathematician who can only think in Arabic numerals. It represents a

paucity of basic elements. It's a fetish. The results gained come from a reformulation of letter values. Rearranging the letters is alchemy.

printer: The Chinese notion of seriality is of individual units: one, one, one, each separate and not a progression.

poet: Right. I was imagining what would be the possible reason to think in terms of one one one one one one. That's so popular now, and I saw that in Creeley. Creeley makes a formal statement of that actually in *Words*: that's how things can be perceived. If you completely reformulate, you deconstruct the various cultural conditions in so far as you are able, or want to, and then you can resynthesize based on one.

A PIECE

one and
one, two,
three.

You can think that however you want — you can think of it as letters, you can think of it as words.

printer: Or drumbeats…

poet: Drumbeats! Oh it's so rhythmic, that's where it comes from.

printer: I was just reading this Williams poem, "The Locust Tree in Flower":

Among
of
green

stiff
old
bright

broken
branch
come

white
sweet
May

again

poet: That's ones.

printer: No, "among" is two. They're all one word per line but the rhythm is a drumbeat because it starts and ends with ba-boom. It has the cymbal smash of "bright" at the end of the first measure so it's like a dance, it's cyclical. The way he breaks it up is defying you to make sense of it as one single long line because he's got it deliberately split into these groups of three.

poet: That's the different beat, "broken" like that. That's a marvellous understanding. The sound is crucial and certainly ones are basic to rhythm in that sense. I think it's built in. I like to think of it that way as having been around for a long time, so the current accommodation to the International Business Machines accident of the Selectric is a bit more...

printer: Well, it's the Trojan Horse of business, or, if only it was. You are the crack in their seamless façade, right?

poet: Anybody living their life is possessed of many cracks nowadays. The ones are built in. We were looking at two skulls, and I was saying that it was quite different from seeing just one, so that the two together and the space between them were essential to the perception of the object. Counting is not an abstract

Robert Grenier, A Day at the Beach, *New York: Roof Books, 1984*

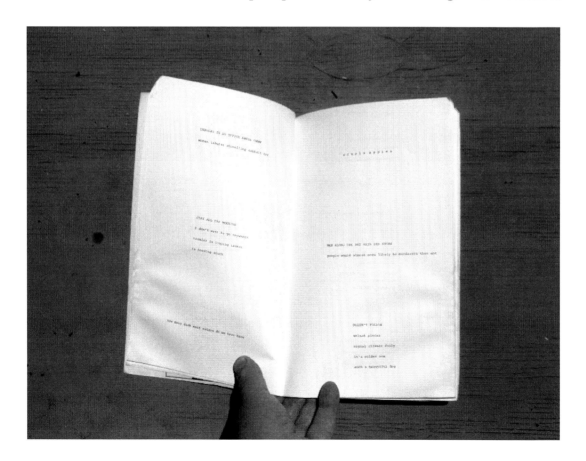

condition at all — it's clear as color or any other sense of the object in its construction as you see it. So to count words or to count letters is a habit of the time, I mean in the particular way it occurs, but the counting is primordial and essential to comprehension and perception of objects. I like the two skulls and would hope to be included as perhaps one of them one day. But you feel your skull alive, like we're sitting together in the car, and the two skulls are in that approximate position right now and there's no real difference. I mean what's the difference? I would hope to be an object in that sense. I like the literal perception of the words next to each other in that functional practical reality of their juxtaposition, and I would see the letters together in the words that way too.

  So that's why I wanted to preserve the ones because if you have proportionate letters then you can't see the independence and togetherness of the letters in the object. Just like looking at the skulls, like "to," *t-o* would be better for them, because you saw the two letters, the *t* and the *o* on the mantelpiece. Together they made the word 'to' by their physical material juxtaposition as letters. Even if they didn't spell it right!

printer: Well, they were Peruvians, they didn't know; they are still learning the language.*

poet: It's very primitive after all, and I hope I can understand that better as I get older.

printer: What do you think about your relationship between yourself and your reader as it manifests on the page?

poet: I have no idea. What reader? I have only my own experience as a reader and I spend a lot of time reading them. We probably read them in the mind while speaking as the reason for selecting them out and writing them down. It should be a little unsettling, and actual, and we look at the objects and they're there and the letter values establish them as objects — in that work, in that sentence, not in the recent stuff, although less so, it's still there. Who knows how much it's still there. How much I'm still sizing up something in relation to its composition by number/letter value. You can do it faster as it becomes habitual. What would be the possible use though? You could run around a swimming pool underwater. I don't know why I'm doing it and what the use is.

printer: Your book *Sentences* has quite a few possibilities for the reader, what about the more controlled landscape of *A Day at the Beach*?

poet: There's a few more of them at least on the same page.

*The skulls on the mantelpiece were ones I brought back from Nazca, Peru.

That was a structured narrative, laid out six poems at a time on the ping-pong table with these various arrangements of six pages set up and various possibilities tried, so that was a structured narrative very consciously constructed. It's great to be able to make a narrative rather than fall into it as if you are on a cliff or something and there's nothing in front of you but spinning around.

printer: Like Gloucester, and you can't see that you're actually standing on the beach...

poet: But think how unnecessary that sequence would be. Once you started spinning around you wouldn't be in any position to alter the circumstances. I wanted to ask you, what was it for example, the typewriter focus — quite apart from whether it had any organic base in the life of any individual — was there more interest or less interest than this other...

printer: The possibilities of typography? My whole comment about your limited bag of tricks?

poet: I wanted to ask you what it was that you could foresee that I could be doing that I wasn't doing that perhaps meant the world to me?

printer: I think I've come to understand why you want to retain control over the final product through its looking as close to your original as possible therefore it being offset from your typescript. It makes a lot of sense because I think in typewriter like you do too. I don't think in terms of the handwritten manuscript page as much as the final typed-up form, whether it's IBM or whatever doesn't matter as long as it has that crisp cleaned-up corporate look. As you said, "to abandon the IBM typeface is to pierce the corporate veil." I agree entirely, but there's so much more that you can do with the suggestive possibilities of typeface beginning with the relationship of the letters to each other, which is this whole basic argument of the ones, the units: the *i* being as wide as the *w* and the *m*. I think of the *m* and *w* as desiring more space and the *i* as being narrower and it changes all the internal relationships. In the typewriter they're all the same width and it creates this *stoichedon* layout, this very fixed, grid-like layout. You're worried because you know at a basic level the average Joe printer or typesetter is going to make a mess of your word-to-word and line-to-line layout. That's very important to you because you know in a typewriter you hit the return and you get the equivalent of a blank line and there are big spaces between the words, so with a typewriter the layout is much airier. You could in fact achieve that look with certain typefaces such as Stymie, it's kind of mechanistic but would appeal to someone who liked typewriters.

poet: You have vouchsafed considerable determination of heartfelt commitment, and so what I can say is that what I understand that you're saying — and correct me if I'm wrong — is that if one looked at the letters one could see that the *i* was thinner than the *m*, and when you write something the hand sees it, the eye sees it, and so the objection to the typewriter spacing is that it makes this mindless monolithic grid out of our, in fact, much more measured and weighed and balanced and felt and realized notions of how wide something is, so I agree, ultimately. I could also say I've been blindfolded, I've been prejudiced by the propaganda of the utterance of the commercial usability and accidental quality of the equivalence of letters, and that's me. Some people would say that they're something else, that they're just genetic makeup or they're... I could say that I just happened to fall into the awful corporate grid of my time.

printer: Oh dear. Let me quote you to you: "Look how your moving your hands across the page will describe what you're doing which opens up all the words." So I'd like to ask you one last question on the possibility of extending your horizons...

poet: I can't help but remark on how literal the fact of the tape recorder has become. Whether it's working or whether we have any tape, in terms of what we might say, in terms of how far we can go, and to what extent we're alive, so this is like the Selectric.

printer: No, we've blown it. They'll think we're dead.

poet: No, it's just the way it is. People are always in that condition and they run into obstacles, co-workers, and so on. But this is not bad. It's like Heraclitus: "The world is at war." It's not a negative condition, it's just what you're born into. It's the basic sense of the harshness of boundaries and conditions that everyone lives in. But you see we're still alive and it's all soft grey matter with certain spiritual overtones.

WALTER HAMADY

Like many young poets, Walter Hamady had a vision of publishing his own work, but once he mastered the art of letterpress his vision expanded to include papermaking and experimenting with the form of the book. He founded Perishable Press Ltd in 1964 in Detroit and soon found a base in Mt Horeb, Wisconsin. Among the Press' early publications are Robert Creeley's Words *(1965) and Robert Duncan's* Six Prose Pieces *(1966). He taught Art at the University of Wisconsin in Madison and ignored the banks of type and Vandercook presses in the studio until he would come in and find the students exploring them. Many of his former students fell under the spell of letterpress and produced works that mimic Hamady's own, which are heavily impressed in varied shades in textured, colourful handmade paper. His work in collage led to assemblage and he now creates whimsical boxes containing curious ephemera and fragments of found detritus that engage his attention. He is a pioneer of the artists' book movement and forever changed the appearance of private press books in America. This interview took place in the Hamadys' home in Mt Horeb on 6 June 2011 in the presence of his wife Anna.*

AMJ: Robert Runser was your teacher, right?

WSH: Yes. The iron press. Didn't I talk to you about him last night? Printing on the handpress with Kenji Akagawa.

AMJ: And you were cursing at each other…escalating racial epithets. So what were you going to tell me about Robert?

WSH: The story I was going to tell you about Robert is he had this print shop in a small horse stable out in back of his house. There was lots of type in there, lots of electro cuts, he had a tabletop Albion, and he had some kind of iron press from the Cincinnati typefoundry and the staple had broken so he had someone repair it with steel plate and bolts all the way across the top. It printed like greased lightning: it was great. But the joke always was that when I would leave, because I would work in his shop a lot, that I had to weigh in and weigh out, so I didn't have my pockets full of type. And you, stealing everything you can get your hands on it this house and out in the barn, invoked that. That's why I pointed to that scale in the barn.

AMJ: But then you just fed me a lot of food so I have definitely gained weight. Who else was your teacher?

WSH: Nobody. I am really autodidactic. My example, the guy who really started my interest in it, was of course Harry Duncan. I've written about this and we've talked about it before. I think you asked me to write an "in memoriam" for Harry Duncan. I was asked by Harry to give a keynote address for his fiftieth anniversary…

AMJ: At Omaha? I was there.

WSH: Do you remember my talk? I had a slide projector, and a screen, but I didn't have any slides. They were all atwitter about it. I think that everybody had had enough wine otherwise I would have been tarred and feathered, but I started out with, "This is a view from outer space looking at the planet, and this is the Olduvai Gorge, where man began…" and I made up some fake Latin, *Duncani homo* something, and then, "Next slide: Here's the Nile River, and as the Duncans moved up downriver they passed by the papyrus patches and they saw people making paper. Next slide: We are on the silk road heading to China and Japan and learning about printing, and then, next slide: Here we are at the Sargasso Sea, heading back to the United States…" and someone said, "You've got that one upside down," and they started to catch on: "That one's out of focus!" And fortunately Harry and his family were sitting there and Anna was sitting with them, and lucky for me they thought it was funny. So I got away with it. After I did that foolishness, I said, "You guys have been kissing Harry's ass for days around here, giving him such a big head I think somebody had to talk some sense." And after that, Kimber Merker made some comments, the meaning of which was 'I should have given this keynote talk, not you: I've spent all this time in Iowa City and you're from Michigan or someplace. Even though your mother is from Keokuk and Harry's from Keokuk.' I imagine that was part of the reason Harry and I hit it off, because he knew my mother. He knew my aunts and my uncle. He was about the same age as my uncle, who was a real horse's ass: a military guy who spent his whole life in the army and got out of there as a something star general. I think he's still alive down in Texas. But, Alastair, I don't know what all you want to know with all this stuff, I thought you knew everything.

AMJ: No, I am curious about why and how people become artists. What did you do as a little boy that was artistic? Did you draw?

WSH: Yes, I did everything?

AMJ: Did you make books?

WSH: No. But I think back about my boyhood and I here I am at the other end of my life, and I realize that everything I've ever done creatively my entire life has all been the same. There isn't one iota of difference between digging in the dirt with a spoon, playing with little toys by the side of the house where I grew up, and creating great empires in mud. Defending it from, who the hell knows what? And all of it was just a vehicle to get out of your body, to be somewhere else. And you know, you're making a book, you're setting type, you're writing poems, you're collaging stuff, you're putting stuff together, arranging, anything…

AMJ: You go into a trance?

WSH: Right. You don't know where you are. A friend of mine I don't think I've ever mentioned to you, is an old dairy farmer friend named Ivan Staley. He was a smart guy and a smarty-pants guy, a good dairyman, a good animal husbandman, and we spent a lot of time together doing this that and the other thing, and I learned a lot from him. And one year — every year in Madison they have this World Dairy Expo, and he wanted to know if I wanted to go and be part of, or watch the judging of the Holsteins, and I said "Yeah" and we went and got a seat and they started judging these big huge black and white cows and I thought, Wow, this is really something because they are talking about all these specifics that they are looking for in each animal — for femininity, her hips, her teats, the equivalent of a beauty contest. It was fantastic, and when we left he was shocked. He said, "I didn't think you were gonna like that." I said, "What are you talking about? It's making aesthetic judgment about something — what the hell difference does it make? It could be dogs, it could be flowers." So I told him at one point, I said, "Ike, I think you are an artist." He looked at me puzzled and I said, "If Art is the arranging of certain stuff in a certain space with a certain aesthetic end in mind, you're an artist, because you are working with these Holsteins and you are trying to bear in mind where you are trying to go with shape and color and proportion, all that stuff." And he said in his typically humble way, "Well, I always thought art was something you hung on the wall, but I see your point."

AH: And he lived to be 90-what?

WSH: I think six. He was the guy who came down in the very beginning and drove my old tractor with the tree-planting gizmo on the back I borrowed from the Department of Natural Resources and he would drive and I'd be back on the thing — it's a really cool machine — it's just a trailer with a seat on it and two square buckets on each side and in front there's this huge coulter. Just a plain round sharp coulter. And that would cut the sod and then behind was a plowshare that was hollow behind it, so the plow would then lift the sod up and then you would put the seedling in the slot that was opened for you, and under your seat were two wheels that were facing each other and they would come along and press the opening shut. If you were gonna be anal you could have somebody walking along behind and heeling in anything that was crooked. But it was pretty efficient, and it was so lovely because you were going along and sometimes you'd hit bedrock, or hit a boulder or something, and the plow would scrape and always make a certain noise, and smoke would come out of the hole. Of course, sometimes you'd go flying. And Ike would love that, love to buck you off the damned thing. He loved getting it on a real steep side hill, and in fact one guy was riding, he was pulling the roots apart and handing them to me so I could put them in faster, and it got so steep he got off. This guy had been on a tractor his whole life and he's not going anywhere where it's gonna roll. Anyway, we are up there and it's all open-grass meadow and Ike stops the tractor and he comes back, and he'd always push the bill of his cap up and look at you in the eye and say, "Say…" and that meant 'I am gonna talk to you, so pay attention.' He said, looking around at all this grassy meadow, "Don't you think you should have some drive roads through this woods, so you could take your children for a sleigh-ride?" And I'm looking around and thinking, "I don't have any children. Where the hell's the woods? I don't have any horse, I ain't got no sleigh," and I said, "Yeah, it'd be a good idea." And he proceeded to continue to plant and every time he'd come to this imaginary road he'd lift me up and go across the road and put me in again. Back and forth, back and forth. So, nothing happened for years — it takes like seven years for the damned trees to get up over the grass and then they get bigger and bigger — and every forester who has come here to inspect the planting and all this stuff, they always compliment me: "Walter you really had foresight. Most guys they just plant from fenceline to fenceline and then they can't get in there and they can't work on their woods." Then I have to confess it was Ike.

AMJ: …and his vision of the sleighride.

WSH: So I think of all these things like that and all these trees that you plant, and so many of them are dying or have died of disease. So many of them are damaged by wind storms and disease.

AH: We went and had a sign made "Ivan Staley Woods" when Ike was still living. Walter and I took him over, very emotional, and we took a picture of him in front of it.

WSH: The typeface was Neuland and it's sandblasted into a inch and a half hunk of ash that was cut here and taken by wagon by Ivan and me to an outdoor sawmill about nine miles from here. That's another lovely story, so this is looping. Anyway, when he saw the photo, he wanted that in his casket and that's where it was. And that day he showed me how you load logs on a wagon: you wrap chains around them and then you use your foot and a front-end loader and it pulls like a yo-yo and the log rolls up and it's on the wagon. So we had a stack of ash and oak and we drove my little tractor and the wagon to this sawmill. It was in November, and it's normally really cold but it was a beautiful day, sunny and great clouds and not that cold. And he was standing on the tongue with his butt on the front end of the wagon and every time I'd look back he was looking dreamy. He looked so happy and I asked him, "Ike, what are you thinking about back there? You look really happy." He said he was thinking about when he was a boy, his dad had a hot temper and they would rent a farm and then the father would invariably get into an argument with the landowner and they'd have to move. They'd load all their worldly goods onto a wagon and he, being a little boy, would get on top of all the worldly goods and he'd ride to the next farm, and that's what he was thinking about.

AMJ: Remembering the promise of new horizons.

WSH: We were sitting out on the porch and he waved his hand and he said, "This is my church. All it needs is a few Holsteins."

AMJ: A congregation. Did you know Robert Shaftoe?

WSH: Yes, he was a friend of Robert Runser, and that's how I knew him. In Detroit those two guys and another half dozen more, they were all guys who seemed old at the time but were probably in their forties and fifties, and they were all involved in the printing business, in one way or another, either with presses, type or paper. They met on a regular basis in Dearborn, Michigan, where the Henry Ford Museum is, in Greenfield Village, and they went there and they restored all those antique presses to perfect working order. Every month they had someone come and speak to them about printing or typography, and every year they did a little calendar. They called themselves the Monks & Friars, and each one of them did a month. They were all pretty bad, lousy printers.

AMJ: Right, but they loved it.

WSH: They loved what they were doing, very enthusiastic, and they were very nice to me. And I was, you know, a punk kid, half or a third their age, just starting out, not knowing very much if anything.

AMJ: But you taught yourself. How did you learn about typography?

WSH: By doing it. I'll tell you how I started printing. Robert Runser, his day job was he was the chief of the technology library of the main public library of Detroit, and the main public library was right across the street from Wayne State University where I was an undergraduate.

AMJ: What were you studying?

WSH: Studying? Right, yeah. Chasing girls and important stuff like that. All I wanted to do was make art, chase girls and make art. My mother had a friend who was a librarian, a musicologist named Larry Brown and he gets mentioned in *Gabberjab Number 4* on the bastard title-page because one time at the dinner table he said to me, "Walter you are a real bastard," and my mother who was sitting there puffed up and she said, "He is *not* a bastard. I know who his father is, and we were married at the time!" Anyway, Larry was in the music library and he fed me lots of great ephemera and junk for collage because people would leave the library scrapbooks of their great European tour, and so anything that was duplicated they'd just throw it away. So he gave it to me and I harvested lots of tickets and cool stuff.

Anyway, when I found out that books were printed, that somebody made books, like Harry Duncan, if you don't know that story I'll tell it to you. Larry said, "this guy in the library, Robert Runser, knows how to print. He lives out in the country, he's an eccentric and a recluse and maybe you should go see him." So I went over to his office and I said, "I understand you know how to print." He said, "Uuuurp, uurrrn." Not very talkative. I said, "I want to make a book, I want to know how to do that," so he excused himself, went into the stacks and came back with John Ryder's *Printing for Pleasure* and one of the Pitman bookbinding things that was done by Sandy Cockerell's father, so he sent me away with these two books, and I arranged to do an independent study in the Art Department at Wayne. There was a Chandler & Price printing press in there. So I bought some type from the Detroit Typefoundry. I read in the book, "Type is set upside down and backwards…" So I get the jobstick and I put the type with the face down and the feet up, and I set a line and I go to the book and I say, "How the hell can you tell what you're doing?" So that's how I started. When the time came in typography to show the kids how to set type, I'd say, "You know, it says in the book 'Type is set upside down and backwards…'" and I'd tell them the story!

I was also taking creative writing with Keith Waldrop with whom I am still in touch. He's a lovely guy, and his wife Rosmarie. You know the poet Donald Hall? Every year Keith had a poetry contest and that year Donald Hall came over and was the judge and I won, so I was encouraged that my poetry was not god-awful, so I thought I would do a book of my own poetry and did *The Disillusioned Solipsist*.

AMJ: That's your first book?

WSH: Mmhmm. And I bought some shitty bond paper, I had no idea really how to bind it. And I started making my first 10,000 mistakes. You know, typos, and imposing incorrectly. I illustrated it with two original hand-wiped etchings and two linecuts of drawings I'd made and a print of a color photograph I had made on the Staten Island Ferry. I bound it in French pastel paper. And I printed the ad for it before I printed the book. I didn't even have that typeface. I went to a type shop and said, "Could you set me some type in Craw Modern?" And they said, "We don't have it but we can get a font and do it for you." So they bought a font and had enough to do three lines, and they'd tear it down and do three more lines. Then I gave them a print of one of my drawings and they did the paste-up and did a mounted plate.

AMJ: A zinc?

WSH: A zinc, and I printed it and I sent it out to people and said, I am going to do this book and the price is ten dollars until May the 15th, after that date the price goes up to sixty-five dollars. I didn't have any money, so believe it or not, a whole bunch of people sent me checks for ten bucks. I mean a font of type wasn't even ten bucks, it was like five dollars or something, so I was making money…

AMJ: And you hadn't done anything?

WSH: I hadn't done a thing!

AMJ: It's a racket.

WSH: Definitely. So then I started learning how to print on this clamshell, and eventually through trial and error started learning about inking, how to lay the ink, and line tension. Robert Runser was not a good printer. His eyesight was not very good, number one, and he had the early signs of Parkinsons, that finally carried him off. And he was also very frugal, and he and Shaftoe and their wives would travel the backroads, all over the Midwest — Ohio, Indiana, Illinois, Michigan — looking for old newspapers and old printshops. They'd stop in every little town and they'd ask, "Was there ever a newspaper here? What happened to it?" And they did their research (before the age of the computer) and they'd haul back incredible stuff. Mostly they were after type: wood type and antique metal type. Not so much equipment because by the time I knew them they already had all the equipment. So that was fun. Robert Shaftoe was also conservative and I remember I made a Lebanese meal for Robert and his wife at their house, where I spent a lot of time working at his shop, and Robert Shaftoe came in. I made some tabouleh and stuff and he said, "What's the matter with plain lettuce?" I said, "There's nothing the matter with plain lettuce. What's the matter with chopped tomatoes and parsley and cracked wheat and onions? And cinnamon and allspice and lemon juice and olive oil?" He was a sweet guy but kinda, you know…

AH: Didn't the University at Madison buy his press?

WSH: Well, Shaftoe died young of leukemia, and his wife was unloading a lot of that stuff. She was selling wood type and selling old cuts and job cases and Robert felt badly, he didn't want all that wonderful collection to be dispersed and so he tried to place it. The Detroit Historical Museum had just bought another guy's complete collection: they didn't need it, so that's when I got the bright idea to see if the University of Wisconsin would buy it and set up a print shop in the library that would be an interdisciplinary shop. Because the one thing, obviously, binding all the disciplines are books, and the printed word. It was at the time. So, it took a lot of doing, but the amount of money wasn't that immense. I think it was twenty grand max, and it was easy to get because the director of the library went to see the chancellor for a special Excellence of the University fund, and someone had just gone in there from the music department and had got approval for a fifty-thousand dollar violin. One little violin. This guy walks in: it's a whole print shop for only twenty grand! So it was got and all kinds of booby traps and shit happened and it never did fly. The closest it ever got to flying was when Barb Tetenbaum was the proprietrix, and she was shrewd and savvy — she was tight with the money — she's skillful, she knew how to print, she recognizes a good impression, knows about manipulating ink and so on. And she actually created a surplus of funding in the Silver Buckle account and they took it away from her to use for moving the press from one place to another, which is illegal. The University has another fund to move anything. And they wouldn't let her teach so she went off to the Oregon School of Arts & Crafts. She took a knock in pay but she wanted to teach.

AMJ: So how did you go from being self-taught, working with type upside down, to getting in touch with people like Hermann Zapf, Reynolds Stone, Sandy Cockerell? I mean these are big names in the fine book world.

WSH: They were just people doing stuff.

AMJ: So you just wrote to them?

WSH: No, as a matter of fact, somebody was in the US Army, and they were in Germany. And they must have been loving poetry.

AMJ: Are you talking about Jonathan Williams?

WSH: No. He is old, man. Hell no, he was never in the army anyway. He could never pick up a backpack, let alone shoot a gun! I don't think he ever saw his penis for forty years, he was so fat!

AH: Pardon my ignorance, but how famous was Bobby Shaftoe? I mean, we used to jump rope to that song, "Bobby Shaftoe's gone to sea..."

AMJ: The guy you jumped rope to lived in the eighteenth century. They just happened to have the same name. He probably didn't go by Bobby but he was smart enough to use the name for his press.

WSH: When finally the Silver Buckle Press became an entity, they invited Robert Shaftoe's widow to come over and they presented her a silver buckle with some words on it that they'd made in the art metal studio. She was very impressed with me: she had thought I was just a scatter-brained wild crazy-assed liberal guy.

Anyway, somebody visited Hermann Zapf in Germany and showed him some of my books, and I was using…

AMJ: Palatino. All your books for ten years were in that.

WSH: Exactly. People would say, That's Mr Hamady's favorite face. Well, it's not my favorite face at all.

AMJ: It's all you had.

WSH: The reason I got it is, I went on a trip for Robert Runser to pick up some type and some equipment: a small treadle press that had a very ornate casting on it, from some guy somewhere in Delaware. So I had a big Ford station wagon, and I picked it up, and those cases I have in the other room were from that guy's basement, and Robert said, "Just lay newspapers on the floor and dump the type on the newspapers, roll them up, put them in the car."

AMJ: Good God!

WSH: How else are you gonna do it? I had tons of wads of all this guy's type. So I got back to Robert's and unloaded all the stuff, and he starts sorting through this type and he said, "This stuff is Palatino, it's too modern for me, maybe you should have it." So I sorted out all this goddamned Palatino.

AMJ: It didn't get bashed up?

WSH: Not noticeably, not that I know of. But at the time I wouldn't have known, all that stuff you're not tuned into anyway at the beginning: chips and dings and missing serifs. So that's how I wound up with the Palatino. Each bundle was one size. It wasn't total pie. So I sorted it out, put it in a case. When people wanted me to do something for them printing-wise, I wouldn't charge them money, I would say, "Buy me a font of type," so they would buy me a font of Palatino. So pretty soon I had a lot of Palatino. I did this book on handmade Shadwell paper. This guy showed it to Hermann, Hermann flipped, he went bonkers. He never saw his type printed so clearly in such rough paper. I think he got in touch with me, to make a comment. When he visited here he said, "I showed printers in Germany your work and they said, 'Ah, he printed it damp.'" And I said, "No, I printed it dry." He said, "You do? I wish you'd put that in your colophons so I can show them." So after Hermann's visit a lot of the colophons say "printed dry…" So that's how I met Hermann and we corresponded. And Paul Duensing knew him, because Paul went to school in Germany. I don't think he studied in Frankfurt, I think he studied in Hamburg. So he knew Hermann because of his interest in letterforms and typography. I actually met Hermann for the first time over there; we met twice. The guy in whose house we met the first time was a professor in some Schule. They had taken all of Stempel's matrices and sample castings and everything, and they'd put it in the basement of this school. The basement was the size of a football field. Walter somebody.

AMJ: Walter Wilkes?

WSH: That sounds like it. And he, I think, got it on with the curator lady of the Gutenberg Museum in Mainz. But you go down into that basement, and talk about saliva! It was dreadful. Not only for the reality of what it was, and the beauty of the casting of that stuff, all the patterns for the pantographic engravers and stuff, oh, I could make collages out the gazoo with this stuff! Give me a screwdriver and a drill press and some epoxy and turn me loose!

Then Hermann was coming to the States going to Kansas City on a regular basis, advising Hallmark Cards and doing shit for them, so I picked him up at the airport and he had a bee in his bonnet. He wanted to go to Parker Pen Company down in Janesville. He wanted this ballpoint pen that they'd just come out with that would make a mark one half of a millimeter; a little fine point. He said, "When can we go to Parker?" I said, "We don't have to go to Parker, we just go to a bookstore." So I get him in there, and he's like a little kid, and he starts writing all this stuff in like three point size with this pen, and he shows me and says, "Look what this pen can do!" And I say, "Look what Hermann can do! Wow! This is really cool." He stayed for a couple of days. The kids were all little. He had a cold. And [my daughter] Laura was suffocating in the car. We had a little Volvo. Did you ever see that film *Five Easy Pieces*? I had a Volvo like the one in there, a little squareback station wagon, a beauty. Two carbs, four cylinders, you couldn't get that thing to spin out. Anyway, there was a hole in the floor in the back. The windows were all up, so Laura's got her face down breathing highway air that was better than the car air!

Hermann could fold his arms behind him, he'd walk along like that. I remember we were sitting on the porch, it was very hot so I asked him if he wanted a beer. And I brought him out a St Pauli Girl, and he said, "Pauli Girl, you know what this is? This is a red light district — these are prostitutes!"

The trip with Paul to Germany, we were in Hamburg. We

stayed with a guy there, a fine printer, though it was all done on a machine. And he did all the printing for the opera, so they had courtesy passes for the opera, any performance, any time. And Paul had lost his *Gepäck*, his suitcase. I refused to change my clothes until his suitcase showed up, so he was traveling in dungarees and looked like a shop rat, and I was traveling in blue jeans too, so here we were at this opera and these people are looking at us, Oh Americans! How snooty can you get? It was great.

When Paul Duensing and this man… His wife's name was Floride. They had this big printshop in downtown Hamburg and they told me about this street that was all prostitutes.

AMJ: The Reeperbahn?

WSH: I don't know. The old guy said, "We'll go down there, and Walter can go in and do his stuff and he can tell us about it." They take me down there. They had gates at each end of the street. All the windows were a little above street level and in each one was a woman, dressed in a white whatever. She's sitting in there waiting for business. I'm looking, thinking "this is ridiculous," I'd never been in such a situation before. My poor old peeny didn't know whether to go up or down. So I didn't have the guts.

So that's how I met Hermann. Then continuing stuff with Hermann, I asked him to calligraph the title-page for my paper-making book, and he got the title wrong. He gave it another title, so I had to give it a double title: I used his piece, then I put my title.

And then back to Robert Runser — these things all loop — Robert hated contemporary poetry, thought it was all jibberjab. One of his tricks was he'd take a newspaper and cut words with a scissors and then he sprinkled them on a piece of paper and glued them down. And he typed it up and sent it, anonymously, to me. He never got a comment from me, and months and months went by, and he finally said, "Did you ever get an envelope with a kind of stream-of-consciousness poem in it?" I said, "Well I did get something that was a piece of shit, and I threw it out." He admitted he'd sent it and was damned sure I was gonna publish it. That's how little he thought of it. He said, "Look, Walter, I really love your printing, I love your paper, and I love your typography, why don't you print something in Greek so no one can read it?" I said, "Come on Robert, people read Greek. It's not dead." So that didn't satisfy him, and some time went by and he said, "Well, what about the Sequoyah syllabary?" And he showed it to me and I thought, "Well, this is pretty interesting." So I got a big brainstorm and I thought, "Why don't I get the world's greatest living type designer/calligrapher, Hermann Zapf, to redesign the Sequoyah syllabary, find a living person who is fluent in Cherokee, who's writing decent work, and do a book, in the Cherokee syllabary, with footnotes, or interlined with English?" So I got a bunch of grant money. Hermann did it. Got more grant money, I found an author: My friend was the chairman of the English department at the University of Oklahoma, and he found this poet named Robert Conley, a genuine Cherokee who had some poems. Got more grant money to get it all digitized, put into the computer, and that got done. Printed it out and looked at it, and it looked like shit. It visually looked terrible. And I thought, "What am I gonna do?"

AMJ: Was it because Zapf is not in touch with the syllabary enough to make a significant improvement on it? I mean it's a weird alphabet, because it's all based on 1801 letterforms, so there's backward fours, upside-down *J*s, and Bodoni Bold *W*s, so you'd really have to take it to another level to make it readable, to make it attractive.

WSH: Well, Hermann did make it attractive. As a specimen, his work is beautiful, he based his redesign on Walbaum. It's beautiful. But the problem is, it turns out — I never would have been able to figure this out on my own — but my friend Patrick Flynn who is a typographic designer, said, "This is a display alphabet: this is not a text alphabet. There's no kerning, there's no fit, there's no flow, and it looks weird.

AMJ: It's an all-cap alphabet.

WSH: There's personally nothing that I can do with it. My friend Flynn is a procrastinator and a slowpoke and it's not gonna happen. He has it, he has the manuscript and it's all in the computer... It would probably make a succesful book: you could start with the story, and you could show Hermann's drawings, and blow some of them up, they are just gorgeous. And do Mr Conley's poems. Another player in this is a former student named Lester Doré. And Lester is a magnificent wood-engraver. He's from Louisiana, and he actually went to look up Robert Conley and his wife to see the scene of the poems and all that, but it's not gonna happen, I don't think.

The other one was... As a result of a show at the Center for Book & Paper at Columbia [College, Chicago], curated by Bill Drendel. I called him up and I said, "You know, Bill, out in the barn I've got several boxes full of student books that were done in my artist book classes, what the hell am I gonna do with them?" And he immediately said, "Let's have an exhibition," and I said, "OK, that's fine." I think within two weeks he was up here with his curator, and we were taking them out of the boxes and showing them, and their jaws were on their chests. They said, "How do you get them to do this stuff?" And I said, "Well in art classes we make up problems to solve, and everyone works to solve the problem. Everyone's solution is different, but can be satisfactory." And I explained about having critiques and cross-critiquing, and making it perfectly plain and clear that

Cherokee alphabet by Hermann Zapf, 1977

it's perfectly OK to steal some of this and some of that to make your book better. So they were amazed. They said, "What were the problems?" So I told them a few. And before the whole thing got done, I wrote them down, and Anna transcribed them, and then she read them to me, and I would make corrections verbally, back and forth.

AH: In the car on our way to Chicago…

WSH: So I wrote out all these problems from all these classes that were all invented, that all had to do with personality and, personal things, and things to do with design, things to do with typography and things to do with structure, and it worked great. So this show happened. They filled up this exhibition space. They asked would I do a talk. I said I won't do a lecture, but I would come and be in the gallery a week or a month after it's been up so the kids have a chance to look at the stuff and have questions.

AMJ: How many books were on show?

WSH: At least fifty, seventy-five. Tons of them. All kinds of crazy shit.

AH: There were students writing down the questions and answers.

WSH: We'd taken a list of my problems, with no explanation, and made a big poster-sized thing and had them on the wall, so the kids were copying all that shit down. So there's a book there. And it's been set by Michael Bixler in 12 point Gill Sans. My problems from thirty years in the classroom.

AH: The only thing that's not done is his snooty spacing.

WSH: I haven't run it through the stick.

AMJ: Snooty spacing, is that what you call it?

WSH: Yes. I run it all through the stick.

AH: Copper thins here and paper thins here…

AMJ: It's gotta look right.

WSH: Well, coppers are too thick sometimes, and some magazine pages are too thick. You know in German type you can buy metal — white metal and yellow metal — and the white is quarter of a point, and the yellow is half a point. Because the paper I cut is in thousandths, it's a little less than a quarter of a point. I would use *Aramco*, a Saudi Arabian publication, for making paper thins, but their paper changes. So the last time there was an article about Walter in the *Wisconsin Academy Review* and that paper was perfect. That was compoundedly crazy because I am picking little pieces of paper out to put in between letters and I find the word Hamady or names of friends. Some of it I've left standing, because I think I am going to give my 12 point Gill to Patrick Flynn, because he's kind of nagged me about it, and I thought to let him have the curse of having this type from four different foundries because the x-height is okay on three, one x-height's…and then the shoulder on them is different. It's terrible. I know that some of the first Gill I bought was Riscatype from Yendall in England.

AMJ: You've got more books in you, Walter.

WSH: I'm not saying it's the end, but probably. Doing that last *Timeline (of Sorts)* was a race with time. It's degeneration of my retina, macular degeneration. You just lose your central vision, period. I don't want to talk about that, it's stupid. What is is, and what ain't ain't.

My friend Bunce once said about these *Gabberjabs*, "They are Walter's autobiography, but they are in code."

One of the things about Bill Bunce was he would buy books, all kinds of interesting artists' books and he'd leave the invoice in them. He'd leave them on a table in front of his office [in the UW Madison Art Library] window. Nobody's gonna steal anything. And every once in a while someone would look at these books and they'd notice the invoice in there, and say, "How can this book be three hundred dollars and this one be fifteen hundred dollars and this one for fifteen hundred dollars be a piece of crap that even an uneducated eye can see…and they would

Desultory liftings from the journals of WSH Hamady / First segment 1963-72, *2010, 80 pages, 80 copies*

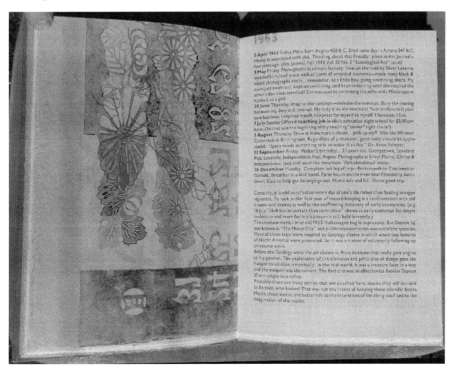

have a discussion, and Bill got to teach somebody about artists' books and cause and effect and value. A good guy.

AMJ: How did you get interested in the Black Mountain poets?

WSH: I didn't know I was. I didn't know what the hell Black Mountain was. I started just loving Robert Creeley. I didn't know where he came from, I didn't know anything about any of that stuff. At Wayne State University that had this Miles Modern Poetry Festival. It was at first one week of poetry readings at noon and in the evening lectures to go with, and then they stretched it to two weeks. And I mentioned I was taking creative writing with Keith Waldrop and he was involved in organizing that stuff, and so Robert Creeley came and gave a reading.

Robert Creeley, Divisions
& Other Early Poems,
Perishable Press Limited, 1968

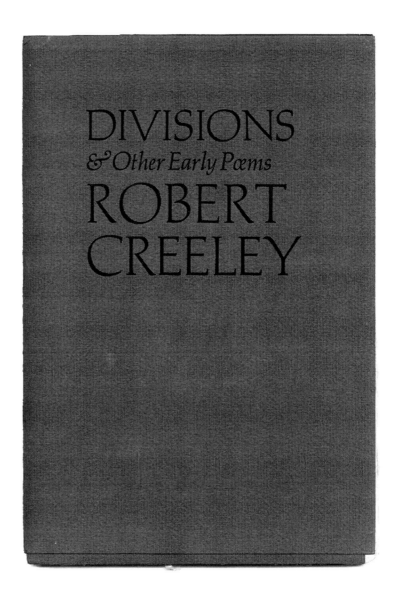

I went to the Black Mountain school. I met all those guys because I was the repairman of the printing press.

AMJ: You're making it up.

WSH: Of course. I only knew Robert Creeley because he came to Wayne State during that Miles Poetry Festival and he gave a reading and I bought his book and I looked at it and there were like two words to a line, or three, and I thought, "What the hell is this?" You know? I went to the reading and listened to him read and it was incredible: it just completely changed my life. I never heard such a thing. The rhythm and the cadence… and he started off on one poem and he didn't get it right and he stopped and said, "Excuse me." And he recomposed himself and he began again and he had it the way he wanted it to go. And after that reading, there's gonna be a reception across the street in this esoteric used bookstore. They would sometimes let you in and sometimes wouldn't. So I went over there and out in front was my teacher Keith Waldrop and his wife and I went up to them and I am just standing there and I started to gush about what an incredible experience I had just had, what a fantastic reading. And I said, "I'm not going in there because I don't know what to say," and Keith said, "Walter I want you to meet someone" and I turned around and Creeley was standing right behind me, and he heard every word I said, and he said, "Come on in, I'll buy you a drink." So we went in the bookstore and he signed my book, and I told him I was learning how to set type and how to print and I was working on a book, and he said, "I would like to see that book," just matter of factly. And when I finished it, I sent him a copy, and I received a very encouraging response. And I think he was that way with everybody, I mean he was extremely encouraging for young people, and then *he* said, "You should read Denise Levertov," and I did, and I wrote her a letter and asked could I publish something. And Levertov led to Nemerov.

I met Paul Blackburn because I read one of his poems in a magazine called *Choice* that came out of Chicago and it had poetry and photographs and other stuff, and I read this poem: the narrator is sitting in a coffee shop in New York, down in the Village probably, and it said the reflection on the glass is reflecting everything inside and there's a Ballantyne Ale truck outside on the street the guy is unloading, and he's talking about the movements of this man and the movement of the waitress and his hands and her body, and so on — it's an absolutely glorious poem. And I thought, "This guy must be an artist, who the hell is this guy?" I didn't know him, I didn't know anything, so I wrote a letter to Paul Blackburn care of the editors of that magazine in Chicago, and goddamn I got a letter from him. He was excited and I must have sent him some stuff that I'd done up 'til that point, and I asked him if he had anything I could publish and he said he had a cycle of poems about a friend who had been beaten to death in the Village and the focus was that bar called McSorley's. That's a wonderful very famous old pre-Civil War bar. It's on a street by Cooper Union, on East 7th Street and Paul lived the eighth door down that street and they were the sixth door. It had sawdust on the floor and an old potbellied stove, everything hanging on the walls was Civil War. They made their own ale: light and dark. They had the biggest urinals you've ever seen in your life, and for years they would not let women in there. So when I was going to school at Pratt in 1959 it was fun to take your girlfriend dressed like a guy and go in there. You were really getting away with something! I mean they knew what the hell was going on.

Now this Black Mountain stuff. Paul gave me that sequence to publish called *The Reardon Poems*, which I did, and I drove to New York and I met him at McSorley's to pay off author's copies. I didn't know about paying off, I mean how do you do that, is there a percentage? Anyway I learned a lot about that from him. And he turned me on to Joel Oppenheimer, and I got to publish a poem by Joel called *A Sirventes on a Sad Occurence*, and Paul explained that a sirventes was a specific form with a sequence of observations on weather and specific rhythms and lines, but Paul said, "I showed Joel this form and he went ahead and wrote one of the best ones that's ever been written." And it is absolutely gorgeous: it's about an old woman coming down some steps on the Lower East Side and she's lost control of her bowels and her daughter is rushing around cleaning it up and then the narrator sees this and he makes a soliloquy about getting old. It's just, in my opinion, absolutely gorgeous. I never knew about Joel's father, but Joel's grandpa was a printer, maybe in the Bronx. Joel fussed with the printing press and was the printer at Black Mountain. Maybe the Oppenheimer affinity for printing skipped his father's generation, but Joel had a fascination with printing and the press, so I think that when he knew what I was up to we had an extra-special handshake.

But I wasn't following anything. I had an arrangement with the bookstore near Wayne, around the corner. Every new book of poetry that would come in they would just set it aside, and when I came in I would look it over and if I liked it I could take it away and keep it and pay for it. So I got to read a lot of stuff that otherwise I wouldn't have known about, so that was helpful. So what else?

AMJ: Is that how you discovered George Oppen?

WSH: I'm not sure, that was through James Laughlin I think.

AMJ: And how did you know him?

WSH: Through Denise Levertov. See it's all scrambled up. I did something of Denise's, a broadside to start with. I went to New York for some reason, Denise invited me for lunch to her place down in the Village. It was in the winter with tons of snow, very snowy. I went in and shortly thereafter appeared this very tall man in this very shaggy sheepskin coat that hadn't

Paul Blackburn's The Reardon Poems *(Perishable Press Limited, 1967) was set in Palatino and Michelangelo and bound by Elizabeth Kner*

THE
REARDON
POEMS
PAUL
BLACK-
BURN

———————

THE PERISHABLE PRESS LIMITED
JANUARY TWENTY-FOURTH
MCMLXVII MADISON

been trimmed, covered with snow. It was J Laughlin. So Denise introduced me as a good young poet and he said, "I would like to see your work," and I said, "Well I just happen to have my life's work in my car! So I went out in my little Volkswagen bug and brought in all the books that I'd published. Not many, but one of them was the *Plumfoot Poems*, so that would have had to be '67, something like that. He started looking them over right away, and he said, "Why haven't you sent me something for my *Annual*?" I said, "I don't know about your annual, what annual?" He'd been doing an annual since forever putting young unknown people together in there, so he wound up putting my "Plumfoot Poems" in the next *Annual*. And he insisted on buying all those books, and I tried to insist on giving them to him, I said, "In homage, in respect of what you have published and who you've published, and how many New Directions books I own." He insisted, absolutely not, he said he knows what it's like to publish on a shoestring. So he bought all those books, and placed a standing order. I published a book of his poetry too. It was good.

AMJ: Where did he get his money?

WSH: He inherited it from his dad, it was the Laughlin-Jones Steel Company in Pittsburgh, so he came from a very well-endowed family. There's a great book about him called *The Way it Wasn't*. You should read it. I'd show it to you but you'd get distracted and I would talk about him and not talk about me.

AMJ: Did Jonathan Williams have independent means as well?

WSH: Slight. He was always whining and chiseling and begging for money.

AMJ: That's because he published really obscure writers. Some of whom were great — Lorine Niedecker, Mina Loy, Gilbert Sorrentino's first book — but remained great obscure poets.

WSH: I learned about Paul Metcalf from Jargon. But I don't want to talk about him either.

AMJ: You mentioned this show you had in Chicago of your ex-students, and when you think about people like Amos Kennedy, Michael Myers, the Red Ozier guys [Ken Botnick and Steve Miller], Barb Tetenbaum. Can you really say there's no Walter Hamady School of Books?

WSH: Absolutely. There's a Walter Hamady school of bullshit, of bullshitters who say there is this school. There is no school. Amos Kennedy is a great bullshit artist who learned from another bullshit artist.

AMJ: He learned from the master.

WSH: We had a lot of fun in the classroom. Every class he'd bring up something about the racial inequality going on. When he left I said, "Amos, I am really gonna miss team-teaching with you." He always had something to the point. All these white-bred kids, they didn't know nothing. It was great because he had stuff that was sometimes pretty damned shocking, but totally relevant. Anything that ever came up in the classroom was game to me. He published *Nappy Grams.*

AH: They were wonderful.

WSH: It was right on; it was damned good. He was always fun.

AMJ: Did you ever experience racism against you?

WSH: Yes, I still do, but sometimes it's not quote "being Middle Eastern," it's being Jewish! They don't know what the hell I am! *He ain't one of us!*

There's a painter named Sam Gilliam. He's pretty dark. I said, "Is your real name Sam?" He said, "When you're Jewish your name is Samuel, but when you black your name's Sam! At one point he said, "Walter — he ain't one of us, but he ain't exactly one of you neither." That's a pretty good compliment.

My biological father wanted to show his new bride from whence he had cometh. He was a pork-barrel government guy. He had a diplomatic passport and had to travel first class. He wouldn't fly, so he took me and my sister, I was sixteen or seventeen. We went across on the *SS United States*, first class, and went through Paris and Geneva and Milan, Venice, Bari, Piraeus, Athens, Alexandria and then Beirut. And everyplace people would come up to me and talk to me like I was a native. This happened over and over, and I get to Lebanon and I am with my cousin, and a friend of his says to him in Arabic, "Who's the Jew?" How do you like that? Talk about stupidity and prejudice.

AH: But the girls were crazy about him on the ship. He wore suits and ties…

WSH: The ship coming back was one class and it carried freight and passengers, had a swimming pool, maybe 125 people, and it stopped it all these ports in the Mediterranean and you could get off in one port and train or however you wanted, and catch the ship at the next port. I was the only eligible guy. That was fun but I didn't get anywhere. They were all too clever.

AH: But there was one girl who was crazy about you?

WSH: That was on the first ship, and she wasn't crazy about anyone but herself. Her name was Lilly Claire Berghaus and she was one of the many heirs of the Budweiser thing, and there was a waiter named Nick, and my dad had crossed back and forth on this ship so many times he knew everybody. And so this waiter would come to me and say, See that blonde over there? She's dying to dance with you. Then he'd go to the blonde and say, "See that young man over there in the tuxedo? He's just dying to dance with you." So I thought, This dame is dying to dance with me! So with all the confidence in the world, Mr Braggadocio himself, I go over and we go dancing. I didn't know the guy was playing both ends. I wound up drinking champagne out of her shoe in the lifeboat. And of course making a point, any time beer came up, of saying I hated Budweiser. Anything but Budweiser.

AMJ: So you got her in the lifeboat?

WSH: I didn't get anywhere. Just dumb, you know, you're drunk, and this waiter kept bringing the champagne out.

AMJ: And she was paying for it?

WSH: No, my dad was paying for it. The next day my dad asked, "What were you drinking?" "Oh, Piper-Heidsieck '49." "Oh, and how much did you have?" "Uh, several bottles." "And who paid for it?" "You did. I don't have any money." He didn't say "Dutch treat."

So let's go back to these students.

AMJ: What about Michael Myers?

WSH: Michael was a good guy.

AMJ: Hell-bent on self-destruction.

WSH: Yes, but still a good guy and a good artist. He made wonderful linoleum cuts. My colleagues gave him shit for being psychedelic or whatever, and I said I don't give a damn, look at this carving here! This is accurate wonderful linoleum carving, I don't care what his imagery is. He loved printing, he loved drawing. He was extremely bashful, almost to the point of painfulness to hear him talk, but I don't think he ever thought of working in that typography classroom as the School of Hamady.

AMJ: It was just access to equipment?

WSH: Exactly. That'd what it was: it was a forum, everything was on the table. I've written about that in that catalogue Karen Heft did. Karen was a student in 6451, the number on the classroom. She commuted from Racine to Madison to take typography and artists books and she added so much to the class because she was smart, she was older, had a great perspective, and she had a lot of connections. When we got to pop-up books she knew those people in Western Racine who made pop-up books. She brought one of the paper engineers over and showed examples and the guy explained all this shit was done in Cali,

Colombia, in this certain industrial building by Colombian women who wore white gloves, and they assembled all these damned pop-up books. And that's where all the pop-up books at that time were being made, before even Singapore.

   Anyway she thought there should be a show of all the people who had worked in 6451, so she curated it and left herself out, and got donations to produce a catalogue. And of all the people in there, there aren't many of them who are still printing. Some of them are dead, some gave up the ghost, some went commercial, and I'm told there are a lot of people who weren't in there were pissed off thinking they should be and I keep saying, over and over, that "taking a class with" does not constitute "working with." "I worked with Hermann Zapf." I did? It doesn't mean anything. It's annoying because of all this great robust army of the School of Hamady people all over the place, if any of them are in institutions, not one of them has ever invited me to come and be a visiting fireman (for an honorarium), not one has ever had their library buy copies of my books to have as a teaching example or something. That's what a great teacher I am in this School of Hamady.

AMJ: You did a lot of work with Bill Anthony, the bookbinder.

WSH: He was a honey of a man. He was an Irishman who trained in England, at a time when there was a lot of prejudice against the Irish by the English.

AMJ: There still is.

WSH: And he wound up in Chicago. Once I made the mistake of thinking I was being considerate about time and cost and stuff and I said, "Hey, I don't know what your schedule is like, but maybe you could bind half of these and bind the other half later, or maybe I could help in some way." Thank God I wasn't here to answer the phone, because he called up and said, "You tell that goddamned dah-dah-dah…" and I was reduced to the size of a…

AMJ: A Leprechaun's toenail.

WSH: Or less. He said, "Just tell him there's one hopping mad Irishman at the other end of this line!"

AMJ: Did Elizabeth Kner bind books for you?

WSH: She did the very first hardcover book, that Robert Creeley book, called *Words*, there were thirty five; she did that Robert Duncan book, oh my, she did a lot of books… She was no Bill Anthony, believe me. She could do incunabula very well, but edition binding not so well, for a whole bunch of reasons.

AH: Being repetitive is not easy.

WSH: Of course not, it's very hard. Sandy Cockerell loved to get an edition in to bind, he said, because it loosened up his crew. They were used to doing incunabula for Cambridge, so to get an edition for these guys to do one hundred or 125 that was great, because they had to kick ass and pay attention.

AMJ: So they didn't just do marbled paper, they did edition binding, and you hired them?

WSH: Absolutely.

AMJ: That must have been expensive!

WSH: Yeah, very expensive! I told you, my mother never balanced her checkbook, and I never learned to say, "How much would that be?" All I knew to ask was, "Can you do this?"

AMJ: So that book, *Maps*, by Toby Olson, with leather spine, marbled boards, that's by them?

Robert Duncan's Six Prose Pieces *was printed on Robert Runser's press near Rochester, Michigan in 1966 (drawing by the author)*

WSH: Yes, and they did a WD Snodgrass book under his pseudonym of SS Gardons, and they did a Paul Blackburn book, one called *Gin*; I think he did five or six books: Galway Kinnell, *Collected Poems*.

AMJ: So you would ship the sheets to England? And they would sew, case and ship it back? Weren't you afraid something would happen between here and there and back again?

WSH: No. But something did happen once, and it's in that book *A Timeline of Sorts*, where the US customs stopped a shipment because Sandy insured it for some outrageous amount of money, and so customs impounded it saying it couldn't come into the country because it was of foreign manufacture, because it was

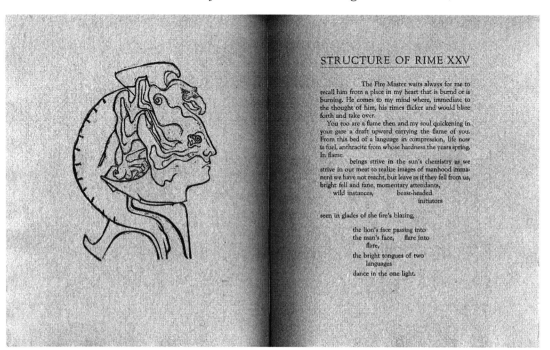

STRUCTURE OF RIME XXV

The Fire Master waits always for me to recall him from a place in my heart that is burnd or is burning. He comes to my mind where, immediate to the thought of him, his rimes flicker and would blaze forth and take over.

You too are a flame then and my soul quickening in your gaze a draft upward carrying the flame of you. From this bed of a language in compression, life now is fuel, anthracite from whose hardness the years spring, In flame

beings strive in the sun's chemistry as we strive in our meat to realize images of manhood imminent we have not reacht, but leave as if they fell from us, bright fell and fane, momentary attendants, wild instances, beast-headed initiators

seen in glades of the fire's blazing,

the lion's face passing into the man's face, flare into flare,

the bright tongues of two languages

dance in the one light.

Toby Olson, Maps, *Mt Horeb,
WI: Perishable Press Limited,
1969*

bound in England. I couldn't believe it. At that time my father was a big-shot government official in Washington, and so he pulled strings and made lots of trouble, and I was able to get it through customs, pay whatever I had to pay, got it to Mt Horeb, and a whole box was missing, so the US customs people owed me a fortune and they had to pay. And I thought, "That's what happens when you fuck with the Druze! Fuck with North-American Druze mutations, you no win."

It's almost as bad as seeing a guy with a kilt in downtown San Francisco. You don't say, "Hey! what are you doing down here?" You just say "Ah, oh yeah, the Shrine circus is in town," whatever you want to say, and you just pass by, pass by: you don't say anything.

And, Alastair, you'll be pleased to know the second time I visited Cambridge and stayed in Sandy and Elizabeth's, he had a hydraulic gold stamping press in his personal shop, and it was the hydraulic landing gear from a German war plane that had been shot down. He was a clever son-of-a-bitch, and his cousin invented the hovercraft. Not a dumb family. So the second time I visited Cambridge, I took this very long hot soak bath in the bathroom and went to bed and during the night the ceiling caved in.

I am sure the steam loosened it after hundreds of years. That was a very lovely old country house. The plaster had to have been an inch and a half thick. And if somebody had been in that bathtub you would have been injured, no question about it. Crash! The thing I learned from Elizabeth Cockerell, when she got excited she'd say "Blow me!" And I thought, "What the…?"

"Blow me!" They had a great Aga stove in their kitchen, and I learned the word "joint." "We have a joint in the oven." She was an absolute honey, and so was he.

 You know, Alastair, I have had an extremely fortunate life. You know that, I can tell it, because your complexion has gone from caucasian to reptilian green. People would say, "Walter, you've had such a tragic life because of all these terrible things, your parents divorced and so on." Come on, man, the important stuff really sticks.

 Did you ever read the book, *The Gnostic Gospels*, by Elaine Pagels? Look, I don't give a rat's ass about organized religion, and I read a profile about her in *The New Yorker*, about the loss of her Swiss husband who made a mis-step off a Swiss mountain. The writing and the story about her and the loss of her husband in that way it just broke my heart. And it talked about her book that was the first scholarly book ever to become a best seller, so I read it and it was fascinating, it was very interesting. It was about the evolution of Christian testament, and I couldn't help but think, in the ninth and tenth centuries there was all this struggle going on to try to regularize all this stuff, and that's about the time that the Druze got their shit going, and I always wondered where did those guys fit into all this stuff.

 This business of keeping a journal. When Anna started transcribing, after she transcribed '71, which was big motor mouth, I said, "Hey, I don't know what this is, I need to find a professional editor to tell us what this is." So I wrote a letter to the only professional editor I knew, who was Peter Glassgold at New Directions. We did a book of his, I don't want to get off the track, but it was fascinating it was called *Hwæt!* with an exclamation.

AMJ: From Anglo-Saxon. It's the first word of *Beowulf.*

WSH: Exactly. He had back-translated poems by Black Mountain people back into Anglo-Saxon, and lots of those concepts did not exist in Anglo-Saxon language, and of course the typographic figures don't exist except in Icelandic nowadays, so I was stuck doing this book. And I thought, "Wow this is crazy, everybody translates from ancient shit into now, but who the hell takes now back to ancient?" And he did it. And when I got to setting it, and Paul Duensing cut and manufactured the letters that I needed, so I could do this book, it was kick-ass, it was brilliant. Not only a hoot and hilarious, but intellectually incredibly significant if you think about it.

 So I wrote to Peter and said, "Hey, I am doing the transcription of this journal and we need some help, could you recommend an editor." So unbeknownst to me he sent my letter to Sara Blackburn, Paul Blackburn's first wife, who was an editor at Pantheon. So next thing I get a letter from her saying, "Hey Walter, here I am. I got your letter from Peter, and I am just what you are looking for," and of course she knew me and knew the work. So we connected. I sent her the transcription and she went through it and sent back a selection of what she edited from there. I would not have continued with this project but for her. And she went through all this chaos and pandemonium and she delivered a sensible narrative that she found in there, and so we kept going, and then she died.

AMJ: How inconsiderate of her.

WSH: And if I could have told her that I would have. She was so enthusiastic and sharp and on the ball, and so human, it gave me a lot of courage to keep going. That's part of the reason that the *Timeline (of Sorts)* as a book got done. She reduced all this material from a quotidian pedestrian slobagoody recording of day-to-day junk, and so I am very sorry that she's not here any more.

DAVE HASELWOOD

Dave Haselwood, founder of the Auerhahn Press (later Dave Haselwood Books), was born in Wichita, Kansas in 1931. I interviewed him before an audience at the San Francisco Center for the Book, on Tuesday, 28 January 1997. This transcript was originally published in Ampersand *vol 16 no 1 special issue* Beat: A Dead Horse, *under the title "Glabrous & Egoless." The Whitney Museum of New York was touring a huge show about the Beat Generation which, naturally, curated the life out of it and missed a lot of the writers, so the tireless staff of* Ampersand *put together our own informal history, with an article by Joanne Kyger on Allen Ginsberg, photos by Harry Redl, articles on Bashō and Wallace Berman, and an appropriate Zippy the Pinhead cartoon by Bill Griffith. Steve Lavoie, Roger Wicker, Steve Woodall, John McBride, and Holbrook Teter were among the members of the audience who commented.*

AMJ: Despite my greatest efforts as a bibliographer, the person sitting here is still relatively unknown in the history of printing and publishing.

After the Auerhahn Press ran its course from 1958 to the mid-sixties, Dave Haselwood left the Bay Area and, like George Leite,* cultivated his garden, as a landscape architect. He recently has been ordained as a priest at the Sonoma Mountain Zendo. Since he has given up not only his hair but his ego as part of this, I'll ask him to restore a little of the ego tonight and talk about his work which I believe may be the most significant publishing endeavour that we've yet seen in San Francisco.

Dave, I'd like to know a bit about your background, growing up in Kansas — your parents, your youth, things like that.

DH: I'm really a country bumpkin. I grew up in Wichita in the midst of the Depression on a farm. All of the people in my background are farmers, but my father's side of the family were very clever people: they were also musicians, and did beautiful cabinet-making and things like that, so there was some strain in there that was preparing for somebody to be outrageous. I'm thinking of *Buddenbrooks* by Thomas Mann — remember? — which builds up until you get these effete characters that do something kind of interesting, but that's the end.

AMJ: The end of the line.

DH: My mother was an educated woman and she was very fond of poetry, so from the time I was a baby she read poetry to me and I was given poetry books, so I grew up with a great love of poetry and books, and I was always — it's interesting — I don't know why, I was also as much interested in the book itself as in what was in it, so I remember — tactilely — I remember books from my childhood. I remember how they looked, how they felt, the kind of paper that was in them. So at some point obviously the fascination was so great it pulled me into this.

AMJ: Are you talking about Longfellow and Browning, or TS Eliot and the moderns?

DH: Well, of course when I was a child it was the American poets because that was the only thing available. It would be people like William Cullen Bryant. I can still quote poems by him: dreadful stuff. But it was okay. Actually a little tiny bit of Whitman, what was acceptable in those days, which would be the poems that we don't read anymore: the sort of boring ones. And Stevenson — people like that.

But anyhow it whetted my appetite for poetry. Also when we lived out on a farm I became fascinated by The Bible — mainly

*The same issue of *Ampersand* had an article on George Leite, Berkeley publisher, by Steve Lavoie, entitled "Beatnik Zero?"

as literature. So that again was beginning to track me into how Bibles look, they have a certain kind of beauty — especially the ones printed on India paper. Those were basically from my childhood; what got me into it. Then when I went to the university I immediately dove into the library — this wonderful place — and at one point worked there for a few hours a day and spent the entire time going through the collection finding wonderful things. I found Patchen's *Panels for the Walls of Heaven* and I didn't steal it — but I wanted to steal it! That became a precious thing to me. I was about sixteen or seventeen at the time. Somebody at the university there, even though it was out in the sticks, in Wichita, was into very hip literature.

AMJ: Michael McClure and Bruce Conner were both students there at the same time?

DH: No, Bruce Conner was actually a high school friend, and I got to know Mike when I started in college and he was still in high school.

AMJ: But you started college a year early, right?

DH: A year or two early. We already had a bohemian scene going by the time I was eighteen years old, in this university that still had all the earmarks of an Episcopalian college, which is to say a very liberal type of Christianity. I don't think many people out here know...wait, it must be Congregationalist. Many of the teachers were still these aged people that taught morals with whatever else they were teaching. I remember my chemistry professor would give us long lectures on how we should morally behave as good Christians.

AMJ: How did your form of rebellion manifest?

DH: I was kind of a little precocious and snotty and I would do things like wander around the campus with a copy of *Nausea* by Sartre. I was madly taking French so I could read all these great things. It was a pretty precious little scene, but we all became very well-read. Everyone read just about everything that you could think of that you'd be interested in reading, so it was an educational experience.

AMJ: You joined the army in the 'fifties when it was relatively okay, between the Korean War and the Vietnam War.

DH: No, the Korean War was still going on, but my desperation to get out of the academic world was so great that I risked it. I joined the army and was sent to Germany for two and a half years.

AMJ: You'd already visited New York before you enlisted?

DH: Yeah, in 1950, my girlfriend and I went to New York and that was the point at which Greenwich Village had its great flowering. I don't know what that part of New York was called — the old Jewish settlement area down on Henry Street; every other building was a *shul* — and there were a lot of these bohemian artists living down there in the Village. I must have had the right contacts because I met an enormous number of people who later became the New York end of the Beat Generation, about eight years later, including Carl Solomon — he was quite crazy, but he was the brilliant one who inspired *Howl*, which was dedicated to him. And William Burroughs, who was the most fascinating human being I had ever encountered till that time. I can still remember him talking: he just talked and talked one day and it was all about his trip to South America and his taking *yagé*. And here was this little virginal boy from the sticks of Kansas and I'd never heard of psychedelic drugs. Who'd ever heard of psychedelic drugs?

  At one point there was a big bust in the Kansas City jazz scene, so some of the musicians came to Wichita and I got an early education in jazz going to their jam sessions at night. They would smoke marijuana which was a very exotic substance, but they wouldn't give it to me because I was too young.

AMJ: Do you remember who else was part of that New York scene?

DH: Huncke was around, but I didn't meet him until many years later. But you ran into everybody. It was a very compact scene. There were certain coffee shops and constant parties going on — there were people who had parties going on for weeks in their flat, and you'd just go in and hang out for a couple of days, sleep on the floor. This was the real Bohemia. In some ways much more outrageous than even the Beats were. The Beats were a little more middle class!

AMJ: So having tasted this life why did you join the army?

DH: I was on this track to become an English professor at the university, and I was firmly on that track. I mean I was being given teaching fellowships and I was being groomed, and one day I realised that I hated it to the bottom of my soul. There was nothing wrong with it, but I hated it, and yet I was being sucked into this thing. I remember I read *From Here to Eternity* just before I took off to Mexico, and somehow whatever happened in that novel went around in my head, and during that summer in Mexico I thought, "Oh, I know how to get out of this, I'll join the army because this is the thing I have avoided doing: this is the thing I least have wanted to do in my life! That's what I'll do!" Actually it was just right, it was perfect.

AMJ: So you adapted okay to military life?

DH: It was a great challenge. I went through basic training in Fort Riley in the middle of winter. The snow must have been about five or six feet deep and it just turned into this vast poem. The whole experience was quite a beautiful poem that I found myself in: getting up before dawn and going out in these open trucks into the snow and then laying in the snow and firing rifles. All the white and the sky, it was just one big poem.

AMJ: While you were in Germany were you aware that Jonathan Williams was also there — I think he was also in the army — and publishing his first book, which was McClure's *Passages*?

DH: No, I didn't know it. Michael sent me a copy of that book, but I didn't know that Jonathan was there. As a matter of fact, during my last year there in Germany, Michael wrote to me and said, "Why don't you publish this poem of mine while you're in Germany?" and he sent me a beautiful etching by Bruce Conner, and he said, "German printers are supposed to be very good, why don't you design it and put all these things together and we'll do a broadside," and I really was working on it, it came very close to happening, but somehow it never quite jelled, but that was my first publishing attempt.

AMJ: At this point you decided that you wanter to be a publisher?

DH: No, I had just decided that I was going to live in San Francisco! I had seen it for two days before I went to Germany and decided that this was where I wanted to be, and so when I got out of the army and came to San Francisco I immediately told Michael, "Let's go ahead, let's do a project," so he was going to have me do the book then that was done by Yugen, but in the meantime I did the book by John Wieners and I did the next book of McClure's.

AMJ: The Wieners book, *Hotel Wentley Poems*, was printed by a commercial printer and they left out the word "cock" in the title of "The Poem for Cocksuckers," so it just says, "A Poem for ____suckers" which really changes it!

DH: Olson was furious. He wrote both of us these letters saying, "Don't do that again!"

This was very interesting. It was Henry Louie, a Chinese-American, and Peter Bailey was his partner, who later was a book designer and then very active in the Zen community here. He used to work on the Zen books with Shoemaker. Later he was at East Wind printers. I worked with them at first.

SL: Did you know Wieners in New York?

DH: No, I was living in the Hotel Wentley, and there was a big scene that went on downstairs every night in Foster's cafeteria. You know in those days Polk Street was an artists' community and there were also a lot of old European intellectuals who hung out in that neighbourhood: old ladies who had Russian pedigrees, who'd sit at tables late at night. I overheard one old lady say to another, "Yes, but she doesn't have your great intellect."

And John appeared on that art scene. I guess the person who was really the center of that was the painter Robert LaVigne, who has since become fairly famous, because he was sort of *the* painter of the Beat Generation. If you saw the Ginsberg film [*The Life & Times of Allen Ginsberg*], all those paintings of his were shown and they interviewed him.

As a matter of fact, one big painting called *Natalie at Foster's*, of this blue ghost floating through the air of Foster's cafeteria, showed all of the Beat poets sitting around looking at this blue ghost, floating. Foster's was all mirrors, hundreds of mirrors, so you could sit anywhere in there and see everybody. It was the perfect place for a literary hangout.

AMJ: There was a PBS documentary that appeared subsequently that had footage taken at the Wentley Hotel, which then burned down I believe.

DH: Well this photograph [*on the cover*] was taken in the hallway of the Wentley Hotel.

AMJ: By Jerry Burchard.

DH: This was the chandelier that hung there; but this was actually not John Wieners. Bob LaVigne drew this [*portrait in the book*] while he was writing the poems. This is always what I'd get involved in, like the project I'd begun in Germany. We'd get together and a thing would develop. A poem would occur and then a book would occur and drawings would occur and the whole thing would be one, and that's really what I wanted to do. I think it's quite boring just to crank out books. There's no poetry in that. The whole thing happening is the point. And that's what John Wieners thought too. One time a policeman stopped him and said, "Do you work? What kind of work do you do?" and John said, "I make it on the poem."

AMJ: And he got a ticket for loitering, right?

DH: He was probably taken to jail…which would have delighted him!

AMJ: So you were working at the post office on the night shift, sorting mail, and making the scene during the day?

DH: Buying a printing press and beginning to get the stuff together.

AMJ: This is kind of a ridiculous question, but were you at all aware of the fine press tradition in San Francisco? You hadn't come here to be part of that scene.

DH: No. My familiarity with beautiful-looking books really was when I was still back in Kansas. Are all of you familiar with those editions of poetry that Boni & Liveright used to put out? I found a copy in a used bookstore there of Pierre Louÿs' *Chanson de Bilitis*. I don't know if you've ever seen that book. It had a black cover and black and white drawings. I vaguely remember it was probably Bodoni type they liked — and it looked perfect — and I loved that book and I think I see something in my early books from being influenced by the way those Boni & Liveright books looked.

AMJ: Aspiring to that level of decadence!

DH: That would have been hog-heaven to me: just to be truly decadent! Michael McClure used to always accuse me of belonging to the Cult of Experience, like that guy in *A Rebours*.

AMJ: Des Esseintes.

DH: Yeah. The guy that would buy a turtle and have it gilded so it would look right crawling across his Persian carpet.

SL: But you didn't hang out with the Hell's Angels, did you?

DH: Through Mike McClure I got to know some of them. But that was later on though. I call that — now don't get me wrong, I never was into cocaine — but I call that the 'cocaine-glitter scene' that occured in San Francisco at one point. I think it was quite fashionable to snort cocaine and sit in North Beach cafés and watch the reflections off of the black limousines that went by, that's what I associate with that. The Hell's Angels were part of that. Somebody once coined the term "the Glitterati"…

SL: Sounds like Tom Wolfe.

AMJ: Here's a book you've probably never seen before. But if you look at it, it may seem strangely familiar. It's Henry Evans' Peregrine Press. Now you bought your press and your Caslon type from him. This is a book he printed on that press and in that type you bought from him.

DH: I never saw it before.

SL: Now who is this?

AMJ: Henry Evans. He was a well-known San Francisco printmaker. He did wonderful botanical prints from woodcuts.

DH: That's what he became famous for.

AMJ: He had a bookshop called Porpoise Books and a press called Peregrine Press and he published a series of books called *Painters & Poets* that included Creeley and Duncan.

DH: He was actually an important part of the printing scene here, but again he's kind of one of those unknowns.

RW: He's known for his books and his portfolios of his prints. But he was also known for a censorship thing. He was busted for selling *Tropic of Cancer.*

DH: This book looks like Henry, this is a good example.

AMJ: In order to finance this, in addition to working at the post office, you organized this famous "Mad Mammoth Monster Poetry Reading" that was one of the great events in San Francisco in the summer of 1959. [*reads press release*]

DH: It sure was. I've got a few photographs of it, taken by Wally Berman, that are some of the most beautiful photographs I've ever seen, because Bruce Conner and a woman artist, Beth Branaman, made these incredible costumes and masks and objects that were carried down the street.

AMJ: Did they stop traffic? I guess Green Street's pretty quiet.

DH: No I think they walked across Columbus and did the whole thing.

AMJ: There were about one thousand people there, according to the next day's paper, so it must have been huge.

DH: It was packed. One of the people in the audience was Rexroth. He'd been out of the country so he did not know at all what was going on with this thing, and he was furious when he got back because he hadn't been consulted about any of this, and he did like to be consulted. So he sat in the audience dead quiet, scowling, and then afterwards just proceeded to rip the whole thing up, and started a rather vicious rumor that I was this extremely wealthy man who was trying to buy his way into the poetry and publishing world.*

AMJ: If only! The accounts in the papers are really hilarious. Lewis Lapham wrote: "A few of the blonde girls wearing black fishnets slouched against the wall in the back, obviously missing the nuances in the poems, but dug it." And they have Ron Loewinsohn saying, "My poems are like the gaps in the freeway, or the silences in a Miles Davis solo," and it's completely saturated with this hip jive talk.

DH: A good chunk of that reading is on the Fantasy four-CD set [*The Beat Generation*].

AMJ: So with the proceeds you were able to get to work, with *Ekstasis*, which, although it's a beautiful book, you were unhappy with.

DH: Well, it got trimmed wrong by the binders.

AMJ: Did you have any previous printing experience?

*Haselwood later told me he had been determined not to gossip or say nasty things during this interview, but got carried away when Rexroth came up. "I really admired his poetry, but he turned my stomach," he said.

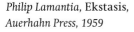

*Philip Lamantia, Ekstasis,
Auerhahn Press, 1959*

DH: One of the things that needs to be set straight for the record is that it's always said that I was Auerhahn Press. But that's not true. I had help from the very beginning. A man who's name I don't even remember, who worked as a ship's printer on the *Lurline*, obtained some type for me that they were selling off the ship and then showed me how to set type and operate the Hartford letterpress. He just volunteered and came in and helped.

And then one day, Jay McIlroy, this young man from Philadelphia, just walked into the shop. He was a printer, and he was interested in what I was doing, and I said, "Well, why don't you join me," and he sort of became my partner. He really knew how to print and taught me how to print.

Whatever happened to Jay I do not know. He was married and had a couple of kids, and a few years after I moved up to Sonoma County, he had a bad nervous breakdown. He was an extremely fine person and really was heavily responsible for the good things that happened at Auerhahn and he's never given any credit.

AMJ: Was he sympathetic to the poems you were publishing?

DH: Absolutely. He was a typical South Side of Philadelphia, not educated beyond high school, salt-of-the-earth kind of person, talked with that wonderful working-class Philadelphia accent, no pretensions, but just loved this poetry, and wanted to work

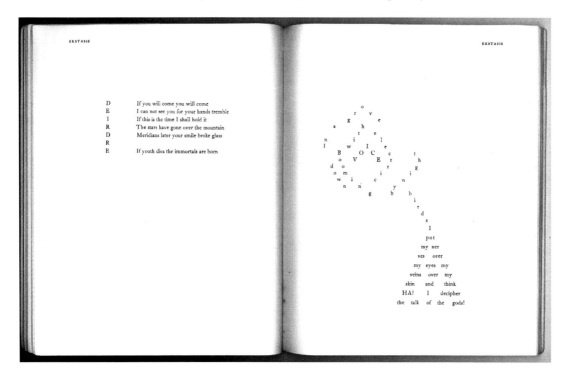

on it. Quite a strange thing actually. He really was the one who got it off the ground. I don't think I could have ever printed this. For instance in *Ekstasis* there are all these shaped poems, I look back: [*reads The Volcano*]

That's Lamantia at his very best.

AMJ: Was Lamantia in Mexico at this point?

DH: No, he was living here and he was going through…you know, Lamantia has always had a big problem with a bipolar condition — manic depression — and was going through a really serious problem with it. But at this period he was on the upswing, and when Lamantia was on the upswing there was nobody on earth more fun to be around. He was just this font of energy and poetry constantly spilling out and excitement and so that was what was going on while this book was being written and printed and so it really was 'Ekstasis.'

I love this book. Imagine naming a poem, "Les Langueurs Allongées"! Only he could get away with something like that.

AMJ: He was exactly what the *Life* magazine writers were railing about when they talked about the decadent pot-smoking bongo-playing wasters, he epitomised everything that they hated about the Beat Generation.

DH: Well, Lamantia (I use the past tense though he's going strong right now, though I haven't seen him for years) in those days — in this swing that would go in him — it would swing when he would get down he'd become a very, very devout Catholic — the kind that would crawl to kiss the bishop's ring, and have some kind of ecstatic experience. I remember the time he said he met some Catholic functionary who was a mystic of some kind, the whole room was filled with the scent of violets.

But then when he was on the other side of the thing, he'd get addicted to heroin. He had a very serious problem with that so he'd go back and forth, but it's all in his books, it's right up front.*

AMJ: Someone asked him once about his Catholic devotion, and he said, "To tell you the truth, I cultivate the vibes and let the theology slide!"

You finally got to do your old buddy McClure's *Hymns to St Geryon*.

DH: McClure had done a series of these huge enamel paintings. Anyhow we decided we'd put one of those on the cover of the book, reduce it way down, and I said, "You know, I want it silkscreened, I want it to stand up on top. The print'll be punched in and I want this thing to be shiny and on top." So I looked around and found a silkscreener, and he took the painting and he took my money and disappeared forever!

*Haselwood relates that after this interview appeared in *Ampersand* he was invited to an art opening in North Beach by an old friend. Lamantia was there and said he was really hurt by these comments in the interview. Dave says he took Philip's hand and said, "I love you. I would never hurt you. Those were all things you told me." So Lamantia said, OK. "And so we stood there holding hands," Haselwood recalls. "He and I had endless conversations while we were working on the books: he'd bring hashish and tell these stories about everybody. It was wonderful, if only I could have recorded them."

I found Lamantia's letters to Haselwood from Mexico to be one of the most interesting parts of the Auerhahn archive at The Bancroft Library, but Lamantia refused me permission to quote them, saying, "I wish to forget that period of eclipsed activity."

McClure did another one, and we got a real reputable place to do the silkscreening on it.

AMJ: McClure came here initially to study painting with Hans Hofmann at the Art Institute, didn't he?

DH: He was very into the New York school of painters when we were still in Wichita. And when he went to New York, Jackson Pollock was his absolute hero, and Franz Kline. It's interesting, like Frank O'Hara, his big inspiration was painters, not so much other poets. And you see it in his poems, there's all those wonderful…he can describe colors like nobody else I know of. It'll be like some sort of chartreuse-color cloud and then this loud ringing of a bell comes out of it. It's kind of a Rimbaud "derangement of the senses" thing in McClure's poetry of those days, although it was Lamantia who was called "the Rimbaud

Michael McClure's Hymns to St Geryon *and Philip Lamantia's* Narcotica *(cover by Wallace Berman) both published in San Francisco by the Auerhahn Press in 1959*

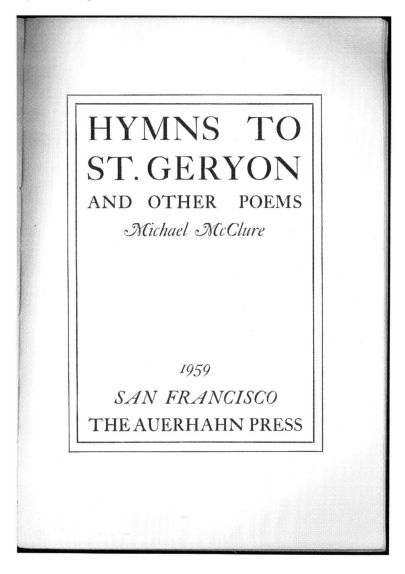

HYMNS TO
ST. GERYON
AND OTHER POEMS
Michael McClure

1959
SAN FRANCISCO
THE AUERHAHN PRESS

of the Occident" by André Breton!

AMJ: Your next book was probably your most controversial book, and that was *Narcotica,* which was Lamantia's translations of Artaud. Herb Caen even wrote a little piece about it where he said, "the cover shows the poet mainlining a shot of heroin. But when it came out he took it on the Lam to Mexico."

For the time this was an outrageous thing to do, to publish a book in 1959, where the very first line says in all caps: "I DEMAND EXTINCTION OF THE LAWS PROHIBITING NARCOTIC DRUGS!"

RW: Is this before or after *Junkie*?

AMJ: *Junkie* is '54. But that was just a novel about the depravity of these drug dealers: it wasn't in your face saying we demand the right to use heroin. Though they both have lurid covers!

DH: Those Wally Berman photos are beautiful.

AMJ: Did you work with Berman on this?

DH: Lamantia got the photographs from him, I didn't know him that well at that time.

AMJ: That's a great title-page, that Christmas tree of type!

DH: You see Liveright & Boni in there? Now I see it in those books.

SW: Whose design idea was the cover?

DH: Those were collaborations. Wally undoubtedly arranged the photographs and I would have set the type.

AMJ: At one point you announced a couple more Artaud translations by yourself.

DH: I worked on them; I don't know if they still exist.

AMJ: Then as a prelude to your big Whalen book you did this very nice broadside: Phil Whalen's "Self-portrait from Another Direction." This was just to get warmed up to the complex typography that Whalen is famous for?

DH: Yes, I'll tell you, it was complex, but it was simple compared to McClure. McClure's poems — every line had to be exactly where he wanted it to be. Handsetting his poems was the only way to do it, I mean, if you'd set those on a machine you'd have

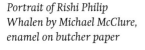

*Portrait of Rishi Philip
Whalen by Michael McClure,
enamel on butcher paper*

to do it about five hundred times.

AMJ: How did you meet Phil?

DH: I had seen some poems of his in *Yugen* — that magazine that LeRoi Jones brought out in New York — and I loved them. Plus the fact that by this time I had met people like Snyder and Lew Welch who were around San Francisco. I decided I wanted to do a book of his definitely. He was living in Newport, Oregon, at the time, working as a bailiff in the courthouse there. A friend of his from Reed College was the judge, so he convinced Whalen to go up and be his bailiff and give him plenty of time to write. He had a little cottage fairly near the sea, it was very pleasant there. So Bob LaVigne and I hitch-hiked up there and just appeared and convinced Whalen to give us a manuscript.

He is a jewel among human beings, and wonderful to work with. If you want to talk about profound, he's a truly profound poet, not to everybody's taste: hard to read, almost impossible to read out loud. He does a good job, but they are operas, almost every poem is an opera, so you have to have a lot of different voices and you have to know which voice to read that in, and some of them you toss off and some of them you bellow out and it's a production, a whole dramatic production. So they're quite hard, if you don't know that, they're almost incomprehensible at times, if you don't realise that they are a bunch of different personae.

AMJ: I think the consensus in this room, at least, is that Whalen and Welch are by far the best poets of the Beat Generation. That was the odd thing about the Beat show at the De Young (just for a little aside): clearly Lisa Phillips [*the curator*] hadn't read the books. Someone had told her: This is who counts; this is who's in, this is who's out. There wasn't really any understanding of what the contents of those books was. Certainly there were books in cases…

DH: There were books *tossed* into cases.

AMJ: There was one Phil Whalen: *Highgrade*; we didn't even find Lew Welch.

DH: But everybody's books were tossed in there, helter-skelter. It was the pits, as they say!

AMJ: Right after Phil's first book, you did Lew Welch's first book, *Wobbly Rock*, as a little pamphlet.

DH: Again it was a typical shot. Lew and I hung out together for a while and we produced this book. Again, like Lamantia, Lew Welch was a very up and down person. He had a serious problem with alcohol at times, and he could get very depressed and sort of disappear, but when he was up he was an absolute delight to be with. He was one of these — I know this is going to sound like a put-down and it's not — but he was sort of a 'gee whiz' person. He was always amazed, like 'Wow! Did you see that?' and then out of this would come a whole huge take on some little event he had seen happen. A very typical poem of his is that one: "Draw a circle and find how many things are inside of it." That was how he saw the world, every little thing was like 'Wow! Look at that label, did you see that? [*picking up Calistoga water bottle*] There's a geyser on it, phew!' and he'd be off and going…

There had to be a little lion, a little red dot. Because he was a Leo; he was obsessed with being a Leo.

So he was really great to work with and, again, Bob LaVigne was also one of the collaborators on a lot of these books and he did a drawing for it, so it was a collaboration: we all worked on it together. I'd have thought…later on in Auerhahn Press, occasionally a book would be done and the author would have serious problems with it — like its design or something — that never happened in the early years, because they were strictly collaborations. If the author hadn't liked what I was doing I'd have dropped it immediately. That would have been it.

AMJ: Was East-West House going at that time, in 1959? Tell us a bit about that.

DH: I used to go over to dinner there and the people who were living there that I really remember were Joanne Kyger, just before she went off to Japan to marry Gary Snyder. There was this wonderful Taoist, Ja Fu was his name, I think he's since gone on to be kind of a famous Taoist, he's from Shanghai. John Montgomery hung out there [*chortles from the audience*]…the infamous John Montgomery, who used to come by the Auerhahn Press and bring me presents, like he'd come in with an old cash register, and dunk it down and say, 'This belonged to Lord Buckley; I'm leaving it with you.' He was always leaving stuff! Let's see, Tom Field was living there and several other people.

AMJ: So it was a Buddhist commune?

DH: Yeah. That's a good name for it. Brian Shekeloff was living there. He was married to Myrtis Shekeloff. She's this extremely handsome tall black woman. She was Rexroth's amanuensis for many years. I had an enormous crush on her. She's a wonderful woman, I ran into her the other day at Phil Whalen's reading at the Art Institute.

AMJ: So then, this is in 1960, you've done this huge body of work in very little time: flying sparks doesn't begin to describe it. Then you did this broadside.

DH: In some ways this is my favorite thing I ever did.

AMJ: …with this beautiful little Phil Whalen drawing, a poem by McClure, a piece by Lamantia, a nice little piece by Wieners: "Bagdad by the Bay." And Bruce Conner did this pressmark?

DH: Bruce did this. This was his idea of the Auerhahn, a bird with a human face and a bagpipe for a tail. The flaming Zoe/Phos [*Life/Light*] by Robert LaVigne: it's a mystical cross in Greek Christian myticism. It's just a catalogue but in some ways I think it's the nicest thing.

SL: Joanne Kyger says that [Jack] Spicer used to hang around that commune you were talking about.

DH: I did not like Spicer. I sort of avoided him. He said very hateful things about the Auerhahn Press all the time. There were these two major factions. And Spicer believed in friction as a way of generating poetry, and actually I agree with him, but I did not like to be around him.

  I think actually he did create a kind of friction that did create poetry and I was in the other camp. For instance at one time in Gino & Carlo's (which was his hangout in North Beach) he wrote on the john wall, "The Auerhahn Press is driving me away from poetry like a fast car."

AMJ: Right before you arrived, there was a series of books that Spicer instigated that Joe Dunn had printed as White Rabbit Press. Did you know Joe Dunn?

DH: He was a very good friend, he lived in the same building as I did on Polk Street for a while. He was an extremely lovable person. I liked Joe very much. But he got very fouled up on drugs.

AMJ: He was a methedrine casualty?

DH: Yes. That was the great bane of the early Beat scene. People were unaware of how destructive speed was, and all of these people got deeply into it, and really hurt by it. I'm afraid it's happening again; people don't learn the lesson. But Joe and I were great friends. We were the printers for the two different factions, but he and I were close friends, and complete admirers of each other, and so that shows what that little thing was about: it didn't amount to anything.

AMJ: The difference was that Joe and Graham Mackintosh (who revived the imprint) were both clandestine printers. They'd been instructed by Spicer to get a job in a big plant where they wouldn't be noticed, and run off his pamphlets after hours.

DH: The printing was truly ephemeral, and I admired that so much. I remember early on, I said to John Wieners one time

(I think it was the day we got his book finished, warts and all, because that's a very warty looking book), I said, "You know, John, I really don't want this to be a fly-by-night operation, I really want this to keep going." And he said, "Fly-by-night? I want *everything* to be fly-by-night!" I thought, wow, maybe White Rabbit should have done it, because they could have just fallen through the cracks at any moment. If they'd lost their job that would have been the end. The boss might walk in and the whole job would vanish into the waste-paper basket.

AMJ: At this point had you made money on any of these books?

DH: Actually, on Wieners' book we went to the coffee shops in North Beach and just went from table to table and sold them to people.

AMJ: The Julia Vinograd approach. Then you tried for the big time with this: you did a relatively slick job for William Burroughs and Brion Gysin's book, *The Exterminator.*

DH: Yes, it has this really incredible back section, which is Brion Gysin's wiping out the word. It's a progression, it's worth getting for this part.

AMJ: Did they think this was going to become a best-seller?

DH: Yes, they thought they would be very rich and famous. Can you imagine, from a cut-up book! God, he must have really been out on smack somewhere at that point. These are almost impossible to read. It was impossible to typeset.

AMJ: Was it all handset?

DH: The little headlines at the top are all handset but the rest of it was set on a Linotype machine. But you can't keep track, of what is going on anywhere, it just keeps…like diarrhea…

To tell you the truth I was pissed off that he sent me this manuscript, because I was a great admirer, and wrote to him — because I'd seen *Naked Lunch* in manuscript — I wrote to him and said I'm a great admirer, I'd met him many years before, and I thought I was going to get something really wonderful, and I got this and I'm afraid I don't think it's wonderful, even to this day.

JM: Then why did you publish it?

DH: Well, I think because now I'd asked for it, I've got to do it. I'm sure there are other publishers that have wound up in that position.

AMJ: The cover is great: they are Brion Gysin's drawings.

DH: I kind of like the cover. This is another Auerhahn mark, it's more like a constipated rooster.

AMJ: I liked your description, in your deposition, of the

Auerhahn: It's a German grouse — the thing about it is a hunter is only allowed to kill one in his lifetime, which is just as well, because when it's cooked it tastes like turpentine! The perfect name for a small press.

SL: A deposition? Was there a lawsuit?

AMJ: Dave wrote a little piece, which was published in his hometown paper.

DH: But I looked at it as if I were being deposed by the police.

AMJ: Explain why you did this, Mr Haselwood. Why would anyone spend years of their life setting this esoteric rubbish and printing it in fine editions of five hundred copies just so bookdealers in twenty years time can grow fat off it?

At this point you've hit all your main authors — McClure, Whalen, Welch, Wieners, Lamantia — did you feel like you'd really achieved something, or did you feel like you were just starting?

DH: You know, I never knew what I was doing from one day to the next, and I think that's probably still true! It never seemed like anything was accumulating or happening, it was just always, 'Oh, here's another thing to do' and I would get completely caught up in whatever I was doing and that was it.

AMJ: Were you still working at the post office?

DH: Probably by this time I had stopped. I had a little bit of job work and it just kept me barely alive. You know where the press was in those days? It was on Franklin Street and that was an interesting address. It was an ugly little one-story shed-like building that went down the street, across from the Women's Club of California. At one time above this had been a huge mansion. In that mansion was where David Park, the painter, and Duncan and all those people lived during that early fifties scene in San Francisco, but it had been torn down. It was between Sutter and Post. And the landlord was very interested in what I was doing so I paid almost no rent. So that was how I could afford to be there, and it didn't require much money to live. Somehow I got by on peanut butter and jelly sandwiches.

AMJ: Then you printed a book which is certainly not your greatest work, although it's nicely printed. Illustrated by Robert Ronnie Branaman, it's *Hellan, Hellan* by Edward Marshall. If anything he'll be remembered as the most obscure poet in Don Allen's *New American Poetry* anthology.

DH: Well, most of the poems in there are not by him. The so-called best poem by Edward Marshall in *The New American Poetry* was by Robin Blaser.

AMJ: You're kidding! How did that happen?

DH: I don't know, I think that Don Allen did it on purpose.

AMJ: The drawings are nice in a proto-comix style. Branaman was someone you knew in Wichita also, wasn't he?

DH: He came from Wichita. He became a favorite artist of Ginsberg, who used him in some of the stuff that he did. And I think he's an extrememly interesting sort of primitive artist.

SL: Who's Edward Marshall?

DH: Edward Marshall is from New England and his mother was quite mad. He was well-educated, and quite mad himself. He was discovered by Irving Rosenthal, who, before he moved to New York, was the editor of the *Chicago Review*, at the time it became infamous when he published the Buddhist issue and the Beat poets, and then was removed from the editorship. This guy, he had something, I don't know what it is: a kind of madness that I've always found very attractive. Actually I did a book by someone even more mad than him — that you've probably never even seen because it doesn't say Auerhahn Press on it — it's called *Dreams of Straw* by Roxie Powell. Oh, you have it! Let me read you a poem by Roxie Powell, the name of the poem is "That Old Lady":

> That old lady you been with
> Make zero plain and cold,
> Her teeth smell like a plumb,
>
> You shoulda let her go before
> She bit it off,
> Her teeth were gone
>
> You're an old lady fucker
> And I ought to invite you home,
> But I ain't got time for
> Celebrities
> And besides my sister's come.

How do you like that for a poem? It's an incredible poem.

SL: There's the link to Catullus.

RW: Who was Roxie Powell?

DH: He was also from Wichita, Kansas. Quite mad. This great big cornfed-looking kid. Looked like he could be Little Abner, totally mad. He came to San Francisco. These were later arrivals: Charlie Plymell, Roxie Powell.

SL: Sort of like when we had to experience the Iowa Poets invasion.

AMJ: You also did your share of stultifyingly boring fine printing on commission?

DH: Well, you know, as straightforward as Andy Hoyem is, he also has been always attracted to truly mad offbeat poets. He's done several of them too, like that guy from South Carolina he did a few years ago…

AMJ: Speaking of Andy, he wrote to you about this time. He was in the navy and was trying to kind of peddle a Paul Reps book that he wanted to get done. You were going to print this book for Reps but Andy was going to be involved in it?

DH: I don't remember these things very well. My memory is that Andy showed up on the scene. He was this very intense, very wound-up person, and he really wanted to get involved in the publishing of these poets, and he was writing poems himself and his great hero was Paul Reps and he had met Reps. So at a certain point he said, "You need money, so why don't I buy into the press?" And I would have been involved with Zen by this time, so Reps was interesting to me too.

But suddenly it was all done in a very different way. The Reps book was printed in Japan by collotype and it is beautiful. You can't tell that these are not original sumi ink drawings because collotype will do that. It's the only way you can do it. But it was done in Japan and it's this elegant book. Has anyone ever seen that one? It's fairly rare. It was boxed and very fancy.

Now I had done limited hardcover editions of some of these books I had done so far to help pay for the rest of the edition. You did a few hardcover editions signed by the author, so these paid for the rest of the books, so you could sell them for one dollar and everyone could have one. That was the idea. But suddenly we began getting into these exquisite productions. I think Andy is a great printer. I don't really want to get nasty about this, because it was just that he really wanted to go in a different direction than I did, and he's done an incredible body of work, but that's not what I wanted to do, so from the very beginning, it was the beginning of the end. When we formed this partnership, it became this tug immediately.

AMJ: Through him you saw the viability of this other world of the collectible book, but at the same time, that wasn't anything you cared about or believed in?

DH: I didn't want that at all.

AMJ: *Dark Brown* was the first book that has Andy's name in it. That's in 1961. But this is still your vision. It's one of McClure's greatest works.

DH: Yes, I set it and did the typography. It's a great book of poems. That's the one where he really hit it.

RW: You taught Andy how to print? He'd never touched type before?

DH: He was just out of the navy. Andy is a lovely person but very self-willed, he will go the way he will go. Once he really began to get his self going he wanted to go in a very definite direction and I realised I didn't want to go in that direction at all.

AMJ: After Andrew joined the press, the next book you did was the Big O: Charles Olson's *Maximus from Dogtown*.

DH: That is one of his best poems. He tells the story in that one about the young man — Merry was his name — who starts out, he was a very strong farm boy, he kept picking up this calf, as it got bigger and bigger, till he killed himself. It's one of his best poems.

I'm not a great fan of Olson's poetry, I don't think I'd ever have solicited that.

AMJ: I don't mean to be rude, but it's kind of overblown. It's really just a big broadside.

DH: Andy was a great admirer of Olson. Andy tended to like father-figure type poets. In a partnership in publishing you're going to do some of what you want to do and some of what the other person wants to do. That's the nature of that. There were a couple of things that Andy wanted to do that I didn't particularly care for. I won't say which ones: one of them you'd be shocked!

AMJ: Well, it's probably not Lamantia's *Destroyed Works*.

DH: No, that's obviously one of the things I wanted to do.

AMJ: It's one of your masterpieces, I think. Cover by Bruce Conner. I love the letterspaced running heads with the little astrological ornaments and the use of the second color: that Jänecke-Schneeman orange for the titles.

DH: And typical of my books: every book is shaped different, and sometimes the shapes are not always pleasing but are determined by the poems. I would look at the poems and say we need a really wide page, or we need a narrow page to present the poems right. The whole idea was always 'what's going to make this poem come alive on the page?'

RW: Was this after you'd set one or two sticks of type?

DH: Yeah…

JM: You only had one or two main text sizes?

DH: I had not got into buying lots of type. That was Andy's thing, especially after he met the Grabhorns. I was really pretty happy with Caslon. I could have worked with Caslon for the rest of my life. And then I really liked Hermann Zapf's Palatino which is what I did *Dark Brown* in, but looking back I think that was a mistake. I would no longer…it never developed into anything. You know you get into a typeface and you begin discovering the beauty of it, and it takes a long time to really find out how to use it. Palatino had the feel of 'you could really get into this,' but you could never get any deeper, it was always right there at the beginning.

 The one that I started using for the last two books, just before I got out of printing, was Gill's Joanna. And that's something I regret, because I think with that typeface you could develop a whole style and really go into it. Maybe not; I didn't get into it deep enough, but I wish I had continued just to experiment with that typeface.

 And nobody else uses that typeface. I don't know why. It's a peculiar typeface because it's really hard to work with and if you begin using italic with it, you've really got problems, it's really hard. But I wish I'd continued with it.

AMJ: You printed another pamphlet, which was David Meltzer's *We All Have Something to Say to Each Other*, which is kind of an epitaph for Patchen, who'd just died in '61. This time it's set in Linotype Garamond, and sold for seventy-five cents. How could you possibly have made any money?

DH: That was the idea, the pamphlets were just practically give-away things.

AMJ: And then you announce on the back that you are going to do *Mad Sonnets* by McClure and *Wafer Neon Papa* by Ray Johnson. Whatever happened to that? It would have been great to have had you do a Ray Johnson book.

DH: It would have, but somehow it just disappeared, it just never crystalised.

AMJ: One of your most beautiful books is Jonathan Williams' *In England's Green &*.

DH: That and the Ronald Johnson books are probably the two most beautiful books I did. He's another Kansan, but I didn't know him there. He was a Western Kansan. Liberal is where he grew up. The drawings in this were done by Thomas George, he was the son of the man who did the 'Toonerville Trolley' cartoon. He does these beautiful line drawings of natural scenes. One of the challenges here was, I wanted to really work them into the text so I printed them in an avocado color, and this book really did come out quite beautiful, if I do say so myself. It was a commissioned job for Jargon.

AMJ: Right now we reach the centre of the tornado, if you don't mind the Kansan simile here...

DH: The Wichita vortex!

AMJ: ...which is the publication of *Heads of the Town up to the Aether*.

SL: If you hated Jack Spicer so much why did you publish his poetry?

DH: I didn't hate him. As a matter of fact I loved his poetry. One of my favorite books of poetry still is *After Lorca*. Oh what a beautiful book.

AMJ: ...a great book.

DH: But I couldn't stand him as a person, because he was so abusive. Actually he was an unpleasant drunk...

AMJ: ...and he was drunk all the time.

DH: He was drunk all the time. I believe Robin Blaser had a certain function — besides being a good poet — Robin got along with everybody, so one day he came into the shop and he said, "Would you be interested in doing this book by Jack?" He said, "We've got a patron who is giving us this money to have it published and I think you ought to be the one who prints it and publishes it." So, yeah, not just because there was the money but Jack Spicer was a good poet. I think Andy especially...again, I say Andy had a tendency to hero-worship. I never did hero-worship poets, they're all a pain in the ass! (I knew I'd start getting indiscreet.) I take that back, they're wonderful, but they can be a pain in the ass! Andy especially thought of Jack as a major poet, and Andy really wanted to do it, he just sort of grabbed it and there was no question: he was the one who was going to design it and do it. He had a very definite idea of how he wanted it to look and he did not consult with Jack at all. I don't believe Jack even came into the shop. When the book came out a lot of people hated the way it looked. Duncan was absolutely outraged, he hated the way the notes were all squinched up at the bottom of the page, was how he put it. I think it's fine: you could argue about it. It's a nice little chapbook, there's nothing wrong with it, but it caused a lot of trouble. It did not sell well. So we were blamed for that and a bad scene started developing. It started getting really nasty with a lot of name-calling and stuff. Stan Persky was the worst: he was a thug.

AMJ: He had a magazine called *Open Space*. Didn't they somehow remainder or take over the edition?

DH: He came into the shop one day and said he'd like to buy the rest of the copies of this because they're not selling well. And

I think his intention was probably just to give them away, or something, and I said fine, because if someone could get them distributed, great, because they weren't going well.

Spicer's reputation at that time was tiny, it was in this tiny tiny area and these people thought he was God, but nobody else knew about him. So I said "yes" and actually gave him most of the rest of the edition. Some of them I left with Glenn Todd, but he took most of them. Well, it turned out Jack really appreciated that gesture. So I got a phone call, I can't remember from who, one of his minions, and they said, "Jack would like to do a poetry reading for you and Andrew" — just for us. He said, "What would you like to hear?" I said, "I'd love to hear him read *After Lorca*." So sure enough at somebody's apartment up on Telegraph Hill, Andy and I went, and there were a couple of other people there, and Spicer came in and sat down and read the whole book. It was an incredible gesture. That also later caused a storm because somebody was writing a biography of Spicer…

AMJ: Lew Ellingham.

DH: And he got a lot of this information from me, when he was writing the chapter on that book, and the minute he showed it round all the Spicerites screamed in agony. This could not be! This never happened! This is not what Jack would ever do — anything like that! They didn't want to see Jack in this way. But it was an incredibly beautiful gesture to make on his part, and it was extremely moving to me.

AMJ: At this point things were in a much worse predicament, because you'd already contracted to do Duncan's *Book of Resemblances* and this would have been one of your great books, I think. All that remains is the broadside announcement. From what I could reconstruct of the story, Duncan objected to the printing of this linecut of this Jess drawing: here's the actual piece. To me it's perfectly well printed.

DH: Apparently Jess was outraged that the lines were too heavy. If you've ever tried to print that kind of line…

AMJ: …with the solid black…

DH: …in a letterpress, that's just unbelievably difficult. Again, what really happened was there was a clash of wills. And that's okay.

AMJ: It seems at this point you're no longer publishing your friends and the books you love, but you've reached out into a larger world and suddenly you've got this other adjunct to your press, Andrew, who is just great at public relations!

DH: Duncan wrote a couple of great books, *Letters* and *The Opening of the Field*. Most of his poems you could throw off the Golden Gate Bridge!

AMJ: But they would bounce!

DH: And they would float…and somebody would find them and print them!

AMJ: But you'd bought type and paper, so that then became Andrew's first book of poems, *The Wake*, which is very nicely designed, has a very discreet little title-page, but there couldn't have been the market for a book of poems by an unknown poet that there would have been for Duncan who had collectors and libraries. This must have been a real setback to your finances, your publishing programme.

DH: I didn't even keep track. I never had any idea of what was going on with the finances. My wife tells a wonderful story. She's a New Yorker and she knew this man who became the "button king" of New York — remember when buttons were big in the sixties? It was the very beginning of the button craze, and he proliferated, but he had no business sense and kept no books, nothing, and one day she said, "How does your business survive?" and he threw up his arms and he said "Every day's a miracle!" That was, I think, a little bit how the Auerhahn Press was run.

But I think this made Andrew quite nervous because he had a much more stable sense of 'you should be making a living; you shouldn't depend on the kindness of strangers' and all that stuff.

AMJ: This was the point at which Andrew got a part-time job at Grabhorn Press, so he was over there soaking up this atmosphere of the gentlemen printers with their clients?

DH: Gentlemen? Come on! No. Bob Grabhorn was a true gentleman, I don't think Ed was.

AMJ: But this was the beginning of the end for Auerhahn. At this point any poet you were involved with, Andy was getting into some kind of major altercation, so your former wonderful relationship of working with the poet and producing the book was no longer viable. You had a whole series of things about trying to make money, trying to do fine editions. You did the Everson book, *The Poet is Dead*, about Jeffers, which is on handmade paper and so on, obviously sucked-up by the collector market.

DH: Lawton Kennedy always called it "pissed-on paper," he thought it was pretentious. He was a great printer…

AMJ: There were two more Auerhahn Press books, and they both have sad stories connected to them. One is DiPrima's *New*

Handbook of Heaven, again a beautiful book.

DH: That's one of my best designs: that title-page is maybe the best title-page I ever did.

AMJ: It's really a pretty book, but then after it came out, DiPrima and LeRoi Jones [Imamu Amiri Baraka] ripped it off and did a Poets Press edition to undercut your edition. They just offset your book, even copying the cover. This must have been a real blow to you after handsetting all these poems to see this crappy printing flooding the market at half the price.

DH: Diane is a good friend of mine now. At the time I could have wrung her neck. She was really unpleasant about the whole thing. This book is about her great affair with LeRoi Jones, so maybe it was good that there was some some of reprise with LeRoi again.

AMJ: And then maybe the last thing you were involved with as Auerhahn was Olson's *Human Universe*, which was going to be Oyez! Press first of all, and then Hawley and Hoyem had a falling out and it ended up being Grove Press.

DH: Which again we didn't get a penny for.

AMJ: So this was basically the end of Auerhahn as a viable commercial press.

DH: I don't know why we never got paid. Our edition was a huge fancy book, I don't know if you've seen it, with parchment spine and elaborate colored linoleum prints for the front and back papers, and this [*Grove Press edition*] is pretty much a rip-off of it, done ugly style, and there was never…Nobody ever said, "Here's some money." That was the end of Auerhahn, but of course then I started printing books under my own name, but the last one I printed under my own name, the same thing happened.

   Ginsberg gave me this whole box of his journals and papers of his trips to India. They were almost illegible. He got someone in New York to transcribe most of them, he got these endless sheets, mainly of dreams and stuff like that, a lot of it almost unreadable stuff. And he sent it to me and said, "Do you want to make a book out of this?" and I said "OK," so I started going through all this material, and I thought, "Yeah, we can make a real book out of this, we can make a statement." But have you ever read this book? It's depressing. It's a death book; it's about Ginsberg's encounter with mortality and obsession with death, and it's really worth reading, but it's not happy going. I spent a lot of time editing it. I took most of the dreams out, I thought he could have a separate dream journal, unless the dream had something specifically to do with what was happening with him in India. So, I got the book down, selected from the photographs he'd sent me, these really incredible photographs, and again, all of it intended to really make a book, which I think it does, maybe not a very happy book, but I got to the end of it. I had it set in type, I had the whole book laid out, everything, and I no longer had any money, so I called up Ferlinghetti and I said, "Do you want to be co-publisher of this book, it's all ready to go to print, do you want to take it from there?" And he said "Yes," and that's the last I ever heard about it. This book is in a lot of editions around the world, but that's the last I ever heard of it, so I guess I do not have a very good business head.

AMJ: Did you set that Holbrook?

HT: Jim Brooke set it and he had a pirated edition in the trunk of his car for many months and gave them to us, and Michael [Myers] did a very beautiful linoleum block with that of a lotus blossom, but I don't know whatever happened to it.

AMJ: So the tables were turned and you went to work for Andy?

DH: It became Grabhorn-Hoyem and he and Bob formed a business and moved over on Commercial Street, and they offered me a job as a typographer and editor there with the agreement I could use all their presses and facility to go ahead and print my own books, so it was actually a pretty good deal.

*Human Universe by Charles
Olson, Auerhahn Society, 1965,
woodcut by Robert LaVigne*

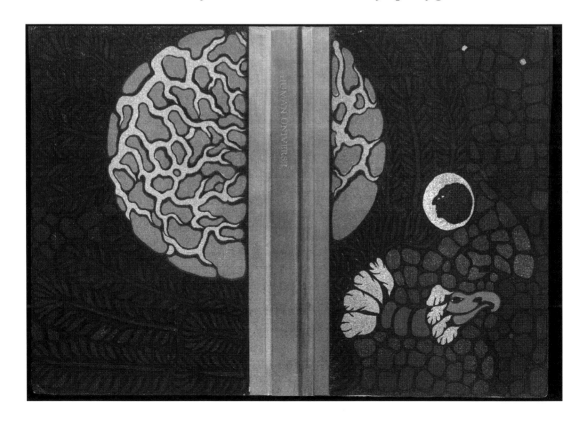

AMJ: This is interesting: Andrew's edition of *Chimeras* by Nerval. Because Blaser had just done one and Duncan did one, so Andrew decided he had to do one.

DH: Duncan, again, just had an unbelievable fit about this, because Duncan was very much into this kind of magic — a lot of baloney — but anyhow I think he saw these poems as some kind of sacred arcana, that these were somehow magical things, these Nerval poems. They're incredible, but I don't think that's what they are. When Andy rewrote the poems and put his own slant on them, this to Duncan was a total outrage. Well, it's called *Transformations*. I think it's a very pretty book.

AMJ: Two final books contracted to Auerhahn Press were published by the Auerhahn Society, and these were completely the work of Andrew?

DH: Yes, and you can see how heavily influenced he's become by the Grabhorns: the wallpaper binding.

AMJ: In some ways the limitations of simple materials and the strictures of just Caslon type really helped Andrew. The books he did at Auerhahn under those constraints are really elegantly done: they are simple. Once he got the resources of the Grabhorns, all of their decorative types and so on, things changed. You were definitely a good influence.

You did still produce some books at their facility. You did reprints of your most popular books, *Dark Brown* and you did another edition of *Exterminator*.

DH: I love the cover on this edition of *Dark Brown*.

AMJ: My favourites among your works are this little series of seven oblong books, obviously done on offcut. These were hobby things done on a proof press?

DH: When I got out of Auerhahn they were a form of protest against what was happening to Auerhahn Press: it was becoming just precious editions. So I thought, I'm going to make these absolutely exquisite books, and every one of them will be given away. They were not sold. They are made on handmade paper.

AMJ: *Courses* [of Lew Welch] is bound in leather.

DH: Magda [Cregg] did them.

AMJ: And there were others. For me that was a real delight finding those. To complete the circle you ended with the book you'd started with which was John Wieners' *Hotel Wentley Poems*. You did it now the way you'd wanted it done, in Joanna type, beautifully handset and printed. That's really the remarkable thing: to complete the circle that way, by saying, 'this is why I started the press, this is the book I wanted to do, and this is how it should have been done.' It must have been a great feeling after that journey of ten years…no it was only seven years — You had a lot of energy: it would have taken me twenty years to do all that! — to get back to where you started and to tie it up.

DH: Yes. [*picking up McClure's* Sermons of Jean Harlow and Curses of Billy the Kid] This is me being absolutely baroque. I had so much fun doing this, with all these funny hokey typefaces.

SL: I remember McClure reading that at a reading one time, and he got hissed!

DH: I can imagine.

AMJ: So then you retired and became a landscape architect. Did you ever wish you'd taken the press in a different direction, or gone on as a designer?

DH: No absolutely. As a matter of fact, I probably got out at the right time, because the poets that I really liked could get big publishers, they didn't need a small press, they needed big publishers. And what was happening, newly on the poetry scene, did not appeal to me at all. You know the Hippie period was dead as far as poetry was concerned, it was not a poetry period. The Hippies were into music, certain kinds of visual art, but not really into poetry so I thought the new poetry that was coming out got very boring. So I didn't really regret getting out of it at all.

AMJ: We didn't mention the last couple of McClure books: *Dream Table* and *Lobe / Key / Stilled / Lionman / Laced / Winged / April / Raphael / Dance / Wiry* that you did. This one [*untitled 'mandala' book*], which was a collaboration again with Conner and McClure — the homeboys reunited — although it looks like a slick offset book, it's letterpress. Very constructivist-modern.

DH: This was done just before I quit. We set out to do a three-way collaborative work of art.

AMJ: It's a truly remarkable achievement.

DH: It's just a little pile of paper.

AMJ: I think you opened a lot of minds, especially with the work of Lamantia, Whalen, *Dark Brown*. You certainly paved the way for, not just a lot of poets, but for other small press publishers. You were the beacon shining. But indeed Auerhahn was one of the last great literary presses in San Francisco.

DH: Do you know that great line by WS Gilbert in *Patience*? "For art stopped short in the cultivated court of the Empress Josephine." Actually, there were probably four really seminal presses at that time, and maybe City Lights should be included though I don't know how.

AMJ: Most of his books were badly printed in England by Villiers Press. He had one book printed by Clifford Burke and one by Wesley Tanner, but he could have found a Chinese printer round the corner in North Beach to keep the work local.

DH: There was Jonathan Williams' Jargon Press; there was Yugen of LeRoi Jones; White Rabbit and Auerhahn. Those were really truly literary presses. I mean unlike Grabhorn or Arion Press, which are 'fine printing,' they were presses where the emphasis was on the poetry and yet an attempt was made to bring out a really beautiful book. I think that what was useful was to show that could happen. It's obviously what turns you on, and I think a lot of other people.

SL: It seems to me that there's an attempt in this latest wave of revival to really portray this scene as happy in which everyone loved each other and sat around playing bongos together. But it seems to me that didn't occur. There was a very deep…basically three Bohemias operating simultaneously all headed in different directions?

DH: Right. I thought the New York section of the museum show was very off-base. There were different people pulling in different directions and trying to become the official boundaries of the Beat. At the time it was going on those scenes were quite different but they cross-fertilized each other a lot. And Ginsberg would come out here, and of course Kerouac came out, and Neal Cassady (who by the way has never been properly portrayed: he was an incredible human being, a great person); Corso — all these people — it was a hard-edged New York thing and Diane DiPrima came out of that and LeRoi Jones. Then there was this much less intellectual and more traditional poetry scene going on in San Francisco. In LA there was a mainly visual arts thing beginning to happen. My clear memory of it is they were all cross-fertilizing each other all the time. The people from LA would come up and they were all close friends with McClure. For a brief time it was very fertile because of all these cross-currents.

SL: But, like what we see as the stereotypical North Beach scene?

DH: Those people were clowns. No one took it seriously, those people were truly clowns: the guy who always wore the pirate costume…I remember the day when the first tourist bus came up Grant Street and all the people were looking at the Beatniks, and of course this was manufactured: it was good old American commerce.

As a matter of fact the famous Gough Street building (which

I also lived in) was in some ways the real place at the beginning of what most people think of as the Beat Generation in San Francisco, when Neal Cassady and Natalie [Jackson], who became the muse of all those people (then threw herself off the Golden Gate Bridge), lived there. Ginsberg lived there, and Bob LaVigne lived there. This was about the time of the Six Gallery reading. So in some ways you could say it was a Western Addition movement.

RW: Was that the Fillmore?

DH: There was Upper Fillmore and Lower Fillmore. Lower Fillmore was black and it was a wonderful scene. Actually, that poem by John Wieners, "Up Above the Cobalt Bomb," was written in a little jazz club on Fillmore Street before there was any tension in San Francisco between the blacks and the whites; it was a very sweet scene.

L to R: Glenn Todd (pressman at Arion Press), Dave Haselwood (Auerhahn Press) and Joe Dunn (White Rabbit Press), at a party at Ernie Edwards' house, San Francisco, July 1986. Photo by Alastair Johnston.

One of the things nobody mentions any more is the Hipster, who is quintessentially a New York type, but they were big heroes of many of the Beats. McClure to this day dresses like a Hipster: dark shades and all.

AMJ: Thank you all for coming, especially Dave, who, starting on Thursday, is taking a thirty day vow of silence, so that's all he has to say. I'm not kidding!

ROBERT HAWLEY

Born in Wisconsin in 1929, Robert Hawley was briefly a student at Black Mountain College. Poet Charles Olson, who was at the time rector of the College, discouraged Hawley from writing poetry and suggested he become a publisher instead. He started Oyez! Press with Stevens van Strum in 1964. When Hawley retired, I called poet David Meltzer and asked him to meet me at Hawley's bookstore, The Ross Valley Book Company in North Oakland on Friday, 19 May 2000, for a chat.

AMJ: Batteries good. There it goes.

BH: There was no oval office!

AMJ: It was square I tell you. Is that your first book, the Bram Dijkstra [*Faces in Skin*]?

BH: No, the first book was David [Meltzer]'s *The Process*, and we tried to live that down for forty years.

AMJ: Who did the cover for that?

BH: That's Bram. He was working at Cody's [Books]. I only knew him very slightly, I think he was a Dutch exchange student. And Stevens van Strum who was my early partner brought in some of his work which I thought was really delightful. A great sense of humor. I think he did several other drawings for the book.*

AMJ: You were working at Cody's also?

BH: No, I was working at Holmes Book Company in Oakland.

DM: Three floors of books.

AMJ: I remember that.

BH: We also had a store at 22 3rd Street in San Francisco: great store and a great staff.

AMJ: I remember the San Francisco store. It seemed like it had been there a hundred years.

BH: The Oakland store started in 1925. The San Francisco store started at that location in 1922, but Mr Holmes had had shops in different locations in San Francisco since 1894.

AMJ: Why did you decide to go to Black Mountain College — what was the appeal?

BH: I had gone through a very nasty divorce, and I went back to the Midwest to get away, see old friends, family, and things like that, and there was a musician — I think he was the director of the Minneapolis Chamber Symphony — it was Tom Mee. I was really at loose ends and probably not terribly rational, and it was Tom who said Charles Olson had been a friend of his and he had been there and I should go. He called and apparently Olson said, "Yes, send him down." Tom loaned me thirty dollars for the bus fare and I got off at Asheville and apparently somebody was there with a car, I don't remember his name now — it might have been Tony Landreau — and he drove me out to Black Mountain College and Charles was having headaches. Russ, er…there was a second-in-command, the drama teacher — Wes Huss — welcomed me and said, "Take any room you want." There were all these cottages and nine people there.

There were no real classes except Duncan was there for two months and we had sort of informal poetry seminars. There was a wonderful student union. Upstairs there was a large

*The Process by David Meltzer is illustrated by the author with cover drawings by Peter LeBlanc. Bram Dijkstra's *Faces in Skin* is illustrated by the author.

study hall sort of place, and Duncan would sit and talk poetry. If you wanted to show him your material you could — and he didn't like what I was writing at all — at all!

AMJ: Were there fees to go there? It sounds more like a religious cult than a school.

BH: I never paid anything. If there were fees, nobody charged or collected.

AMJ: So it was just like if you were invited you ended up there?

BH: That's right, though I think you ended up there even if you weren't invited. There was Eloise and Don Nixon, who I think ended up in Stinson Beach, Tony Landreau, Ebbe Borregaard…

AMJ: Tom Field?

BH: Right. Dorothy, the woman I was with, and I were lying on the porch patio of the student union. The highway was there; there was a gravel road coming up and Dorothy said, "That's the most beautiful man I've ever seen in my life," and it was Ebbe walking up. Anybody was welcome. You could talk to Charles; you could talk to Wes; you could talk to Duncan. But we went into Black Mountain. There was a roadhouse called Peak's Place and we drank beer and danced for two months. It wasn't bad.

AMJ: So that was how you met Duncan?

BH: I met Robert very briefly here, in 1955, at Josephine Miles'. Ms Miles had been a teacher of mine at Cal. I really loved Jo. She had that little house on Virginia with that fenced area and it was so great; we'd sit there and drink tea and she had a maid or companion and George Stewart would come by, dear courtly George…a great time.

AMJ: How did you meet David?

BH: David was working at Discovery Books, next to City Lights, in 1965. We talked, and David had done at least one book of poetry.

DM: Two. But the bookstore had published one.

BH: You either gave one or two to me. And when I thought of publishing, with the encouragement of Bill Farrell who had Farrell's bookshop in Berkeley, and Stevens van Strum, my associate from Cody's, David was the first person we thought about. I really like his poetry. I liked it then.

DM: Don't read it now.

BH: I don't read anything anymore.

DM: I hate the stuff too.

BH: I read Pound and Williams and Moore…

DM: She said, "I too distrust it."

AMJ: Who? Marianne Moore?

DM: Yes, it's a famous poem.

BH: We thought the people we really like should be available in local editions. There was no Duncan, no McClure, no Meltzer. Their stuff was not there. We decided very consciously in 1964, 1965, to start publishing those people we cared about the most. David was our first choice. We did a series of broadsides.

AMJ: The ones Hoyem printed. Haselwood was going to do them first, right?

BH: Haselwood did some and then Hoyem kind of took it away from him. We went because of Dave Haselwood.

AMJ: He was publishing, so you felt like he wasn't publishing the people you wanted to see in print?

BH: Right.

AMJ: And of course there was Ferlinghetti but he was mostly involved with the East Coast school.

BH: And people I didn't care for particularly. Ginsberg has certainly written some wonderful poetry, but most of the stuff that City Lights has done I don't care for particularly. And this was consciously our choice. Stevens and myself. These were people we wanted to publish. And looking back I wouldn't change anything. On my dining room wall I have Duncan's "My Mother would be a Falconress." I've read that poem four hundred times.

  He read it at Cal, at a chemistry schoolroom with these steep stairs, and he said, "I've just finished this. I'm going to read to you." And he read it and I ran down the stairs and almost broke my neck and hugged him and said, "I wanna publish that, it's big. It's a magnificent poem."

AMJ: Duncan was a giant in the local scene.

BH: I wish we'd done more. We did *The Years as Catches*, the early poems, and *The Cat and the Blackbird*.* And I think one other thing. I wish I had done a lot more. Robert was intimidating to me. He was so bright, so articulate, that although I delighted in every moment I studied with him, he really — it was difficult for me to approach him *mano-a-mano.*

AMJ: How did you get involved with Everson?

BH: On Wednesday one of Everson's old, old friends was in town and we sat here almost in tears talking about Everson. It was 1963 probably. We had this list of the ten poets we wanted to publish, and Everson was at the Dominican priory in San Rafael. Stevens and I called and made an appointment to go over and see him and sat outside at a table just talking. I was totally taken by the man. His thoughts, his perceptions, his outlook, his concerns, things like that, and he promised us a poem, which I liked very, very much. It came immediately. Our

*Oyez! published three Duncan titles: *Medea at Kolchis: The Maiden Head*, 1965; *The Years as Catches*, 1966, and *Of the War, Passages 22-27*, 1966. *The Cat and the Blackbird* by Robert Duncan and Jess was published by White Rabbit Press in 1967; however at that time, White Rabbit books were being distributed by Oyez!

friendship was so strong. He was a very lusty man: he liked his cigars and his bourbon, his food. I would say probably once a month he'd call and I would take the bus over to San Francisco, walk up Post Street and stop at Drucquer's tobacco place and get four cigars and walk to the Oak Room at the Saint Francis Hotel. Usually I was there ahead of him. He'd say, "Meet me at four o'clock," and I'd be there at five after four and sit with a drink, and you could hear him coming. On a great day he'd be wearing his robes, the Catholic habiliments. He had this rosary — you could use it to lasso steers — and you'd hear it clicking and he'd stop in the doorway with an immense grin. We would sit there for an hour or two, have a few drinks, stop, and go to Jack's or someplace like that for dinner. He'd take the bus back to San Rafael and I'd take the bus back home. He was very, very dear. It was a thirty-year friendship that I really treasure in retrospect.

AMJ: And how did you meet up with Graham [Mackintosh]?

BH: [*Uproarious laughter*] Graham was in last week. We were just sort of talking about the sixties and things like that. Graham had a house on Jones Street in San Francisco but he was printing in Oakland using a press quite close to Holmes, I think, somewhere on 17th Street.

AMJ: Right. Downstairs from Jack LaLanne's Spa.

BH: I think it was just by chance we met and had a beer. And when I decided I wanted to print and publish, several people said, "Talk to Graham: he's ready to do bigger and better books." I have the greatest possible respect for him as a printer as well as the greatest possible affection for him as a human being. He's very, very dear.

AMJ: I love that thing you did with him at the San Francisco Public Library, the *Ad Interviewum*. That's one of my favourite things.

BH: Graham had an apartment on Union Street: second floor. He was having an exhibit at the San Francisco Public Library and they wanted something to give away. I went up there and he had this typewriter and with traffic down below on Union Street I interviewed Graham. It still is funny.

AMJ: Yes, things like "How did you manage to achieve fifty years of great printing in just five years?" And Graham said, "By taking ten times as long as I should have on every job."

BH: I asked him, "Can you express in layman's terms your aesthetic, your philosophy of the book?" He replied, "I'd say it's ink on paper, and a strict sequence of pages."

AMJ: That's it!

BH: I haven't seen it in years. We did five hundred or one thousand copies and gave them away.

AMJ: The introduction by Dave Kherdian was hilarious.

DM: Oh God, that was such a…I'll never forget him coming up to the place on Jones Street, fibrillating with pride, and presenting a copy of this book they did. I started reading it and Tina [Meltzer] started reading it. What was it called? *A Checklist of David Meltzer* or something. I was too young to begin with. Anyway, his writing was so unintentionally bizarre it was all we could do to hold it back. We would entertain guests with a reading from his introduction.

AMJ: But who published it? [*laughter*] Uh-oh…

DM: And then there was one on McClure where Kherdian talks about his chubby fingers. You can imagine Michael getting really hung up about that. Sitting on his hands.

AMJ: The other classic is the "Artifical Rarity" broadside you did with Graham.

BH: I don't have a copy of that.

AMJ: It really is a rarity.

DM: Didn't it used to be in the toilet at one of your bookstores?

BH: A long time ago, and then it disappeared. But to have it read "Artifical" is pure Graham.

DM: I asked Kherdian why, he said "Otter-brown eyes," and he said, "Well I saw an otter once. " He's a Gurdjieffian.

BH: Isn't Dave Haselwood also?

DM: Dave was, he got started there…

AMJ: But he's into Zen now, which is just "then" in a French accent. He's an abbot and runs the Zendo up there in Rohnert Park or Cotati. He's the big cheese, or I think they call it *Le Grand Frommage*. But Dave is so unassuming, he is so great.

BH: In '64 we went there because Dave had been recommended to us and we wanted him to do this series of ten broadsides. About the fourth broadside, Hoyem took it away and David kind of faded out of the picture. Someday if the story ever comes out…

There was a Creeley, which was number six or seven. The design is too tricky: it's two poems, long and narrow, like Creeley's writing. And the *T* was in diamonds all the length of the broadside. It was being printed on a very warm day so the diamonds were to be filled in with yellow. You could see where they began to go out of whack, when the paper began to shrink, and your good friend Andy went in and hand-colored them in a sort of an orange. It's really ugly. I kept a copy of each: the printed and the painted.

AMJ: That's been a problem since the early days of printing: registering the second colour.

BH: Another bourbon, David?

DM: Sure. I'm just witnessing. When we came in and interviewed about Everson that was the extent of my interviewing chops.

AMJ: Graham tells some funny stories about Everson, or Brother Antoninus, whom he calls Brother Egotinus. He worked with him at Saint Albert's priory in Oakland. Graham had gone over to help him and he had just finished tying up this whole galley for a page they were printing on the *Psalter* or something like that. The thing about Everson was he was a shouter: he would suddenly yell, "Ohmigod!!" as if in ecstatic prayer, and he yells "Ohmigod!!" and Graham jolts and this galley of type goes flying all over the floor. He looks around and Everson has this beatific look on his face.

DM: He had a strong sense of self.

BH: Alan Kaprow did a bibliography of Everson. We were friends for thirty years and exchanged stories but he had the same… Brother was always very good to me, he had an avuncular attitude toward me, but he was so consumed with self it was hard for him sometimes just to see the outside world.

DM: He had great platform manner.

BH: Oh boy, yeah, I remember. He was always confronting the audience. Then he'd pace the stage using the microphone cord almost like a whip…

DM: Something Mick Jagger picked up from the Bro. I remember when Jack Shoemaker and I organized this week-long poetry reading series tied up with a week-long celebration of arts in San Francisco that Glide [Memorial Methodist Church] was somehow underwriting and he was one of the last to read. The reading was in the main church while most of the other readings had been in a smaller area as befitting a shrinking audience for the series we had set up — like the all-star band filling up the big auditorium then gradually the more serious but not as well known — without the entourages, the stretch limos, you know the things that come with being a great poet in America… And Brother Bill with the uniform on was confronting the audience and beneath him, which was where I guess the Reverend Cecil Williams preaches, a lectern, but beneath it were these candles, you know wax candles, not ones with electric light bulbs on them. At one point in the poem Brother Bill puts his hand down like Haldeman and starts hanging it over the candle and continues to recite the poem. You know that it's hurting him, and he had their attention all right.

Then I remember when I was interviewing him for that book [*The San Francisco Poets*], he had just left the Order and came to the place in Mill Valley, in this case in buckskin, you know the 'Buffalo Bill' Everson, with his caribou teeth and eagle feathers or whatever.

BH: His necklace was bearclaw.

DM: One of the interesting things that he said in the interview was that he needed a costume and one of the great things about being in the Order was that you had this great costume and could make this appearance, so when he left the Order he had to have another kind of costume. He was quite candid about that. It was an interesting transitional time for him.

AMJ: He was going from Brother Bill to Buffalo Bill.

DM: That's right: he was more liminal at this point, and I guess a little more honest. He had embarked on this relationship with a woman. He tends to think it was nice, I have heard other stories.

AMJ: So he needed this shell for his persona to protect who he was?

DM: Right. Out of the costume would develop the persona, or encase the persona.

AMJ: According to *Oyez: The Authorized Checklist…*[*]

BH: There are five things that are not in there. Some friends of mine did that with the help of my wife, and they went with what was on the shelf and there were five things that I don't have. But it was very sweet.

AMJ: It was odd that they did it in alphabetical rather than chronological order because it doesn't give you the right sense of how things evolved.

BH: Four of my friends, who got Dorothy's cooperation, took stuff off the shelves. So it's incomplete and not in a format I would like, but it was a sweet thing to do.

AMJ: It says that the first thing you did was a McClure broadside. Was that the "Lion Fight" poster?

BH: Actually, the first thing we did was a checklist for a 1965 poetry festival. We did this little thing and gave it away. Then we started the broadside series. The "Love Lion, Lioness" poster was rather later.

AMJ: That's a really inspired piece. It looks like a boxing poster.

BH: Michael has a great sense of theatre. I sometimes have a problem with his poetry. *The Beard* is a comic masterpiece, and I think that the "Love Lion, Lioness" poster is so bizarre. It's just wonderful.

[*]Oyez! The Authorized Checklist, by Dave Bohn and John Carpenter, Berkeley, 1997, 32 pp., in wrappers.

AMJ: You had that printed at some little printshop on San Pablo Avenue in Oakland that did all the boxing posters?

BH: Right. Dorothy has photographs. Michael was driving a little sportscar that was this far off the ground and we drove around Telegraph, College, Broadway, and we stapled it with a theatrical staple-gun to telephone poles and building sites and they all disappeared right there, they were gone by next morning. I have one copy left and wouldn't part with it for anything.

AMJ: I had heard a story that McClure took it into a store and asked the guy to put it in the window, and he said, "Have you got any free tickets?" And so he went back to the printer and had him print up tickets that also said "Love Lion, Lioness."

BH: I don't recall. Michael did a version of the play *The Beard* at Berkeley High School theatre and we put two tickets on every seat and there's that scene of simulated cunnilingus and the play was busted. Here come ninety-seven Berkeley policemen, 'You can't eat no C*** in my town!'

AMJ: I would have thought that would have been very educational.

BH: I think they were all aware, you wouldn't have taught them anything... What is Michael doing these days?

DM: He remarried: a woman named Amy who is a sculptor, a very good one, and does graphic design. They moved into a very nice place in the Oakland hills.

BH: Well, if we tell the neighbors who he is they'll get him out of there.

DM: There's a nice book that Shambhala Press published that is these haiku-like poems, and Penguin has been republishing a lot of his old books into single volumes, and New Directions...

BH: This is such a backwater. If it's not six guns or horsies, I don't hear what's going on.

DM: The only reason I know is from interviewing him six months ago.

AMJ: You are re-doing *The San Francisco Poets* book from Ballantine?

DM: Right, and adding on a bunch of stuff. City Lights is doing it; it will be the same book with an additional set of six poets. We are going to have Harry Redl — who took all those beautiful pictures for the *Evergreen Review* "San Francisco Scene" — we are going to use those pictures.

BH: The McClure is so saccharine — I really don't like that.

DM: We are going to use photos that he took during that period of all the poets who are in the book. Then we are going to use the photographer who took all those famous photos of the poets in front of City Lights.

BH: Jack Ruby!

DM: Not Jack Ruby…but anyway he's going to be taking pictures of all the poets now. So before and after: it'll be like *The Picture of Dorian Gray*!

AMJ: Oh God!

DM: For once and for all we can dispel this bogus Beat stuff to show that, yes, time does march on: all over you as a matter of fact. And perhaps what we'll do is get all of the survivors in front of City Lights, and parody it, you know, with their walkers…*Night of the Living Dead*.

AMJ: Those Harry Redl photos are fantastic.

BH: Why doesn't someone publish them?

DM: He keeps trying to get people to publish it but no one for some reason wants it.

BH: It seems a natural.

DM: He propositioned Ferlinghetti who seemingly would be the obvious one, but he didn't want to do it for some reason.

AMJ: It's not really his thing. I mean Ferlinghetti has his little niche and won't go outside of it.

BH: Well, his niche is one of the cutest little girls I've ever seen!

DM: Since many people have died subsequently in that book then I thought I'd try to do interviews with people who knew them.

AMJ: Was Lew Welch in there?

DM: Yes, Lew was; in fact Lew was the reason I did the book, curiously enough. I wanted more attention directed to him. He felt he had failed in some way that all of his peers like Phil [Whalen] and Gary [Snyder] had gotten all the glory and he felt that he was in a sense their teacher.

AMJ: That's sad because I would have thought he was a key part of that whole scene. On one hand Phil is so self-effacing it's going to be another fifty years before he's recognised for his contribution to the whole movement and on the other hand you've got Snyder who's out there like Everson with the image and the cult promoting his version of Zen-egotism.

BH: A third-rate poet at best. I mentioned to David that one of the regrets I had is somebody who didn't write more is Ebbe Borregaard. I really loved him and the little bit I could collect was fine, but I wish he'd written more, and I'd published more.

DM: Well let me tell you, he's written an awful lot.

BH: Where is it?

DM: It's all in Bolinas, in trunks and notebooks, in these Blakean handwritten drawings. There's tons o' stuff. But he's disassociated himself, not from writing…

BH: If I had any money I'd publish him first, and Joanne Kyger. Another person whom I really like.

DM: We've talked about this before. Her work is only getting better, and she's at a wonderful place now with regard to her work.

BH: In 1965 during the poetry festival [former UC Berkeley English professor, Tom] Parkinson had a party at his house, and I'm not a Parkinson fan, but it was a good group: Peter Orlovsky was standing catatonic in the middle of the floor, and then Allen wandering around. I ended up talking to Joanne, and I said I really wanted desperately to publish something of hers, and she said "I'll send you a manuscript," and never did. I never followed up on it. I love Gail Dusenberry, but from that period I thought Joanne was the best of the living poets.

DM: She was superb. I've known her probably longer than any of the others and she was, when I first met her, when we were all very young, she was living in her hotel in North Beach…

BH: She was nine…

DM: Well, something like that. But she was very self-effacing about her poetry. She was very much under the sway of Robert. And Robert in a sense is a kind of source of permission, but she always kept her poetry…

BH: Was she in those Thursday evening things at Robert's house?

DM: You mean the Moon… The Moon Society he called it.

BH: I was there. I don't remember her, but I didn't know any of those people. Jess [Duncan's partner] liked Dorothy, and Robert was always very good to me. We'd go over there once every two months, or something like that.

DM: Well, her poetry would be in her dresser drawer, literally under her underwear: that's where it was placed.

BH: I've been there and I never saw it!

DM: It took her a long time to develop a kind of confidence in her own work. I think in the past decade or so it's really turned into…

BH: I'd like to do some publishing again, but the few thousand dollars I have put aside, I really want this trip, I need that first. I'm going to Mexico with the world's greatest woman. Up to Teotihuacan, Toluca, Tascal — we both love Tascal — there's the Empress Hotel there. We'll sit in the garden and drink margaritas for days on end.

*Portrait of Bob Hawley &
Graham Mackintosh by Ann
Charters (Oakland, 1965)*

SANDRA KIRSHENBAUM

Sandra Kirshenbaum (1938–2003) edited and published Fine Print *magazine from 1975 to 1990. Born in Milan, Ms Kirshenbaum's family came to San Francisco in 1940 to escape Fascism. She was a Phi Beta Kappa graduate of UC Berkeley, earning a degree in Italian literature. Following that, she attended Carnegie Library School and received her master's degree in library science in 1960. She founded* Fine Print *in 1975. She received several honors, including the American Printing History Association Award in 2001.*

When Artweek *did a special issue on artists' books in 1991, she interviewed me, and it was an opportunity for us to discuss our ideas about fine press tomes versus democratic multiples. This interview first appeared as "Making Books in Northern California: A Conversation with Alastair Johnston" (*Artweek *vol 22 no 21, 6 June 1991)*

SK: Alastair, first of all, I thought you could tell me a little about your latest book, *Luxorious*. I understand it's a fine limited edition book.

AMJ: No, I hope not. I hate the term "fine limited edition" book.

SK: Oh, you hate it. Then why did you produce one? [*laughs*]

AMJ: Uh…

SK: It's a joke, it isn't really fine?

AMJ: No, it is a fine, limited edition book. I produced it because, in order to use the best possible materials in the book and because of the nature of the binding, which takes forty minutes a copy, I could only produce, realistically, a hundred to a hundred twenty-five copies. If I manage to sell out the edition, I will reprint it. But to me, the notion of a limited edition is anathema. I believe in unlimited editions because that's what publishing is — getting a text out into the world. Having something so expensive or so exclusive that only a few people have it appeals to the worst kind of snobbery and the commodification of the book. It takes it out of the realm of information, which is what a book is, and puts it into this realm of collectability, which renders it as useless as a 1937 Edsel.

SK: So what you're saying is that limitation per se is not a desirable trait in a book, only the natural limitation by a factor such as the amount of handwork or even the restriction of available funds.

AMJ: Right.

SK: But if you carry that idea to the logical extension, then isn't it sort of antithetical for you to deliberately choose methods and materials that will result in limitation and exclusivity, snobbery and all the rest?

Simply to See, Poems of Luxorius, *translated into English by Art Beck (Berkeley, Poltroon Press, 1990)*

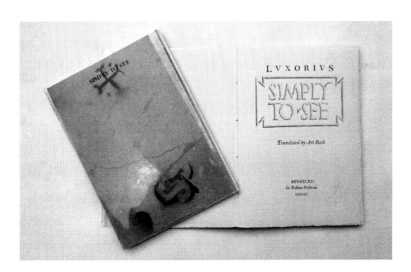

AMJ: Well, I've actually had a change of heart in recent years. Initially, when I started publishing, I would use cheap materials, of which the main single cost is paper and binding. And I would do books on the cheapest decent paper and do big editions, and try and get them out in the marketplace for under ten dollars. I published a lot of books under ten dollars. And people would ignore them. Generally, at that level, you're trying to compete with the trade publishers. You also have distribution problems. And I began to realize that there was no point in putting up all that money and doing a thousand copies of the book if I only sold two hundred. So, therefore, why not spend the same amount of money and do fewer copies and charge a more realistic price for it. I'm still trying to make it affordable. *Luxorious* is eighty dollars, which is a lot of money for a book of poetry, but it was an exercise in the historical period, the fifth century, and I was able to echo that in the choice of paper, in this binding style, in the decoration of the binding. And I was able to give the book an attractive package. And I think that by giving attention to materials, I've made it so that people will notice it, look at it, and go, 'Oh, this is great and it's a book from the fifth century and how appropriate that it has a fifth-century binding style.' If I followed my previous idea of doing it as cheaply as possible, and put it on the market for ten dollars, I think it would pretty much vanish without a trace, like so many of my other books.

SK: Well then, you would seem to be saying that artistry or craftsmanship in bookmaking really is only an attention-getting device.

AMJ: No, not entirely. I think that it's important to craft your books as well as you can, given your financial limitations. I think that the attention-getting aspect of it is when printers use a binding style for its own sake, deciding that it's time to package it in a pizza box, or use some nice bark paper on the binding, and there's no real connection between that and the content. One of the things that I really object to in the *livre d'artiste* world is this notion that you take a book like *Sonnets from the Portuguese*, take an artist like Francesco Clemente, or whoever's fashionable at the time, take a structure like Coptic or accordion-fold, take a novelty material like Mylar or Formica, shake well, and you've got a limited edition artist book. There's not really any artistry or craftsmanship in there that's applicable, because you don't really have the right marriage of components. You haven't brought a writer and an artist together and said, 'we're gonna do a book.' You've taken something off the shelf, a chestnut, that the people have read and are familiar with and has a certain cachet as a work of literature. Then you take an artist who has a reputation for doing interesting work. And then you just say, 'Okay, now how can we put this over?' It requires craftsmanship, but it's in the service of novelty or commerce.

SK: But one can choose a well-known artist and a text of some dependable author, and put them together in a significant way, put them together in a new way which is more significant as a reading object or as a way of appreciating the text than has been done before. Just because you use a novel format or some unusual material doesn't necessarily mean that you're plucking something off the shelf and sort of reaching for some unusual combination that will be attention-getting. You may, in fact, be trying to put the elements together in a way that is significant.

AMJ: Yeah, but inevitably in those cases, the author gets the shaft. Because inevitably what people remember is the format or the wild typography or the illustrations. And usually the text just gets walked over, and the package is paramount, and the text is hammered into shape to fit the package. And, you know, there are many, many examples. When I saw the Kaldeway Press exhibit at Mills a couple years ago, I was really disappointed, because they had the superficial appearance of beautifully made and interesting books. They have Jean de Gonet bindings, for example. And then you open one up and there're illustrations by a well-known artist, Jasper Johns or whomever, but then you get down to the text, and here's this wretchedly printed, badly spaced type that's a poem by Samuel Beckett, without margins, and it's absolutely an insult to the reader or to the person who appreciates a well-made book, when you realize that all the effort has gone into the package and you're buying this ostensibly valuable commodity and when you get down to it, it's a very shoddily put-together thing.

And this is something that becomes more offensive when you have famous artists involved, like Anselm Kiefer, who, like a lot of artists, realize that a book is a better format for a narrative than a canvas. On canvas you're limited to a certain kind of linearity. You don't have the same kind of time sequence that you have in a book.

So he discovers the book format and does a whole series of books and the art world is agog, and it's an affront to books, because he has no respect for the reader. The book falls apart.

You see it in a gallery, there's a woman in white gloves turning the pages every twenty minutes if you want to see the next page and bits of the book are falling on the floor. In the case of Kiefer, I don't mind that he doesn't respect the traditions of the book, because that's one of the great things about artists' books: it's a great opportunity to turn your back on the traditions. But in order to do that, you should know the traditions, you should understand them, you should master them before you flout them.

SK: You're asking an awful lot of what we would call a book artist. You're really extending the definition because you're saying that, essentially, you can't be a book artist without being a craftsperson as well, without having some domination over that craft. Is that correct?

AMJ: Right. Marie Antoinette's milliner said, "There's nothing new but what has been forgotten." So anything that's done, that's new in book arts, there's a precedent for it, and you can find someone else who's done it. But, to paraphrase Stanley Morison, 'books don't require inspiration so much as investigation'. And I think if artists were to really study the structure of the book they would find things like that wonderful Batak manuscript that you have here.* That's a several hundred-year-old shaman's book of recipes that's done on bark or bamboo. The letters are burned on there, and they're recipes, and he's carried it around with him, and it's been wrapped up in alligator entrails or whatever, and it has these recipes in a code that only he can decipher. And to me, that is so much more viable and valid then any number of artists' books. And so many artists' books are attempts at that, but in a modern way. Like Paul Zelavansky's *Case for the Burial of Ancestors*, which is often cited as a key artist's book, which is rubber stamps and a little shamanistic drawings, and so on, but that's a cartoon version of your Batak manuscript book, because there somebody was using the materials at hand, the materials that would be durable, and he was recording something that he needed to record, that was so important he couldn't just commit it to memory. It was the formulae for certain kinds of rites and rituals and so that book is charged with this amazing power and magical energy that this shaman has imbued into it. This is something we can see in Egyptian papyri. But to say, 'Oh, gee, I'll do that,' and to buy a bunch of papyrus and start drawing hieroglyphs on it without knowing what you're doing is just being trendy, being glib. It's not really adding anything to mankind. It's not

*The interview was held at the Printing Industries of Northern California Museum on 3rd Street in San Francisco. The Batak book mentioned was owned by Sandra Kirshenbaum and on loan to the museum.

doing anything to elevate consciousness or enlighten one more person. It's just making a fast buck off something you've seen that you think is a good idea.

SK: Well then, would we say that if a book was to be made in a similar way, using, say, modern sayings or religious thoughts; using materials of our time, would that make it authentic?

AMJ: You mean to have it on a floppy disk [*laughter*] rather than in book format? It would more accurately reflect our time, which would necessarily mean that we would have to admit to a large extent that the book formats are being exhausted, and people are increasingly turning to video and retrievables. But a lot of artists' books are really self-published and that's where you have the opportunity to do things that you wouldn't normally do. Up until thirty years ago, it was considered a derogatory thing to publish your own book. You know, you'd find this little ad in the back of the magazine: 'Poets, do you want to be in print?' You'd send your poems and they'd churn out an edition you could give to all your relatives.

SK: Yeah, well, it's vanity publishing.

AMJ: Yeah, vanity publishing, right. But you know, vanity is a key feature of the artists' book and the small press movement. I mean, there's so much vanity tied up in the presses and particularly the presses that have a recognizable style and you see the ego of the printer on display in every book.

SK: Am I mistaken, or do I see an increasing preciousness in books being produced now, in the nineties? It seemed to me that in the seventies and even into the eighties there seemed to be deep reasons, deep societal reasons why people wanted to make these kinds of books, whether it was expressing feminist yearnings, whether it was to publish poetry that would otherwise have been censored or mangled in some way by a trade publisher. Or to put together art with literature in an interesting way that had not been done before.

AMJ: Umhmm.

SK: But it seems to me that I'm looking around at the books being produced today and very often I see more concentration on the obscure or little-appreciated, perhaps Latin authors. There seems to be a great fad on right now for Horace, for example, and everybody seems to be producing an edition of Horace.

AMJ: Horace is a timeless author. I would like to do a Horace myself. But I would certainly do a new translation if I was going to do it and try and come up with a new approach to it. It's a reflection of our times. There is an increasing conservatism and has been since the sixties. In the sixties, there was immediacy and urgency. The materiality of the transmission didn't matter; it was just the matter of getting the information out there. So there was newsprint and off-cut and whatever else people could generate. But, as you know, we've gotten into this much more conservative social and political and cultural climate, and people have started to turn more toward durability.

SK: Okay, so tell us something about the artists' book precursors in the Northern California area.

AMJ: Well, I think there is a healthy disregard for the traditions that was manifested by Graham Mackintosh, Dave Haselwood, Michael McClure, Wallace Berman with *Semina* magazine, and then Holbrook Teter and Michael Myers. It really opened the door for the whole artists' book movement. And they were the people in the fifties and sixties who during the Beat movement began to experiment with formats and began to explode our notions of what a book was and how it could affect society. That was the point at which people began to have their awareness opened up by publishing in our generation and see that by taking control of the means of production and just having an attitude, political or otherwise, you could influence society. And, in those days, letterpress was just the cheapest means of production. People like Wally Berman and Dave Haselwood were out there producing these revolutionary, radical works that were challenging the status quo. And saying, you know, we need a change.

SK: Well, where did it go from there? It seemed like there was quite a hiatus between what was done by Haselwood at Auerhahn and at the White Rabbit, and what came later.

AMJ: No, I think it carried through. I think Zephyrus Image had a very, very strong impact on the next generation, which was Poltroon Press, Rebis Press, saying, 'Well, gee, we can do this, play around with notions of the structure of a book.' They would go to great lengths to create a letterpress book that looked like a five-cent Woolworth spiral notebook. And that had a very strong influence on Betsy Davids, Jim Petrillo and on Frances [Butler] and I when we first started.

SK: Well, let's talk a little bit about fine printing. Do you think there is such a thing as fine printing?

AMJ: You know, the worst kind of fetishism permeates the fine book market — this notion that a fine edition is so much finer than the others because here's Mark Twain bound in paddles from his own paddle boat. Those kinds of books are so rare that they have this thing that connects the possessor of the book to the author in some kind of fetishistic way. And that's what removes books from the real world, puts them into this other mysterious world, this black hole. But if you mean printers who wear white shirts and ties and never get their cuffs dirty, yes. Those are the fine printers, the ones that never get ink on their fingernails. [*laughs*] But it's a dirty business. That's why it's called the black art.

There is good presswork and bad presswork, but the best presswork in the world cannot compensate for a truly boring book. I would much rather read a Dover or a Penguin book and get the ink on my fingers and spill tea on the margins than sit down with something like the Doves Bible and try to read it, try to live with it. But fine printing, as we know it is usually associated with over-inked and over-impressed type on hand-made paper.

One thing that really makes me ill are people that say 'I love the kiss of letterpress.' 'Cause it's not a kiss, you know, it's *Deep Throat*. It's a heavy wallop into the paper (in those so-called fine press books). And, as one observer commented, the history of typography began when Gutenberg managed to put an inked letter at the bottom of a ditch in a piece of paper and then for five hundred years they were trying to figure out how to climb out of the ditch. Well, with offset lithography they finally got out of the ditch. So the ditch, the impression, the dent in the paper, is what distinguishes "fine" printing from regular printing. But there's no reason why offset printing can't be done on good paper and be just as nice.

SK: Maybe you could tell us a little bit about what you think the relationship of fine printing to book art — can you have book art without fine printing?

AMJ: A book is essentially just a sequence of pages. It doesn't necessarily have to be letterpress printing or even any other kind of printing, although it could be Xerox or rubber stamps or potato prints. So I think that there is definitely a separation that's apparent in the artists' book movement between people who are artists making books, who don't necessarily do any actual printing at all. I have a student [Steve Woodall] who's got a Xerox machine at home and he makes wonderful little books on a Xerox machine. If he needs type, he generates it on his computer or out of a magazine. You couldn't say these aren't fine books because they're well-made. And you couldn't say that he's not a book artist because they definitely are sequences of pages which is what a book is. So I definitely see a divorce there, and I definitely see a retreat on the part of the fine printers to the handpress and the idea of sticking to "the ideal book" and "the book beautiful." Not so much a retrenchment as just kind of saying, 'Well, we'll let this pass.' While the artist book field kind of stampedes through. So there's definitely an expansion of public awareness of books through the artist book movement. But I think that a lot of the fine printers are just kind of hiding out while this takes place and hoping that it will go away.

SK: Mmmm. You seemed to say before, however, that you couldn't really consider yourself a book artist if you hadn't achieved mastery over all the traditional arts of bookmaking, which I assume includes typography and printing. And yet now you seem to be saying that it doesn't really matter a heck of a lot that a visual artist can put a book together in a sequence of images and it doesn't really matter if that "book artist" understands anything about typography and printing.

AMJ: I personally think they should all study typography and printing if they want their books to be well-rounded and whole. But a lot of books are purely visual and a lot of books don't really have any typography in them, or they appropriate typography from advertising and other sources. So that it serves the purposes, but it is a dichotomy that there is this whole movement of self-taught people that have come along and have started to say, 'Okay, we're gonna make books,' and they're looking for the information, they're looking for the background.

SK: Mmmm. I think that my objection very frequently is that fact that young people today or new book artists will pick up on elements that exist in say, the Constructivists or the Surrealists. And they pick up on certain elements, whether it's blocks of color, dotted lines or slanted letters. And then just appropriate them and use them not knowing really where they came from or what the origins were, and they think of themselves as being really revolutionary in their new way of handling text, or blocks of color and letters and so on. And not realize that it was all done before.

AMJ: Yeah, they're getting that from graphic arts, because most book artists' exposure to typography and design comes through the media, through posters, record covers and so on. So it's true they're not really getting that. And they're not really understanding it. A sad thing is we've never really had Cubism as a movement embed itself in our bookmaking consciousness to the extent that it has had an impact on the way books are made.

You could say to a minor extent, some of the Hedi Kyle structures as used by Susan King suggest a kind of visual plane and the altered perspective and the multiple viewpoints. You could interpret that from a Cubist viewpoint, but you know, it's been eighty years. California bookmaking has been so stultified because of the William Morris tradition, and because of the Grabhorn-Nash tradition. People were afraid to break out of that and say, well, let's really examine Cubism, let's really examine Russian Constructivism or Italian Futurism.

SK: You've mentioned Northern California, which leads me to ask: do you think there is a special character to Northern California bookmaking or book art as compared to other regions of the country, or even other parts of the world?

AMJ: I would say that it's in a time warp. And that for the most part you've got this very anomalous group of printers who are adhering to the William Morris school. I don't think it exists on the East Coast anymore, but you've still got that sense of attention to the type and the paper and all of the other aspects of the book, and when you graft a modern artist onto it, it doesn't really make the marriage.

I'm thinking of the Arion Press *Tristram Shandy* or the Arion Press *Ulysses*, which were very traditional and conservative books typographically, with fine materials. And then they have this kind of grafted-on art aspect that didn't really integrate into the book-format. And I think that's one of the things that has caused Northern California printing — with the notable exception of Jack Stauffacher's work — to be an anachronism. People still want the book to be a certain way with certain sizes of type and a certain grandiosity.

SK: So in general you don't see Northern California printers doing as much as they do in Los Angeles and in other parts of the country?

AMJ: Other countries more than other parts of the country. I think we're always following behind what's going on in Europe, in Germany and Holland in particularly. And I mean even Iceland — you know Dieter Roth is one of the great innovators in artists' books and he's in a country that has less than two hundred thousand inhabitants.

SK: So you don't seem to think then that there is a special character to Northern California?

AMJ: It's special in that it's reactionary. It's not that it's unattractive, it's just outdated.

SK: Well then, would you say there has been any contribution?

I'm speaking of your independent bookmaking, the small editions. Do you think that the people who've been doing that for the past fifteen or twenty or twenty-five years — let's just limit it to the last quarter of the century — do you think that they have made any significant cultural contributions, and if so, what do you think it has been?

AMJ: I think the big contribution has been in the work of teachers like Frances Butler, Betsy Davids, and Kathy Walkup. I think that they are the ones who have actualized the whole movement of autobiographical and interesting artist bookwork that has then gone on and spread out across the country. But Frances' teaching and classes in typography and design had a very, very profound impact on them. And I'm sure the same goes for Betsy and Kathy Walkup. But the impact hasn't necessarily been felt in books. Among Frances' students were design majors who were mainly interested in textiles or interiors or architecture, so they've gone on to other fields.

SK: So the influence has been mostly in fields other than bookmaking per se?

AMJ: There've been great students that have come out of the various book programmes, but generally they've just had a glancing effect on the book and then have gone away and done other things. The ball keeps rolling forward a little bit but it hasn't started to gather momentum like we all hoped it would in the seventies.

SK: Do you see it peeling out? I seem to see that a lot of the people who were very bravely making books in the seventies have since left the field.

AMJ: No, I think they left out of personal disappointment, as a result of the failure of distribution and the failure of the market to appreciate their work. I think there's a bigger interest than ever in books as structures and the book format. And I think there always will be. It's just shifting.

When I came into it, it was as a poet who wanted to get published and realizing, at age nineteen, that nobody was going to be interested in my weird poetry. And then discovering the work of Jargon Press and thinking anybody who really wanted to could do it, and deciding then, 'Okay, I'm going to be a printer, I'm going to learn how to do this.' But the emphasis has gone away from self-publishing, because now everybody has access to a computer or a typewriter and a Xerox machine and that's the way to do it. But I think that there's a real interest among commercial designers, commercial graphic artists, people who do interiors and so on, to learn more about the book structure, because those are the people who are coming to my classes. They are coming out of the professional world where they want to get an edge on the competition by having a broader range of things that they can do.

SK: So what you seem to be saying is that there is a definite change in the underlying impetus for this kind of work — whereas once the impetus was largely literary expression.

AMJ: Yes.

SK: Now you seem to be saying that it has more to do with graphic expression, as well as tactile expression.

AMJ: Right. And the more people get access to computers and photocopy machines and become computer literate and start doing stuff, then that's the point at which they begin to realize there's something beyond that, which is the well-made book, where something has been thought-out and there are interesting materials and there's an interesting structure. And so that's helping, that's actually pushing forward and giving people greater awareness of what the potential is.

  It's no longer people at the grassroots level, getting a press and a case of type to start printing their poetry, and then saying, 'Well, gee, I can get linocuts to illustrate it, that's no problem.' It's people coming in at a much more sophisticated level and seeing what's possible with offset printing and computers and so on, and then starting to look around at the whole field and getting attracted to the handmade book.

SK: If you're right, we should be on the verge of a great renaissance in book art.

AMJ: Yeah. I think so. I think it's inevitable. When the computer came along, everybody decried it and said, 'Oh, we're going into the dark ages.' Me, too, when I saw Compugraphic ripping off Hermann Zapf type and the letterspacing was all going to hell and the results coming out of the processors looked so bad — I thought, this really is the dark ages. But you know, Adobe and Bitstream have started to improve things typographically and now people are getting more educated. Twenty years ago, the man on the street had never heard of Hermann Zapf and now you get on the bus and people are talking about Adobe Garamond versus ITC Garamond. The only prior time in history that people knew about typography was in 1790s, when Bodoni started printing fancy books for the royalty of Europe and society was all-abuzz with Bodoni.

ROGER LEVENSON

This interview with Roger Levenson (1914–1994) appeared in the Spring 1987 Ampersand, *titled "Updike Artifacts Catalogued." UC Berkeley had just acquired some of the types and ornaments from the Merrymount Press (the press' archives went to the Huntington Library and Daniel Berkeley Updike's own library went to Harvard). Included were some of Binny and Ronaldson's cuts (they ran the first successful typefoundry in America, 1796) and proprietary ornamental materials.*
  A graduate of the University of Maine, Levenson taught at UC Berkeley's Library School and ran Tamalpais Press from 1955 to 1994. In addition to publishing books like George L Harding's biography of Charles A Murdock, the pioneer San Francisco fine printer, Roger wrote Women in Printing: Northern California, 1859–90, *which appeared posthumously from Capra Press, Santa Barbara. Updike was one of his biggest influences. Elizabeth Reynolds was also present.*

AMJ: How is your archaeological investigation proceeding?

RL: A couple of weeks ago I finished proofing all the wood engravings, photoengravings, electrotypes and binding dies that were donated by Daniel Berkeley Bianchi. What we're doing now is putting them in acid-free containers. Elizabeth Reynolds has catalogued them all. The next step, beyond the items themselves, is to identify their use by the Merrymount Press. Then the next stage would be the archaeological investigation, to use your word, yet we cannot possibly, the two of us, have enough time, to chase the artists back; that will have to remain for a student.

But the more interesting parts of this, I think, other than origin and use, are the techniques of the press, that is, why they did certain things. That was the subject of a recent letter to Mr Bianchi. I keep asking questions and he's done very well helping us. We're gradually reconstructing procedures and I think of interest to you is that a lot of the practices of the Press in its back shop were nineteenth-century practices, and that gives enlightenment to an era when letterpress, electrotyping, wood engravings and woodcuts were all in their flower, even late in the century, whether in books, newspapers, *Harper's Weekly* or whatever.

AMJ: Including your theory that a lot of the material was electrotyped to protect the actual blocks?

RL: Lawton Kennedy taught me about this. I remember one day as he was locking up a forme, he said, "If you want your press name in there, go over and set it in that Romantiques No. 5," and I set "Tamalpais Press" and used it on my checks and still have the electro. That's the way printers of that school tended to think. They'd lock up a lot of material and it would be readily available after electros were made for printing, binding, stamping, and it would stand up better in repeated use and save the originals. For most of the original types that you see here, both the original donation and that which came later, there's no wear on them.

For the Merrymount's original initials cut in wood, the outer rim was left to act as bearer in the electrotyping process. So, our proofs show they intended them for electrotyping.

AMJ: Did Ruzicka do the engraving, or did they go around the corner to some trade engravers in Boston?

RL: There was a much-used Boston firm, and Ruzicka did some himself. They're signed. But his were finished: no outer border, and obviously they were going to be included in a lock-up and the whole electrotyped or stereotyped, or even printed from.

AMJ: Any printer will acquire things from other shops, or collect things he likes that he'll never get to use, and Updike, having an incredible library and command and knowledge of the history of typography, would be able to go to books in his possession and even outside and make photographs and then zincs for his own use, did he in fact have a lot of these?

RL: You mean, à la Grabhorn or à la Lawton Kennedy?

AMJ: Yes.

A wood engraving used by Updike

RL: Little of that. There's one instance that I can trace and these do not look used — in fact, they are unmounted. The point is that Updike was still rooted in the nineteenth century so he tended to think in terms of wood engravings and electrotypes although we also have a sizable number of photo-engravings that appear to be far removed from the Grabhorn/Kennedy style of use of older material from books.

But the Press finally got up to date with its own Monotype and Updike used Times Roman. The job work of the Press is most revealing and the standards of the place never changed from the books to such as the *Boston & Maine Railroad Timetable* designed by Updike. It's the only railroad timetable in history that you could read easily and I'm sure he got a good fee for that.

AMJ: One of the exciting discoveries in the original gift is one of the oldest pieces of type in America, and that's a Caslon ornament?

RL: It's from a wood engraving; it's shown in the 1796 Caslon specimen book, and it's done by some primitive stereotyping process because the image is annealed to a type body. Very few people have investigated the technical possibilities in this process.

AMJ: Any other discoveries?

RL: Well, there are questions, not discoveries.

ER: If you want to get a doctorate we've got you a job.

RL: There's plenty of room to go far. We've got an ornament here, kind of like a branch with a flower. We have it as a piece of ATF type, as a wood engraving, and as an electrotype. Now, you figure it out. There must be an answer to this usage. If you look at the specimen book we've got, they are there, side by side, and one is bolder. It's been copied heavier. Bold is not typical of Mr Updike. He always wanted to lighten.

Where's the box with the one line of type? Here's an example of how he wanted to lighten things up. Rudolph Ruzicka went over those fleurons with a graver and put shading in there to lighten them up. Updike didn't have to put them in a second color as a result. Such manipulation puts a too-black ornament into the grey scale to harmonize with the surrounding type.

JOAN & NATHAN LYONS

Since 1969, over 450 books by artists, photographers and writers in the visual arts have come out of VSW (Visual Studies Workshop) in Rochester, New York. This interview was conducted at the home of VSW's founders, Joan and Nathan Lyons, on Monday, 21 May 1988. I had just completed a month as artist-in-residence at VSW.

Joan Lyons has made work in a variety of media, including, and often combining, silver gelatin prints, archaic photographic processes, pinhole photography, offset lithography, Xerography, photo-quiltmaking, and computer-based work. She has published over thirty editions of her artist's books and is the editor of Artists' Books: A Critical Anthology and Sourcebook, *(1986) and* Artists' Books: Visual Studies Workshop Press 1972–2008 *(2009). Nathan Lyons has exhibited extensively since 1956, and was the recipient of the International Center of Photography's Infinity Award for Lifetime Achievement in Photography in 2000. His publications include* Notations in Passing, *(1974),* Riding First Class on the Titanic! *(2000) and* After 9/11 *(2003).*

AMJ: When did you start the artist's residency programme?

JL: About four years ago.

AMJ: Has it been worthwhile?

JL: It's been wonderful. We've got the unique kind of facility and the space for residents. We'd like to expand it.

AMJ: And have two residents at once?

JL: Yes. That is only prevented by lack of funding for honoraria.

AMJ: You've kept the mix about a third video, a third book artists, and a third other things?

NL: The other things being photography. They are the three main areas. We do have "other."

JL: So that anyone who's interesting doesn't fall through the cracks.

AMJ: Have they been consistently interesting people, or have you ever made a faux pas and invited somebody who was at a loss?

NL: Not in general, but some people have been very difficult.

AMJ: I would think so, dealing with artists who are often temperamental.

NL: I think one of the things that's really dramatically shifted is the assumption that if you are an institution of any kind you are particular in certain ways, so some artists do come who have incredible expectations about being here. It has nothing to do with who or what we are, which should be very evident when you walk in the door. That's the only time — a few instances — when it's created some difficulties. It's curiously based on some kind of strange expectation level.

AMJ: Can't you tell from their applications what it is they think is going to happen?

NL: Not necessarily.

JL: I don't think we've gotten stung too many times, just every so often. Rarely, someone comes who expects more…

NL: A more super-technological playground.

AMJ: You made some interesting comments in the interview with Tom Dugan in *Photography Between Covers* (Light Impressions, 1979), where you said that the potential of the book meant photographers were no longer dealing with the single print but were becoming concerned with sequencing and collections.

NL: I'll have to go back and look at it, but I think that what I was implying was that the book represented a constructive option for the photographer to deal with a more developed statement and being in control of that rather than being curated to death.

AMJ: Do you see the VSW as helping further that idea, of getting photographers thinking more in those terms of producing the body of their work in another form?

NL: I think in a number of ways we've been effective, not just in terms of the photographer, by any means. If you consider a lot of the arguments that are based on frustrations, contradictions, the hypocrisy that artists engage in about audience, about support systems, the book form affords the individual a platform that is not necessarily mediated by dramatic issues of commodification. The real problem is that on the scale that the book arts community exists, no one can survive through those efforts, so there's always going to be a more lucrative base that really has to do with the concept of unique objects, mechanisms of collectors, the valuing of the object in terms of the progressively larger scale.

JL: I think artists' books have not been in the expensive range, and in that they are very different from the fine print tradition.

NL: I do think, though, that it's a healthier proposition, but certainly I don't think we've provided an effective-enough model in our society for that to happen. You could say it might happen with a larger audience. The question is whether you can develop a larger audience, why is it always in retrospect that these things are valued? Why the dynamic of popularity, of exclusivity? That, to me, still seems to be something that really has to be worked out. I think it's possible to a degree.

AMJ: The lag between the art, the media hype, and then the acceptance is definitely shortening to the point where artists are being promoted before they've come to fruition. In terms of the artists' book movement, VSW was founded right at the beginning, do you think it's peaked or reached the point where it's beginning to regurgitate itself?

NL: I think its problem is that it hasn't had effective-enough mechanisms to transmit to a somewhat larger audience the values and activity and certainly in relation to what people value in the art world, in general, it comes in second best, if not third or fourth. That doesn't mean that the value of the activity is a problem, the problem is how we value things. It's evident in terms of the collecting patterns that go on even in the book arts arena, that it's usually in retrospect that people respond and so someone wants something that appears to be of a limited edition, that could be perpetrated in the book arts and still minimally articulated. The support mechanisms are becoming more difficult to sustain. It has nothing to do with the people who are doing it, it has to do with the support systems.

JL: There are problems all along. Artists books are stuck midpoint between artworks and publishing, and they have very little to do with the commercial publishing world where the economics is based on large editions, and low unit costs and that's not even applicable as a model, except in a couple of rare cases. It's tantalizing because it's theoretical. It's not even applicable in the terms that it is in photography, you know, there's a little niche in the book world for photographers' books, but there certainly isn't for the artists' book.

AMJ: A lot of them look like artists' books: Duane Michaels or Ralph Gibson, with handwritten text…

JL: They're not totally segregated. But on the other hand — it's funny — I was reading an interview, and the Sackners were talking about first starting as collectors and how they had to really get used to the idea of paying a great deal of money for a little book work, and at first it seemed absurd because you didn't hang it on the wall, then after awhile they began to like the idea that you ran out of wall space and here's this nice little thing you could tuck away on a shelf. Their collection is unique and quite marvellous, you know, they collected fairly expensive unique works and they're also gobbling up every single example of a certain kind of artists' book that they can find. So that's marvellous that their collection is extant, because most of us collecting artists' books depend on donations and can't begin to match that kind of scope. Artists weren't thinking of collectors when they did books, they were thinking of book buyers.

AMJ: Or self-promotion, or another way of getting out their work.

JL: Maybe in a way, for some artists, but others I think really are committed to making books, because they feel that the work they're doing requires the book form.

NL: But I'm not sure that really addresses the question, if you are looking at how effective it is, you have to look at poetry publishing and say, yes, poetry publishing has a precarious survival rate. So that the issue you're addressing is an area of activity that is not popularly supportable by its very nature, then it seems that the assumption that conventional publishing expectations or factor seems to me to be a little strange, if you think even artists assume they're going to do a book, and it's going to generate something in terms that other works that they might produce would generate support, still, it doesn't take into account that you're dealing with a very small segment of a response to what it is they're doing. It doesn't mean that what they're doing is invaluable or has its relevance, but the book arts community has proceeded with certain rarified assumptions, hasn't been able to use commercial publishing as a model, for obvious reasons, hasn't found an effective enough way in which to function.

JL: Because it can't function within the economics of publishing. The other thing you have to realize is that an artist's book that has a $10,000 budget is an extravagant artist's book and $10,000 is nothing in terms of publishing.

NL: Artists, in certain circumstances…

JL: …raise tens of thousands of dollars for projects, but no artist is able to raise that kind of money for a book. Maybe we should start thinking about books as "Art in Public Places."

NL: Technically it is.

JL: We should start applying to do fifty thousand dollar projects. If an interesting artist had fifty thousand dollars to spend, it could be a pretty impressive book which would probably be commercially successful.

NL: But to begin to talk about artists' books in terms of a sense of two very different traditions. You know generally in the fine print tradition a lot has been called artists' books. The thing that's lost is the motivation in terms of cheap, inexpensive, non-pretensious, accessible publishing. If you project that model on where we're at now, it's a model that's not going to necessarily work unless its almost sort of an aside, an aside in a sense that it's a work that one doesn't have expectations about in terms of how it will support the effort back. We're entering a period where that is even less and less a possibility, unless what one is doing is distributing to twenty-five friends, and then one presumes that there's a readership out there.

JL: I was wondering what the circulation of the Dada publications was.

AMJ: *Courier Dada*?

JL: The Dada and Surrealist manifestos in little magazines, that were stapled together, that were done in somebody's basement. Those were minimal publications.

AMJ: The Futurists used newspaper presses, they must have printed thousands of copies and given them away, but most of them ended up like the daily paper — as fishwrap. I don't think people said, this is going to become a priceless object in fifty years, let's archive it, which is precisely why they cost twenty thousand dollars a pop today. But I think the difference between the artists' book and the *livre d'artiste* is one of intention, as well as the manufacturing costs. You know Ambrose Vollard did those books like *Parallèlement* by Verlaine, illustrated by Bonnard, and they weren't cheap. They were phenomenally produced fine prints. They were a way of making the work of a successful artist accessible to the next lower stratum of society that wanted to hang it on their wall, and stuff Verlaine into the bookshelf.

NL: But that's not what the contemporary artists' book movement has been about.

AMJ: Well, that starts at the other end with nickel Xerox and stapler, and giving it away, or selling it in a bar for the price of a drink or whatever, and just trying to promote your ideas at the grassroots.

NL: And in effect there's a different kind of coinage…

JL: Which has more to do with the early modern, the information publications, the manifestos, which had more to do with that kind of attitude.

AMJ: You don't see a trend with artists' book-makers, when they become more successful, towards that kind of elitism and an attempt to increase the value?

JL: I think different people do things for different reasons. You've got the whole spectrum of mail artists who are committed to that kind of throwaway, inexpensive Xerox idea, and networking, you have the comic book movement, where people are interested in couching the idea in something that looks like a popular medium and getting out huge quantities, or the person who's going to the color Xerox machine because it's all one can afford and making twenty or thirty copies and getting those out somehow, or the Ed Ruscha books that miraculously sold tens of thousands of copies.

AMJ: Because they were so different.

JL: I don't know why. The timing was right and the Pop Art stuff was getting popular and so forth, and he was a good marketer.

AMJ: And he was the only one doing that kind of thing at the time. You know, those were really the first artists' books, when you picked them up at first glance they were incomprehensible. You said, 'what is this? It's a bunch of pictures of gas stations, I don't get it.'

JL: But why did so many buy them? I still can't figure it out.

AMJ: Well, they were cheap!

JL: Whatever. So you always had artists whose *shtick* was mail art or disposable art, or you had artists who were cooler in terms of communicating through their artwork, and you also had people who were committed to the book form and felt their work just worked that way. You have somebody like Paul Zelevansky who did some inexpensive throwaway books, but basically his work for a long time was the book form and he worked for three years on writing the manuscript and producing a bookwork. So he was working fairly exclusively as a book artist and what he was doing for a period of three years was meant to be the content of a book.

AMJ: That's *The Case for the Burial of Ancestors*?

JL: Yeah, and that will eventually be a three-volume work, which is a very different kind of thing than an artist who is working in a lot of different media and tosses off a book as an aside. There are artists who chose to do a book for one reason or another, you know, documentation, publicity, or just that a piece works well in book form.

AMJ: Like Claes Oldenburg's *Notes in Hand*, which is a by-product.

JL: That was a by-product published by a commercial publisher.

AMJ: But it looked like the archetypical artists' book.

JL: Maybe. But it was a slick, four-color reproduction, and it was very different from the atypical artists' book of the time. I think that people have always made books in different ways for different reasons. Whether that was their primary media, secondary media or whatever.

AMJ: In the last ten years have you seen any cross-fertilization as a result of work by people like Paul Zelevansky, Phil Zimmerman, or Keith Smith getting out into the world. Have you seen people picking up their ideas and developing them, or pollinating them with different ideas?

NL: I think you have to back up, because you've identified some people who have a longstanding commitment to the possibilities of the form. When you think about it, there are probably two groups of people that are identified in the book art movement: those who've had some kind of glancing blow at it, done a few things and disappeared, and some people who have maintained an ongoing commitment to the form. I think you'd be hard-pressed to find two to three dozen fully committed book artists whose work is growing, developing, they're tackling something else in their progression from what they've done in the past. You know it's a nice place to settle in periodically for some people, but it's a difficult task for other people to stick to it and really work on it, but I'm not sure that constitutes the kind of community you need or that will ultimately generate critical interest in what's occuring. It would seem to me that until you start identifying those contributors to the form, you have an amorphous form. A lot of what one sees is the result of somebody doing a book, two books or three books and they disappear so it's almost in one sense, in fact, an aside for some people, it's a serious preoccupation for others. The degree to which it's a serious preoccupation I'm not sure we've experienced yet.

AMJ: Well, someone like Dieter Roth, while he hasn't been working in a vacuum, he's been certainly isolated for almost thirty years, producing books in Reykjavik. There can't be a huge supportive community there. Or Hansjörg Mayer. They were the torchbearers, in my mind, in the late sixties and early seventies before the artists' book movement was identified as such.

NL: Sure.

AMJ: They've progressed along at their own rate, but there seems to have been a huge burgeoning in the last few years, whether in the access to print, or the access to distribution. I see all this fresh stuff like Kevin Osborne and Warren Lehrer coming along: suddenly there's an explosion of new exciting ideas in the book. Whereas before it was puttering along at a predictable rate. Whether that's a communication thing, or suddenly the artists' book has ascended to another level and there's more of an exchange, more resources…

JL: Well, Kevin was a student here.

AMJ: And Phil Zimmerman?

JL: Zimmerman was here at the same time and they both worked with Keith Smith and John Wood and me and Nathan. Phil has had a big influence as a printer, as well. He's done the negatives on two of Warren's books and some visual input has filtered in through Phil's sensibility. There's cross-fertilization, and all kinds of collaborations going on. I think someone like John Wood, who isn't primarily a book-maker, has been an influence to some of us. He was my teacher; he came and taught a workshop at VSW, Kevin Osborne and Phil Zimmerman worked with him. His tradition was from the Chicago Institute of Design, which was very involved with books in the forties and fifties.

AMJ: So there's the connection right there to Moholy-Nagy.

JL: Absolutely. There's a direct link from there to a lot of book-makers and that gets totally left out. My college roommate went off to ID [Institute of Design] to do a master's thesis in books in 1957. Maybe they were somewhere between artists' books and *livres d'artistes* but they certainly weren't strictly *livres d'artistes* because there was another tradition there, that came through the Bauhaus artists, that was unbroken. So someone like John, who always had a great respect for the book, had ideas about visual flow and sequencing and little cinematic things. As his students, we always worked with sequential images. I made my first adult book in his class as a freshman in 1953. There are a lot of those kinds of lineages that go back. There were an awful lot of people who came through here and went other places: Janet Zweig, Scott McCarney — a number of those people were very influenced by Keith Smith who decided sometime in the mid-seventies or maybe earlier that he was going to do exclusively books. He'd done a lot of photography and a lot of printmaking and at some point he got obsessed with books and started doing books exclusively.

AMJ: Doesn't he do mainly one-off books?

JL: He still does. He has made, I think, fifteen editioned books as well. Books just seemed to be an idea whose time was right. I remember when Franklin Furnace started showing a lot of one-of-a-kind books and all of a sudden, tons of people started making these one-of-a-kind *potchki* books because it was now an acceptable, exhibitable form. That became an accepted almost genre to make these tactile…

AMJ: …particularly awkward…

JL: Yeah. Just the permission to do something is often enough. A lot of people now are teaching book arts courses in colleges and high schools and elementary schools. I think a lot of them are finding that book arts courses are a wonderful way to teach, because somehow students are less precious about making a book than they are about making a painting or a drawing or a print. You can talk about a lot of things through the idea of a book, maybe because each image becomes less precious, so maybe a number of people are teaching or adding bookworks to their curriculum.

NL: I'm still trying to figure out what it is we're responding to in your question.

AMJ: Just keep talking.

NL: It dissipated about twenty minutes ago, but to kind of bring it back: The minute anything is institutionalized academically it seems to have some problems to it. You know there's a broader base of interest in the artists' book within the university presently. We haven't seen yet if that's producing practitioners, or if that's producing a potential audience. We still seem to be short on certain mechanisms using the wrong kinds of expectations. What or how affected were the original ideas by a broader base of acceptance: it's a curious, enigmatic problem. It seems there's some advantage in the fact that you're producing for a limited specialized audience and you have a lot of latitude in doing what it is you really want to do. The minute you feel there's a market out there for what you're doing, how to satisfy what it is you're doing. There's a whole range of creeping questions.

I don't know; some of them are edition sizes, how well things are going out there. I still think it starts with, 'Is that the best client?' Where did we get those expectations? Similar to things we've experienced amongst artists who seem to have vast expectations about doing a book and what it's going to mean.

AMJ: What about grants? The NEA seems to have backed off its support.

NL: Well, the whole book arts area has been minimally supported, I think that's because there's been an absence of attractive work in that arena. I think the problem there is that if you are going to be obtuse about the activity, they don't really see where it's going, and if you don't see where it's going, you don't get that sense of support. You can't think that there are more practicing video artists at work than there are book artists, but the video community seems to command a lot more support. I see parallels between the two communities. If you can accept that surface as another kind of page, a lot of the activity of video artists shares many of the same concerns as book arts.

JL: Except the video people have a unified front, because they all need similar kinds of access: they need broadcast, they need distribution, etcetera.

NL: The book artists need production facilities, they need distribution facilities, they need a basic critical concern for what's going on.

JL: They're a different community, because there aren't that many people who exclusively do books. That's a very small number. Most people who make books are artists who work in other media and sometimes make books.

NL: There's that group, and there's a nucleus of very committed book artists.

JL: Yes, but it's a very small number, in fact.

NL: The question is will it grow? Can it grow? If those are factors, then it seems to me that there are other models that the book artists should look at to gain either support or a response to what they're doing. It's a very individualized base, much in the same sense as other disciplines, represented by exclusive literary proto-support mechanisms. When was the last time *Artforum* did a major exploration just taking the ideas of what's going on amongst book artists? Who are the prominent book artists?

JL: And that was with an editor who was very committed to book arts.

NL: You can't discount the need for those mechanisms. It has nothing to do with how you may regard them. I may feel that there's been as much or more interesting discourse within artists' books than there have been in a variety of other forms, but they're certainly not positioned that way in terms of the kind of attention that the activity is getting.

AMJ: So you would urge a book conference as soon as possible?

NL: I think the community should regroup and stop complaining, and start setting up a program for itself.

AMJ: To get more visibility, understanding and dialogue?

NL: To the degree that it doesn't compromise the concerns. We could say, certainly, that we'd like to see book artists — in terms of the kind of commitment they're making to what they're doing — recognised more strongly, realize a stronger support base for what they're doing. Because if that started to connect to a degree, we wouldn't be under the constraints that are becoming more and more apparent. There's a lot that's been lost in the book arts community over the past ten years, not gained. There was a lot more active potential ten years ago than there seems to be now. Well, you could say, all right, all those people who register concern, or are paying attention, a number of them are teaching now, there may be another generation of people coming forward, maybe not out of the same motivation as in the past, but if there's no foothold for them to engage and continue with you're going to lose what that represents. That to me seems to be the tragedy of any kind of emerging form. I don't see book arts as an emerging form in the same sense I might see video in its history as an emerging form — there's a much longer tradition of the distinctions that everybody has identified. Certainly, if you want to, you can go back to illuminated manuscripts as the start of the whole thing, but the tragedy I think is what seems to happen every time there's a book conference, there's the model of commercial publishing.

JL: Listen, if I ever have another book conference, there's no distribution panel. That is the first thing: no distribution panel.

AMJ: The artists can give each other their books.

NL: What you need is a half a dozen decent critics paying attention and a lot more would be happening. Certainly, we need more archives. We need more being done, historically, about the whole movement.

AMJ: Is there anything beyond book arts?

JL: There are a lot of interesting people who are not exclusively doing books. I think the thing that's really important about the book arts movement is that, like video, it is a good place for people who are working in verbal language and visual language, so that maybe the strongest people in book arts are interesting writers in some respects.

AMJ: But most of the thrust of the Visual Studies Workshop seems to be from the visual aspect rather than the linguistic aspect.

JL: I wouldn't say that.

AMJ: How does VSW chose the books it publishes?

JL: First of all, we're a job shop. We're not publishers in the sense of having a planned title list, because we don't have the funds to do so. If you are a publisher you capitalize the books that you produce and unfortunately we can seldom afford to capitalize books, so therefore all we can say is we're an artist's access shop and if you have a legitimate and valid idea, you can come here and print your book and you will have to pay for most of it, but we'll support you in what ways we're able. So that's very differ-ent than being a selective publisher with a particular point of view. We're open to a lot of different kinds of ideas.

NL: Our general attitude has had a number of interesting people show up at our doorstep and that's probably what we accomplished because we've been fortunate in the number of interesting book artists who've shown up with interesting projects. Even, in a way, the least successful, I don't think that there are that many books produced by the press that we are not interested in, no matter how they arrived.

JL: There were only one or two real dogs.

AMJ: Everybody has those in their list.

NL: Of course everybody has those, but we need those too, it may be important. And it may be important that we are not publishers for the same reason because we would probably start setting up criteria under which we would respond.

JL: Basically the press is very democratic in that we are a job shop, an open-access shop and that's something I think that's been thoroughly important.

AMJ: Is there anyone you would automatically turn away because of their project?

JL: I must admit that there were one or two books that I thought were so awful or the politics were so grotesque I found some way to discourage working on them. For the most part, things sort themselves out. If somebody comes to me with a project that I think could be printed a lot more economically somewhere else, I tell them. Or if it's a project that's just too extensive for us to handle, I tell them.

AMJ: What about people who apply whose work you like but don't like the project?

JL: Well, we do books other ways than residencies. That's a difficult problem, because I would like to open up further conversation with some of the people who do apply for residencies where I think the work is pretty interesting but the development or the particular project isn't right.

NL: The residency works in a couple of ways. One of the things we may be more enthused about is somebody comes who doesn't necessarily have a finished product in mind, can come and explore some possibilities and the situation and maybe leave with a strong direction to pursue a future project.

AMJ: What sort of things should potential residents consider?

JL: They should just get an application together. I see the residencies as a way of helping along, a little bit, projects that might not happen otherwise. We always give priority to things that are unique to this place. You know, there are a lot of residencies where people go and have access to a darkroom or a studio with four bare walls, fortunately we have access to a print shop or to video production. We're looking for projects that match what equipment we have, and what access we have, and is it possible to do this thing? I like to encourage people who have some printing background and who want to get their hands into as much of the process as possible and don't have the facilities, I think that's the primary consideration. Our funding for residents' honoraria is limited, but artists may have access to the shop without a residency grant. We can accomodate more projects that way. I wish some funding agency would get up there and say, 'You have a great track record, you've consistently produced interesting stuff for seventeen years, here's $30,000 to re-grant or distribute to interesting projects.' This is the thing that really depresses me, when I look back over the books we've done over the years, I realize that the really substantial books we've done mostly have been done because they had some grant support. Like Warren Lehrer's *French Fries*, done on a very generous New York State Council on the Arts grant of $10,000, or Scott McCarney's book, *Memory Loss*, done with a state-sponsored project grant. If somebody has $1,000 to do a book, they do a $1,000 book; if somebody has $10,000, they do a $10,000 book, and not many artists can finance those kinds of projects themselves. And the sale of the book isn't going to finance it. So unfortunately there's a direct correlation between support funds and the outcome of the book. Not to say there aren't some wonderful minimal books being made, there are, and there are some wonderful low-budget books, but that's why there are so many one-of-a-kind books and editions of five and so on. I've always had this theory that commercial publishers should support us as a ladder to evolve — I mean it would be a pittance, right?

AMJ: Absolutely. But they're all struggling to avoid being taken over by mega-corporations.

NL: If you consider the fact that we've gone through almost a complete cycle, where do you have to be next in this whole process? And how do you get that represented out there, in order to get different levels of support for the activity, to develop a moderate supportive audience for what's going on, that there's a feeling of appreciation, and a relevance in the activity which grant sources have made possible, and the chances are that an artist is going to do what they're going to do no matter what, there's been more art history than there's been sustained support of ten thousand dollars for a project or this, that and the other thing. But I'm not convinced that the community supports itself, it's still very fragmented and very diffuse, it's hard to see a focus. If you don't have something people can gain access to you are always going to be struggling in the process, and the fact that we have these little flurries of attention, it's going to take more than that. I don't know what your take is, but I think the book arts community is losing ground.

GRAHAM MACKINTOSH

Graham Mackintosh is a printer whose White Rabbit Press stands in the front rank of small poetry presses. White Rabbit, and later presses like Auerhahn, Cranium, Zephyrus Image, and so on, constitute the lineage of Bay Area fine presses which have been devoted to the production of poetry books and ephemera. On the occasion of a retrospective book show, "White Rabbit in Context," at San Francisco Public Library in July and August, 1986 (which was part of a week-long, city-wide series of events "The White Rabbit Symposium and Jack Spicer Conference," sponsored by the Pacific Center for Book Arts), Graham agreed to answer a few questions about his work in front of a full house in the Library's Commission Room.

This interview appeared in the Ampersand Winter 1987 issue under the obtuse title "Two Newspapermen from Cincinnati." Graham loves droll jokes, even those with non-punchlines which he is capable of turning into oracular Zen-like pronouncements. One lame joke he enjoyed telling was about two bums trying to get into the adult theatre to see a porno film. One says to the other, "Leave it to me, we can get in for free." So they go up to the box office and the first bum says, "We are two journalists from Cincinnati in town for a convention and we would like to check out your theatre for a story we are writing..." And the woman in the box office turns back and yells to the manager, "Hey, Irving, it's two newspapermen from Cincinnati..." That's the end of the joke. The point is, that in the world of adult theatres, gentlemen who sit in the audience with something in their lap are called "newspapermen."

AMJ: How did you get into printing?

GM: Joe Dunn was printing White Rabbit and the main person in that as far as I could see was Jack Spicer. There was an interruption and Joe stopped and I took over as the printer. Jack had told me that the way Joe got into it was he'd taken a little trade school class and learned how to run a Multilith and was working at Greyhound running the Multi and *sub rosa* producing books at his place of employment. So I took a little three-week trade course to try to learn the Multilith and began finding jobs where printing was involved — mainly as a source of employment, but with the secondary aim of actually producing these little books. So I knocked around doing that for a couple of years and had a lot of employers because I didn't know how to print very well and, as my main motive was to print the things I wanted to print and not what I was supposed to be printing, as a person that represented himself as having several years of experience but was totally dumbfounded by the machines, what came out was very fortunate.

AMJ: Spicer was a great poet but wasn't himself a printer. In fact he wasn't very practical.

GM: No. His idea of the book was always metaphysical. The actual technical parts of the book, if they coincided with what he thought was important about the book — he wasn't involved in any way with the printing aspects — it was an informational process, if there was certain information he wanted which could be included in the design of the book.

AMJ: Was it true that he lived on Rainier Ale?

GM: Just about. And brandy in his coffee, and later, a little coffee in his brandy. I worked for him at UC Berkeley when he was compiling the *Linguistic Atlas of the Pacific Coast*, and he was living on one roll, one piece of lettuce and two Rainier Ales a day. He explained that contained all the necessary nutriments for a healthy diet: the green group, the bread group…and the Rainier group.

AMJ: While you were in the Army he wrote impassioned letters to President Eisenhower demanding that you be demobbed. What was the strange charm, or position you held in Jack's life that prompted his campaign? Was it like Alexander Graham Bell's needing Watson?

GM: I knew Jack before I was in the Army. I got out of high school with a scholarship to California School of Fine Art. He left Berkeley as a teacher and Minnesota as a teacher: he was an instructor of English there. They were trying to start a

Humanities program. I had one year before I knew I'd be drafted, because everyone was being drafted then, and we became good friends there. He was horrified that I was going into the Army so young, but I'd been drafted. The letters were all advice on how to get out. None of them were really very practical. I'm really happy about one thing: I did hang on to the letters and did manage to save them all.

AMJ: And they're in The Bancroft Library now.

GM: Right.

AMJ: Well, you studied art at the Art Institute…

GM: I didn't really study art. That was one of the reasons I got along so well with Jack. I was very slapdash. He gave a very open-ended class. He was a person of tremendous background and mind, and he was teaching English to art students, so the course was always fun. I guess you'd say it was sort of a 'free school.'

AMJ: Your first White Rabbit book was Spicer's *Lament for the Makers*. Did Jack like your cover?

GM: Yes he did.

AMJ: What was it supposed to represent?

GM: A cover.

AMJ: And the title-page?

GM: I've always liked that. It says, "Po" and "Ill." The copyright on the left hand side was cut out of *The Opening of the Field*, a New

Lew Ellingham, Paul Alexander and Holbrook Teter at the "White Rabbit in Context" opening at the San Francisco Public Library in July, 1986. Opposite: Graham Mackintosh & Alastair Johnston.

Directions book by Robert Duncan, and put in there to have a copyright page.

AMJ: Did Jack feel he needed some credits?

GM: I don't know that Jack knew anything about that.

AMJ: Doesn't it usually go on the back of the title-page though?

GM: Well, see, I was just learning. Like a lot a people, I'd never really looked at a book.

AMJ: Are you still reluctant to discuss your association with some of our finer printers?

GM: Yes. Well, I printed with Antoninus (Bill Everson) at St Albert's Church in Oakland, in the basement which had a rounce and coffin-type press — I think a Washington — and set type there. I always got along, I think, pretty well with Everson. A terrific printer. What is there to say? He's a master. He never tried to interfere with anything I was doing on his book. He was appreciative, or not appreciative, but never attempted to interfere. He was always willing to take what I did with the books as it — so I liked that part.

AMJ: As Bob Hawley asked you, "You started in letterpress and switched to offset, do you intend to continue this way?"*

GM: I don't think at this point you can really get back what you put into letterpress book production. You can't get operators to run Linotype machines. You can't get machinists to repair

Linotype machines. Handsetting anything but poetry is essentially out of the question, if it's any length at all. Fine offset work is the future of what I'm doing.

AMJ: You published something like sixty titles for White Rabbit Press, which sold for twenty-five or seventy-five cents. What's the secret? I'm sure many young publishers would like to know how to make their poetry presses work.

GM: Well there was no economic base to White Rabbit books that I could see, at all. I was working sort of as a commercial printer. It was always haphazard when books, just as they did, appeared. The ideas of setting up a heavy distribution system never really came about. The limited edition part was very limited. Like the book Joe Dunn did, *After Lorca*, one of the first full-scale White Rabbit books. There were only five hundred copies and they were sold mainly by Jack who carried them around in a paper sack and sold them to people who'd ask. And a few other people, and a few bookstores. Of course Jack was fighting with City Lights then which was the only good outlet for a book in San Francisco. Yet the books all did get moved somehow. They sold for a dollar. Any kind of distribution I had with White Rabbit Press I wound up with was about eight bookstores: 8th Street in New York, City Lights, Margy Cohen in New York, one or two others, and that was essentially the distribution. There wasn't Bookpeople. We never got that formal.

AMJ: In every one of your books there's a cleverly constructed typographical error, as John Allen Ryan has pointed out. Would you comment on that? Is this like the Mohammedan belief that nothing is perfect but Allah, and therefore it has to have an immaculate flaw in it?

GM: Well, immaculate flaws, no one has discovered those. But things like *s*'s turned upside down, I could do that without even thinking about it.

AMJ: I guess that is the genius of your style.

GM: I can do the same thing with *I*'s.

AMJ: After about 1965 you printed most of the books for Bob Hawley's Oyez! Press and then started printing for Black Sparrow Press, and now you produce about one title a week for Black Sparrow, and have for the past ten years?

GM: Well, the Black Sparrow thing has slowed down. When the books were smaller it was almost that rapid, not quite. They've found that it's easier to do reprints of people like Wyndham Lewis than to take a flyer on some unknown. Their avant-garde poetry is Diane Wakoski.

*Martin bought a collection of cheques that had been signed by Gertrude Stein and cut out the signatures to tip into the limited edition copies.

Although I have to say that John Wieners was the last book published. And that was the complete Wieners. But that's a press that has a real serious economic base to it. He started off by lining up libraries. To get any Black Sparrow books at all, you had to get them all. And he had a policy of no returns, plus a few other things. He made it a much more serious economic venture as a small press.

AMJ: He also managed to get Gertrude Stein to sign fifty copies of a book published five years ago.

GM: Right. Yes, that's true. There are signed copies and it is Gertrude Stein's signature.* The same thing was done by Noel Young who printed Henry Miller and who managed to get several books signed after Henry Miller's demise, because he got the colophon sheets signed in advance. It's money in the bank.

AMJ: The ton of blank Arches paper signed by Salvador Dali that was impounded by French customs a few years ago I think of as one of the great Surreal arts works of the century.

GM: I might add that I've signed a few books by a person's author of choice.

AMJ: In fact there is a marked similarity between your handwriting and Jack Spicer's. That's very fortuitous.

GM: It was lucky coincidence.

AMJ: Let me ask you about typographical finesse, because I know you've reached the point now where you must be approaching your thousandth book, perhaps. Certain things which the average reader or writer will not be aware of take on enormous dimensions, such as marks of punctuation, and so on, in typography. Perhaps you could elaborate on some of those?

GM: We got a manuscript in to set for Black Sparrow from Joyce Carol Oates. She uses a lot of ellipses. Sometimes there are four dots and sometimes six dots; sometimes three dots. So I said to the person who was setting type for me, 'Set it as the manuscript.' He said, but these are all wrong. What it is was three dots means there's something missing, four dots means it's an end of a sentence with something missing, according to the standard *Chicago Manual of Style*. Se we set it as the manuscript and sent it on, and the Black Sparrow proofreader sent it back saying, 'This is crazy — reset.' So we reset it, to get the ellipses right and sent it to Joyce Carol Oates' reader and when it came back she said, 'But the manuscript had four dots some places, six dots, and so on.' So we replaced the four, five and six dots, took out the three dots, and some places the four dots, and sent it on. It finally came back from the author and she said, 'Why aren't you using regular ellipses?'

Which is only fun because some people use a dash in place of punctuation and she was using these like thinking at the typewriter. While she was thinking she was tapping out the dots...

AMJ: Which is your favourite book that you've printed?

GM: *Holy Grail.* And that was a hard one, because when I was printing the book I really didn't know how seriously Jack took a lot of things. One of the things he took most seriously about *The Holy Grail* was it had to be three colors: red, white and black. White of the page, and type in red and black. The first couple I did, when I was printing the cover and the seven divider sheets in there, I had purple ink on the press and sort of a gold ink and it looked very heraldic to me. I thought it looked real good and I printed off some covers like that. I brought it down to Gino & Carlo's to show Jack. He looked at it for a long time in private. He went in the back and came out and told me that it looked like shit and threw it on the floor. He said it looked like an Easter egg — and so the cover was quickly changed.

AMJ: In 1964, the *Open Space* period, when you printed a lot of books, you used a lot of diphthongs in large Centaur. Were you particularly drawn to that *OE*? It seems to appear a lot.

GM: Well, I may have been totally off the wall at that.

Robin Blaser: [*from audience*] Yes. Spicer said that the distance between the *O* and the *E* is not visible. Anyway, we got a new word out of it, Graham: "pœm."

AMJ: Why did you mix Centaur with lowercase Bodoni?

GM: Well, I had limited amounts of type.

AMJ: One of my favourites of your books is Spicer's *Language.* The cover has lipstick handwriting over Xerox which seems very proto-punk to me. Was this a midnight inspiration?

GM: Probably.

AMJ: You collaborated with Richard Brautigan on *Please Plant this Book* — poems printed on actual seed packets which were supposed to be planted.

GM: It was a flower children-type proposition.

AMJ: Do you think many people planted them, or did they end up in Jack Shoemaker's basement?

GM: I think a lot of people did plant them. A lot of them also realised they could put them in glassine and they'd 'grow' a lot more.

AMJ: Jack Thibeau's *An Open Letter to Che Guevara* is a facsimile of a letter, which he mailed to Marie Henri Beyle (Stendahl) in Paris, and the Post Office returned it saying, 'Please advise your correspondents of your correct address.'

GM: It was a concept.

AMJ: Who were the Natoma Tap Dance Society?

GM: Walter Dusenbery and Janet Stayton Wiley. Walter was an artist and came up with this concept book, *The Story of the Bed.* Just last year there was one called *The Red Velvet Couch* — hi-tech photography and everything, but just the same idea. There's another called *The Airstream Trailer* with views of the Colisseum, and in the corner you see the trailer parked. This was a bed that Walter Dusenbery, who was in the process of getting divorced and staying in a sleazy hotel, kept looking at. Finally he started taking the bed apart and got it out of the hotel and went about the city re-erecting it in various places, the Palace of the Legion of Honor, etcetera.

AMJ: You've rubbed shoulders with writers as diverse as Charles Bukowski?

GM: Very diverse, yes. I met Lawrence Durrell the day he had a tooth extracted. Better not say he drinks two fifths of gin a day.

AMJ: Do you have anything to say about your close association with Jack Stauffacher?

GM: He's the best guy going with type.

AMJ: Why do you eat Häagen-Dasz ice cream?

GM: Because I have Trump and it comes with the umlaut over the *a.*

AMJ: I thought it was something to do with their brilliant marketing strategy. That it used to be Hermann's ice cream, and as soon as they got this convoluted name, it took off.

GM: No, that was Bartles & Jaymes wine coolers, which in Mexico are called "Dos Oakies."

AMJ: I understand you are something of a cinéaste?

GM: No, a cinematatist. Getting a movie scenario from concept to handset type has always been a dream of mine. I'm working on a thing called "Birth of a Nation" at the moment.

AMJ: Are you planning any fine limited editions in the future?

GM: Yes, a miniature stamp catalogue done in miniature. The Hokusai miniature I did was the bestseller of them all.

AMJ: Will you print on a small press?

GM: Yes, and since everyone's getting printing done in Japan, I'm importing bonsaied pressmen.

DAVID MELTZER

David Meltzer, a poet and musician, was closely allied with Wallace Berman and Asa Benveniste. In the sixties he fronted a psychedelic band called Serpent Power. His many books include The Agency Trilogy *and* The Brain Plant, *among nine works of agit-smut published by Brandon House in 1968;* San Francisco Poets *was reissued as* San Francisco Beat: Talking with the Poets, *a collection of interviews, revised and expanded for City Lights 2001;* Beat Thing, *an epic poem was published by La Alameda Press in 2004, and his* Selected Poems *was published by Penguin in 2005.*

Interviewed at the poet's home in Oakland, August 2008.

DM: What do you need to know?

AMJ: The first thing that comes to mind is what inspired you, or was it even your idea, to do the interviews with the poets for the *San Francisco Poets* book?

DM: It was my idea. I was contacted by George Young who was an editor at Ballantine Books and he thought it was a good idea at that particular time, which was the mid-sixties, which was an immensely turbulent period. And, I proceeded to go out with this very heavy portable Sony tweed-covered tape recorder, reel-to-reel, and did these various interviews. A couple of interviews were excluded at the request of the poet.

AMJ: Once they saw how stupid they sounded in print?

DM: Well, Lamantia was the first one and he was very much involved at that time with Schwaller de Lubicz, this European Orientalist who was deep into the Egypt thing, and Philip was deeply enmeshed in this metaphysical universe and so he would keep reading the interviews and doing more and more and suggested cutting and adding more and more and suggesting stuff about De Lubicz and this and that, and he then finally called up, just at the last minute, and said, "I cannot have the interview appear in this anthology." I just wish he had not made me work so hard over the months. And then Gary [Snyder]… Jack Shoemaker was working with me as he had on that press we had, the *Maya Quartos*. Jack and I went over to Gary's. He was living in the City. We put the tape recorder down on the floor and began this interview with a lot of deep drinking going on — wine, sake — and things were getting lighter and lighter and looser and looser.

AMJ: Great for conversation but not to be recorded for posterity.

DM: I guess Gary at the point was either on the California Arts Council or getting on it, and he figured this would look bad, for the image of artist as citizen and so on, though almost all of it was okay. And then [Richard] Brautigan at the last minute decided he didn't want to be interviewed but he'd send something, a written something that would suffice. Again this was all last minute. I don't know if this is the most exciting backstory, but the most dramatic of the interviews was with Lew Welch. We went up to…he was living in Marin City with Magda Cregg and they had this place somewhat up on a hill, with a living room with a picture window of Mount Tam and Lew had apparently really prepared, even though he didn't have a list of questions, but he was prepared for us. And we began and it became this incredible emotional cathartic ritual that Lew was performing. And here were Shoemaker and I just watching this guy go on and on about his mother. And gradually the sun began to set and the living room, as Lew began to reach more and more emotional plateaux, it was dark except for the little green light in the tape recorder. That was very powerful. I think the tapes of the interview are at Washington University in Saint Louis.

AMJ: Including the unpublished ones?

DM: I don't think so, I think just because I decided this would be bad form, because neither of them wanted the stuff made public. You know Gary said at one point, I always wanted to be President of the Boy Scouts!

AMJ: Facetiously, right?

DM: I don't think so! He was talking about you know his childhood in the Northwest and that's how that came up.

AMJ: It's funny because it's perverse but it sounds so Gary to be the über-Boy Scout.

DM: Yes, like King Boy Scout. It's nice being King. So yes, *San Francisco Poets* was my idea and was part of a two-book contract. The next one was an anthology on *Birth*, which led to another anthology published by North Point which had nothing to do with the first one but was more of a political piece about home-birthing and midwives and stuff like that. The North Point one was a collection of incantations and so forth.

AMJ: Speaking of birth, it seems odd nowadays that you were not only raised by one parent but it was your father who raised you rather than your mother.

DM: No. first two raised me, and then when I was about fifteen or so, a cacophonous divorce, and I stayed with my mother for a while. I had three sisters, a sister who was two years younger, and we were both surly teenagers and my mother was trying to change her life by trying to find a husband who would be like a labrador, which she ultimately found. So I don't want to demonize my mom, because I mean I understand her position at that point, but she sent me and my sister Nan each to these institutions, up in a town, ironically called Pleasantville, which is also the home of *Reader's Digest*.

AMJ: Sounds like Stepford.

DM: Oh yes. So I was put into this male facility for psychopathic delinquents and Nan was put into, not the female equivalent, but something a little less strident, where she took solace in this ordered life. I, on the other hand, on arriving, had a cardboard suitcase stuffed with books and writing and some necessary clothing. Not much. *Finnegans Wake* which I was trying to struggle along with, I just didn't have the right Irish accent. And I go into this place and these are not nice juvenile delinquents: they definitely had attitude, scars and bent ears and broken noses. So, I don't know, I just checked it out and took my suitcase and walked out of the place and took the subway…

AMJ: You were lucky, you might have been locked up.

DM: Absolutely. It was one of those "bring on the theramin" moments. Anyway, I took the subway into Manhattan and got off at 42nd Street. My father was living in a hotel on 48th and 8th Avenue and he was at that point in his life a comedy writer. He had started out as a classical musician; once a member of the Rochester Philharmonic. He was Second Chair: he always wanted to be First Chair, or better yet Soloist! So anyway, he was at that point working…he had been a radio writer and the whole style of writing comedy for radio was what he had been disciplined in and suddenly television intrudes into that and requires a whole different approach because it's more visual and not verbal. He was working on the Sergeant Bilko show, I don't know if you remember that.

AMJ: I loved the Bilko show! Henshaw, Doberman.

DM: Those thing were written by platoons of writers…and the writers would meet in my father's hotel room and be there till they finished.

AMJ: And were they ex-army guys?

DM: No, they were basically a part of this whole essentially New York Jewish comedy writer scene. He sent me off contemporarily to stay with this woman he knew who came from the midwest to New York to study to be an opera singer and she had a pet skunk that she walked on a leash. And her apartment was painted entirely black. And so I would sort of stay there, and it was great because all these adults would come over. And I was more comfortable with adults, and it was even more intriguing to see people making comedy, collaboratively and collectively like that. But what was even more interesting was going into…there was, around Times Square, one of these coffee shops that comedians liked to hang out at, and that was a revelation sitting at a big round table with all these comedians doing *shtick* back and forth, not a single laugh amongst them. I'd be on the floor! And it was fascinating, the only time that approval was indicated was always very stoically, and usually the praiser would say "cute!" I remember this vividly.

AMJ: So was it because of your father that you ended up a child radio performer?

DM: Yeah, it was a summer camp I was sent to in the same summer that my grandfather was dying in my room in Brooklyn and so my folks thought it would probably be best to ship me out to Nature. For someone from Brooklyn — what is this Nature stuff? I mean Nature to me was — there's this thing called a stoop and on top of the stoop near the door to our railroad flat was a cement planter with this one tormented succulent, surrounded by cigarette butts. So that was Nature. Anyway when I was there I was miserable and got involved in some little camp production, and it sounded good, and my counsellor Uncle Jerry told my dad, and it sparked something in him, that he seemingly wanted. I was never that keen on it but he was. So yes, I was a star of radio and early TV.

AMJ: First exposure to show biz!

DM: That's right, of which there's no biz! Like.

AMJ: So did your grandfather come over from Europe?

DM: My grandfather and grandmother, that's right. And there's this big malign split between Poles and Russians.

AMJ: So which side was your family from?

DM: They said Russia, but the Poles called Poland Russia, so it's Poland. There weren't nation states, that's a relatively recent invention, like passports. So yeah, and on my mother's side she's Protestant and her surname was Lovelace. The lineage goes back to the poet Richard Lovelace and zoom up to fifty years ago in America there was a woman named Maud Hart Lovelace and she wrote this series of books for young teens called *Betsy & Stacy* and so on. So there's that lineage and then there's the Brooklyn contingency.

AMJ: Where's the poetic affinity with Meltzer?

DM: All these people [*indicating books*], then there's more stuff around the corner, you know. Then there's the RH Blyth, the Haiku series. I started writing when I was eleven. I write about it in *Two Way Mirror*, how this all happened and how the first experience of actually writing poetry was (again, "bring on the theramin") almost like a channeling thing because I had no idea what poetry was, I remember. I was in the sixth grade, in Mrs Callahan's class, and right across from me sat Carol Grossman who lived right round the corner from me too. I did it for love! There was a contest opened celebrating some sort of anniversary of New York, so all the public schools were told to write a poem or essay commemorating the glories of New

York City, and Mrs Callahan announced that. She said, Meltzer, you're pretty good with words, why don't you write a poem? All I knew about poetry was it didn't fill up the whole page, and I liked that, so I said, "Sure, Mrs Callahan, I'll write a poem." And she said it can be free verse, and I said, Sure, free verse, and Carol said now you've got to do it, and that's how it started, and I felt like I had invented poetry, but obviously… So where I would put myself, I don't know.

When I was eighteen I was skulking through LA City College, I had taken a two-year sabbatical from high school. I never graduated from anything: grade school, junior high school, high school, college. I swear, no sheepskin. In this creative writing class at night, the teacher, I think it was Mrs Edwards, gave us an assignment to write a haiku. So she lent me one of the volumes of the Blyth *Haiku* quartet, and that was an eye-opener for me because I was also very influenced by someone like Williams, and influenced by Pound the polemicist, so much more than by Pound the big poem guy. I think it's ironic that Pound, Olson, Williams even, never were able to ever finish…

AMJ: Deliver what they promised?

DM: That's right, whereas HD was knocking them out and some of them are really high material.

I remember I used to work at an open air news stand at Hollywood and Western Avenue. And I remember we got the first City Lights publications, I think it was Ferlinghetti's *Pictures of the Gone World*, and that was very interesting to me, and shortly afterwards *Howl* came in, and that was definitely interesting to me. Since I was part of this circle around the artist Wallace Berman there was a kind of literature that was passed around there: a lot of it related to the French Surrealists, then we would pass around the Germans, and one of the great iconic tomes was the Dada/Motherwell book.

AMJ: You mentioned in an interview you did, the New Directions books, especially the Eluard and I don't know if they did Jules Supervieille…

DM: That's right. It was the mentality that was so different, but then I remember being interested and still am in these poets who work in a documentary style, like Muriel Rukeyser. This was a kind of poetry that came out of the Left Wing Popular Front movement. It's curious that at one time in popular American culture, fifty to sixty percent of it was Left. And it was internalized, so even in Frank Capra movies it was the little guy versus the big guy and the little guy finally beats the big guy, you know — and then becomes a real prick! Which was also part of my childhood upbringing in Brooklyn. I was probably what you'd call a "red diaper baby" and the Left culture was just so powerful there, and Socialist as well, and so I am experiencing first the radio documentaries, the movies and so forth, and then during the fifties when the McCarthy era comes in, when the Rosenbergs were executed. And also there wasn't that much yet known about the Holocaust. And of course now, like all of these horrible things, it's a cottage industry for academics. I mean Adorno should have said not only lyric poetry but movies about it are unconscionable.

AMJ: You once talked about how important it was for you to check out records of poets reading, and I was thinking, since you are such a musical person, were you more influenced by hearing people like Dylan Thomas read than you would have been say if you had just got their book out of the library? Do you think that changed your perception of Williams and…

DM: I will get to that but I want to just get back to the New Directions books, that small series of classics, the influence of Alvin Lustig doing their cover design. It was always much more exciting because living in Hollywood there was this bookshop called Pickwick and there were three floors of books, and there was a guy who worked there, very avuncular, and very knowledgeable, and once he got my number he would always direct me to where the New Directions books were and where the New Directions *Annual* was, and all of that took on such weight. Then Wallace Fowlie's collection of modern French poets. I was gobbling this down but also getting nourished by the *Haiku* just because when they're really good, you're not there, you know?

AMJ: Didn't New Directions publish Arthur Waley as well?

DM: They may have done, and Waley is very interesting because he translated from Japanese and Chinese but never spoke the languages.

AMJ: He was one of those British Museum academics who could read a dictionary upside down and backwards but couldn't order a meal in a Chinese restaurant!

DM: No, it's true. I remember he was friends with Koestler, and in one of Koestler's memoirs he was talking about going to an Oriental restaurant assuming Waley was the one who would know… Wasn't Koestler the one who gave the sleeping pills to Benjamin? I think at the border. It's very ironic. I mean, wouldn't you call that Kafkaesque?

AMJ: [*laughing*] Oh dear!

DM: All this was happening very quick in the fifties. I think it was '55 or '56 when the LP record was introduced and a year later the 12-inch LP, and there was this anthology on Columbia records called *The Pleasure Dome* edited by Lloyd Frankenberg which was also a book, a collection of modern poetry, and I read some of the poets that their voices were so amazing to me. Listening to Marianne Moore's voice, or listening to Ogden Nash, e.e. cummings. All these different accents and these ways of delivering. And then of course Thomas: forget about it, it's like Jimi Hendrix! It didn't make a difference what he was saying — and such a whole different entity of platform style. Yes. People who disappointed me on that album were, of all people, Williams. He had this kind of little wimpy delivery, and I think Langston Hughes was surprisingly lackadaisical, at least on that album. I just got an album of him culled from Folkways that Smithsonian did.

And Whitman is on record. Whitman's from Brooklyn, so that's not what you're expecting, that Brooklyn accent. 'Take me! I'm adorable! Smell my armpits!' All of that! It's fantastic. Whitman was something.

I mean, I came to everything in a non-systematic way. And usually that made me easily surprised. I had no plan, really.

AMJ: A piece of history I am dying to fill in, and you can probably enlighten me, is Robert Alexander.

DM: Yes, Press Baza, for that particular piece [*Bazascope Mother*] which was a tribute to him, actually it was a letter to him, it was between he and I, and he in this great manic enthusiasm knocked together and presented me with a bunch of copies. And I said, Well, why didn't you tell me? So he took it to heart and destroyed it.

AMJ: Was he an actual publisher and printer with a press and a shop?

DM: Very much so. Ever since I knew him in the fifties, I forget when I got to LA, but it was either '54 or '55, I fell into the Berman circle. Bob Alexander — Robert Irwin Alexander — he called himself Baza — just like Basil King signs his things BAZ. Alexander was a mentor figure, came from Chicago, had done a lot of stuff, radio disc jockey, carnival huckster, also a poet with a particular sense of literature. He and Berman became… because they met each other at the same age, seventeen or eighteen, and they were two freaks in high school and they met each other because they knew what each other was talking about. And they loved hanging out because they were were hipsters, too, which is much different from Hippies or Beats. So they were hanging out in the Central Avenue area in Los Angeles, which is black inner city and there was lots of music going on there, with ballrooms and jazz clubs, with a whole contingency of LA players like Mingus, Zoot Simms — it was much more intercultural during a certain period. But all of these — Dexter Gordon, Wardell Gray, was a particular friend — the music was very central too. I remember one of the things that Baza told me was, he said, you know we go down there and this was the first time in our lives that the creative artists that we admired not only got what we were doing but gave us respect, which was very emancipating for these guys because Bob was ultimately middle class and Berman came from a working class background. He was born in Staten Island; his mother's first language was Yiddish. Berman, you know, was born into the sound of that, then acquired English. Bob Alexander, both he and Berman had a print shop they both had first these... Wally had this little handpress, Baza had a regular platen press. So Alexander and Berman opened up this print shop on Sawtelle Blvd like three or four blocks from the VA hospital and they called it Stone Brothers. In fact in the window of the printshop there were all of these artfully arranged Berman stones.

AMJ: [*laughs*] This is mid-fifties? That's incredible!

DM: This was mid-fifties. And so they would be doing calling cards, whatever kind of job work they could get, in between stepping in the backroom for a little whiff or smoke. And then they branched out and started a kind of reading series in this place. That was the first time I read. And I was reading on the platform and Alex Trocchi was there, I recall. Yes, they had cultural events. Baza had a particular eye and style for setting up type and using color and geometric forms that was always very distinctive. He was much more of the printer than Berman. Berman was very basic but had of course the vision sense. But the fellow that you would bring your cards or stationery to would be Alexander. When he was manic (I found out he was bipolar: I think of him like a bear with problems), but anyway when he would be up he would produce an awful lot of stuff, not only jobwork, but he would print books for people he knew. His book called *Collectanea*, that was in collaboration with Berman, I think they did that at Stone Brothers Press. Berman provided the visual material on the cover, a baby *in utero* from Vesalius, but it has this small wax paper, then you opened it up and it was a collection of poems which was exemplary in terms of his

style of bookmaking, and the same thing with collage-making.
He was one of these people who would use… I remember, he did some of these shoe boxes, like the Duchamp thing…and invariably his work was poem-centered, so he's put one of his poems, and then he would create a mount out of these materials. A very good eye for form, balance and so on and he had eccentricity, so yes in fact it was something. For decades this is what he made some kind of a living by. He had a press on Santa Monica Boulevard for a while, and then in San Francisco he had a press right round the corner from City Lights, in that Vesuvio building, or somewhere right there.

AMJ: I had no idea he had been that prolific.

DM: He had been, but everything…he was very scattered, he did many many things. He wound up managing the Jazz Workshop for a year or so. He was very tight with musicians. He just had that kind of hipster style. He was a big guy and had lots of hair: he was always shaving his head, or making a big moustache. There was always something going on. So yes, he had a print shop and he had a partner, this Israeli guy, and they were doing job printing and an occasional book. I think they published Chris McLean's second or third book, and…poor Chris, really a victim of methamphetamine: a hipster-pothead kind of guy, then there was this one period, but late also during the "peace-man-hey-love-flower-power" era, crystal came onto the scene in North Beach. There's this corner large space that housed a big Italian hardware store and that place became, during the height of all this stuff, Crystal Palace. Chris was of one the first, like a lot of people — John Kelly Reed, was a remarkable graphic artist and semi-poet who played Jimmy Guiffre-style clarinet — as artists, as people who collaged with junk and found objects that was a boon, because people found out you could get so much work done, and then at 6 o'clock in the morning you'd be polishing doorknobs! So at first, it was like when cocaine, when that re-hit the scene, it was a lot of energy: "I can drink a lot and not feel it."

AMJ: You can't afford to come down. You've got Joe Dunn, as well.

DM: Right, I know. Joe Dunn — and there was an absolutely lovely guy: really truly very sweet. Those Sunday afternoon salons at his house in the Larkin Street area were a real education for me.

AMJ: Of course I wasn't there, but I imagine it as a kind of Punch & Judy show between Duncan and Spicer, with Spicer as Punch of course and Duncan as Judy, the harpy wife who knows better.

While the drunken Mr Punch is wildly swinging at everything that comes within his range.

DM: It was wonderful. There would be Robert and Jack and they'd usually position themselves right in front of the living room with the window looking out on the street, and there's Jess, and all of these wannabes would come around in this semi-circle, you know, and it was an interesting blend of people who stuck, people like Joanne [Kyger] and sometimes [Michael] McClure would come there. Brautigan came a lot because of his attachment to Jack and Jack's writing style, and so forth, but always wanted to be accepted by Jack as a poet, not as a prose writer and novelist — and Jack wouldn't. Just would not. Now that doesn't excuse Richard's bad drinking and he was, you know, one of these people who'd drink and become bad, just like [Robert] Creeley for many years, who'd get drunk and become belligerent and pick fights with people, but usually with people he knew could kick the hell out of him. You know that's weird — I've never figured this one out — but then, when they are in Marin, living in Bolinas, when the Creeleys are in Marin, he and John Thorpe became very convivial buddies. And so John, or Shao, started popping acid with Bob and after a few days with that Bob's whole attitude towards drinking changed, and he became the happy drunk, you know, spaced out and smiling: no more fights. Richard couldn't.

AMJ: Graham Mackintosh took over the White Rabbit Press. I think he had been Spicer's TA at Cal? Jack had the hots for him as far as I can gather.

DM: Jack was interesting that way. He always categorized things between hots and cold. And then sheer self-destruction. He and Lew Welch were the only two drunk poets that could always awaken if you were talking poetry. They could be face down on the bar and if some guy came in and had some poetic problem, they'd just leap up and go at it, and be very lucid and then: back down again. Or in Jack's case sometimes the pinball machine… Auerhahn did that great *Heads of the Town up to the Aether*, which my only complaint was the book should have been bigger and the type should have been bigger.

AMJ: Let's go back to LA for a minute. Because it seems that there wasn't the same poetry community, other than people like Stu Perkoff. I think of LA in the fifties as an incredibly important art scene and it seems like, as a poet, it seems like you were able to morph into this art world quite well: you are not an outsider, you are part of this group with Billy Al Bengston, Ed Kienholz…

was Ed Ruscha part of that? I think he was influenced by Robert Alexander, maybe even worked there?

DM: I am sure Robert had a lot of influence, as did *Semina*. Even then it wasn't even collectible, it was always a great gift and a great mystery to unlock. Berman loved mystery so he and Alexander were completely interesting in the sense of Berman being small and Alexander being this big six-foot-two guy, leather wrist band, shaved head — so they created a visual style. Then there were other people. You mentioned Ed Keinholz: he had set up this Constructivist atelier in this shack behind the fiberglass car repair shop on Santa Monica Boulevard that belonged to, initially, my high school girlfriend. She was going to be a sculptor there, you know tormented clay things that reminded me of a succulent. Ed stumbled on it, and the door was always open and within a week he had put together literally a worktable and easels and all of this stuff from scrap he had found in the alleyways along Santa Monica Boulevard. So there it was. The doors were always open, and Ed would be there: he was one of these guys, very Falstaffian-looking — the big goatee and the eyebrows — and he'd be banging away at constructions he would be working on, and he could literally take a six-pack, I thought, and just *gllmmp*! There are these mattresses on the floor and people would just fall in, like ex-child-star actors…

AMJ: Dennis Hopper was part of that?

DM: Dennis, yes. And he gravitated to the art, it was much more of an art scene than a writing scene. Very much so. It was a screenwriter's place and probably a fiction place, but the only kinds of poetry groups that were there were very much older and much more traditional and completely alienated from anything that the younger people were doing. And I guess Venice is where they tried to construct a Beat Scene… I remember meeting [Lawrence] Lipton with Jonathan Williams and some other friends of the Ferris Gallery. He came to the Ferris Gallery in his van because he was going to art galleries and putting books on consignment.

AMJ: That was smart, except of course you'd never get paid for them.

DM: It was the idea that counted. And so we all drove in his van to Lipton's place and Lipton was even older than…he was an old guy: he may have been around…like fifty! A baldheaded guy with thick glasses chewing on a cigar. He's a newspaper guy from Chicago with the eyeshades. But he cashed in. He wrote *The Holy Barbarians*, which was bogus, as the car guys would say, but it was fascinating, in a way. He said, "The book is dead." There's this reel-to-reel thing in front of him, and apparently he never went anywhere without his reel-to-reel going. He and Nixon. Now it's the age of the voice, where we are going past type, past paper. We are now going to the beginning, the preliterate, and then he proceded to read some of his own rather twitty verse. Anyway that was the closest I got.

I knew Stuart [Perkoff] earlier, in '57 or so, when he was up here. And I always knew that he was one of the bunch: he was the real deal. There was one other guy named Tony Scibella who was a very interesting case, an interesting writer. And they'll never...they were all published by this Black Ace Press in Oregon or Seattle, they just do one hundred-fifty copies or so and bound with this glue thing so when you open, *plughhh*!

AMJ: The book as performance. I recall that during the production of your agit-smut books for Brandon House the Linotype operator quit on the third book, rather than typeset another one of your books. That's an achievement!

DM: I thought so, but the editor there...now one of the top two book scouts for Peter Howard, a guy named Brian Kirby, who is also from Chicago, and had been a rock drummer, but he loved pulp and sleaze and all that, so he worked as an editor at Brandon House. He had worked at the Free Press and done some kind of administrative, editorial work there. And so he drew up a list of about ten writers sort of sci-fi, or just literary-type writers and then asked each one if they wanted to get into the field and this would be the literary wing of Brandon House. He published *Notes of a Dirty Old Man*, Bukowski. He had some interesting science-fiction, I think [Samuel R.] Delaney was one of the people.

AMJ: So he was trying to be like Olympia Press with a mixture of books that would pay for the rest? The loss leaders.

DM: That's right. It's true. And Jack Hirschman, or as he was known there "Jack Hirschman, Ph.D.," wrote lots of introductions to them, to *The Garter Belt of Madame Fifi*, etcetera. And when I got to know Jack it turns out they paid him more than they paid me for the whole book!

So yes, I did have this printer quit. I wrote and published I think nine within a year's time.

AMJ: So you weren't really thinking about them, you were just writing them.

DM: Well, it was the time, though. I think they came out in '68 and '69 and so there was much going on, and to me, why I call it agit-smut is because I figured pornography is politics, and just all of the issues of power exchange…but also the Vietnam war, civil rights, students getting clubbed at Columbia University, at Berkeley, getting shot, but the surge of revolutionary activity in all of these different sectors: Feminist movement, Black Power Movement — and I realized that poetry, in terms of anti-war, anti-materialism and consumerism, it doesn't do it. In fact when it does do it, it is often like teletypes, like headline writers of the obvious. But to me, pornography, this is the ideal form to do politics through, and to deconstruct, to make it anti-porn. And this is all of the complaints I got from both people who buy it — at Greyhound bus station kiosks — people abroad, and then some friends of mine, like notable poets — with the exception of McClure, who says, 'Ah yes, these are beautiful fairy tales!' Otherwise they'd say, 'Meltzer, we can't get off on these!'

AMJ: Was this intentional? I mean some of your poetry is very erotic, and it seems like you're capable when you are being a poet of writing something that's exciting and erotic.

DM: Sure, but I wasn't writing erotica. Because I perceive pornography, not only as the abuse of power, but sort of like the Fordism, the industrial model, and I mean just so many things about just the porn. Especially things as elusive as loops, you know, and how the bodies are dissected in such a way that you never seem to see much other than the piston going in and on, but the woman is always…her face is always…so. There's just many things, it was a way of focussing a lot of rage and anger at what was at that time. And it was very satisfying. I got off on it, in a different way. It was…and I'd be doing it to this day. I suddenly realized it can be funny and disgusting.

AMJ: And nobody has expectations as a literary form. You know John Cleland is not high literature.

DM: Well, no. Sometimes, because of the use of language, it is just so alien to the contemporary book, when you and I read that. I was impressed by the likeness of the language, there's some sort of musicality there I responded to, and also it didn't really seem that exciting. Which is the same thing approaching De Sade's work through translation, after about a hundred things…

AMJ: It's terrible. De Sade has got to be one of the most boring writers ever.

DM: Totally. But then again he is the one who initiated the whole concept of the industrialization of sex. Also the whole thing of the upper class and the servant class and all the sub-genres of pornography. I mean, I've studied this. I was interested in reading Larry McMurtry's new book, it's called *Books*, and you know he is a bookman, book scout and so forth, because we used to know each other when he was first here at Stanford going through a Stegner Fellowship. He and Kesey were in the same class. And I was working at Discovery Bookshop on Columbus Avenue, and Larry came in and we started talking and he told me that his first book would be coming out soon. It's called *Horseman Pass By* — from the Yeats poem — but they made it into *Hud*. But we would go out a lot scouting, and also one of the things that both of us were fascinated by was the work of this man named Gershon Legman. And there's a very interesting section in this kind of scattershot book of Larry's where he tracks Legman down in Valbonne, which is the Knight's Templar name.... Apparently he and his wife, who is apparently the daughter of Henry Evans...and Larry you know was wanting to get access to his collection which is supposed to be one of the most comprehensive collections of erotica on the planet, outside of the Vatican! Actually Legman was at Cal for a while, and he told this heartbreaking story about why he's there. His wife had sent him away. He was offered something and they always needed money and the wife was very adamant that he go away and he couldn't quite understand it, they'd been married for forty-some-odd years; she'd never acted like that before, and it was only when he was over in the States he found out she had cancer and knew she was going to die and didn't want him to be there and see her suffer that way. That's the kind of relationship they had. *Kleenex*! So I was working in the bookshop and he walked in, a small barrel-chested very "in-your-face" kind of guy. And I was of course flabbergasted, because as a kid I remembered *Love and Death* and I remembered the *Erotica Magazine*, I had them all. And that was very interesting to me at that point. Not that I had the brains to know exactly what they were talking about, psychoanalysis, and EC Comics, you know. It just happened that our first daughter had just been born and when he heard that he said, 'I gotta see the baby: I love two-week old babies!' So we walked up Union Street, turned on Jones Street: we were living right in the middle of Jones Street, one of the steepest hills in San Francisco. And we had over the wall... Tina had made these four frames and they had very ornately L-O-V-E, and he sees that and he says, 'Anybody who has that on the wall...ahh!' He said, 'All poets and writers are moralists.' So when he found one of those books I had written, he sends me back this letter and he says, 'Don't tell me this is you, you who had L-O-V-E…' So he was like not only a moralist, but kind of a prude. And yet he was so fascinated. He was one of the finest erotic folklorists on the planet. His collections of the limerick are epical and definitive. And his polemical essays, whether you agree with them or not, are written with tang! So Larry writes about that and of course Legman was very proprietary… and Larry was helping him, Legman was sending out letters for support, because he's writing his autobiography…it wasn't called *Penis Power*, but it had "penis" in it! Larry was very interested, but he realized this book was getting bigger and bigger and Larry didn't have these deep pockets.

AMJ: Discovery was always my favourite North Beach bookstore. I didn't like City Lights. Discovery was indeed one of these great discovery places.

DM: I remember Robert and Jess would come at least once a month because they'd be shopping in Chinatown. And whatever Robert wanted I would practically give to him.

AMJ: Something else I wanted to ask you about, which takes place right there, is the "Way Out Walk of Poets." There was a reading in '57, something Dave Haselwood organized.

DM: At Fugazi Hall, is that the one? As I recall, I wasn't there, and I know that's a typical excuse.

AMJ: You are on the list of readers.

DM: The parade I think happened in the late afternoon, it was a separate event. I was there, John Wieners, Allen Ginsberg, Ron Loewinsohn, Kirby Doyle might have been there, and that's the first time that Allen read "Kaddish" and that trumped everything else. And yes, Fugazi Hall was such that there was a balcony where all the poets sat, and the people would be sitting down in the pit. [*laughter*] Shades of Mussolini! So Allen being the consummate performer really took advantage of that height differential.

AMJ: I also wanted to ask you about Patchen. Given all this interest in book arts and self-publishing today, why has Patchen fallen off the radar?

DM: I don't understand that either. I don't think the influence of some of his key works has desisted. He was never really incorporated into any kind of canon. He was always problematic. I remember seeing, as a bookdealer, his first book was published by Random House, called, *Before the Brave*, and on the back of the dustjacket they had all of these blurbs, and the general consensus of all of these blurbs, because this was in the thirties, was that Kenneth Patchen was going to be a new emergent pro-letariat voice. Which he was and retained that, kind of, became more fantastic, but still was coming from that world view of the thirties that there would be the possibility of a Socialist revolution. You know there was a lot that was going on gaining momentum until World War II, then the Left decided to join, and fight Fascism, and let the politics... Patchen's work is so remarkable when you think about it. James Thurber, he did... but he wasn't as graphically adventurous at all, as Patchen was. Again like Blake he was a *rara avis*, there was no other. I've seen his archives, aren't they up at [UC] Davis? There's some amazing things.

AMJ: I think Santa Cruz.

DM: This interesting record company that I am in touch with in Chicago, it's called Locust Music, they reissued the Patchen Folkways LP with the Canadian quintet, so it was a much more sort of formalized arrangement. And I wrote the liner notes for it, but then before I wrote the liner notes, I started going back to Patchen and realized how the books, the prose books, like *Sleepers Awake*, and *Journal of Albion Moonlight*, and the various point sizes, and the insertion of graphics, and so forth, and also just the persistent passion of the way he'd unroll this thing...

AMJ: It was Sternean in a way, and like Sterne he's someone that comes along and is so amazing that he has to be put on the shelf for a couple of hundred years.

DM: It's true. I'm thinking of someone like *The Third Policeman*, Flann O'Brien, that's a kind of Sternean work too. But Patchen, absolutely. Yes, I'm sure — using as exemplar Blake, who also... When you read Blake it's always amazing: He said that? Wow!

We had Sterne in our house. I remember when I was nine or ten pulling this book off the cupboard with all of its blanks and inserts and type things going on, and I was instantly intrigued. Like one would be intrigued with Apollinaire, with his *Calligrammes*. He'd come in as a typewriter poet, that stuff, because it was what was being done to the page, which is different from standard type, and also it's very linear. And then you've got, who's the fellow, a British guy who takes books and draws over them?

AMJ: Tom Phillips' *A Humument*.

DM: That's right. Didn't he do...? There was a thing that Asa [Benveniste] did for Jonathan Williams that had illustrations.

AMJ: Called *Imaginary Postcards*.

DM: And that was squashed.

AMJ: Asa told me the problem was Williams thought the design had overpowered the poetry, which it certainly did, and Williams was notorious… Haselwood said to me, talking about that book of poetry he did, *In England's Green &*, he said the more insecure the poet, the more he demands a beautiful edition for his work. So there's always this inverse ratio between a really beautiful book and generally crappy poetry, which is true.

A story you told me that was intriguing was how Asa had served in the Army in Europe, and then he had come back to the US to tidy up loose ends and then had shipped a container of Levis in order to finance his return to Europe.

DM: That's how he financed that, and then he got involved with the quarterly magazine, *Merlin*…

AMJ: In Paris, right?

DM: That's right, and I believe he was involved with that. I don't know exactly when he came to UK.

AMJ: He was in Tangier for a while?

*Jonathan Williams,
Imaginary Postcards,
illustrated by Tom Phillips,
London: Trigram Press, 1975
(Not issued)*

DM: He could have been. I don't know whether he had married Pip at that time or not, but she talks about meeting Baldwin and people like that in Tangier.

AMJ: So you must have met Pip and Asa in London in the late sixties.

DM: Yes. *Yesod* was the book that helped us to decide to go to Europe, to flee, to go back from the New Land to the Old Country, because I was hoping to work for Asa and to continue doing some sort of freelance work, like anthologies, agit-smut and stuff like that.

AMJ: So he asked you for the manuscript?

DM: Yes because of the Jack connection. You know Jack and his first wife Ruth had a very intense time when UCLA bought him out because of his anti-war activities and gave him a deal he couldn't refuse. So he and Ruth and the two kids went, and that's where the relationship to Asa deepened even more. And during his time there Asa published some remarkable Hirschman material.

AMJ: *Yod*, the big silkscreen. And *Jerusalem Limited*.

DM: That's right, this incredible piece of bookmaking or poster-making. That was very elaborate, and then of course, the Hirschmans went to Greece, to Hydra. Leonard Cohen was a friend of theirs and he has a house there and he let them stay while he was on the road. Much happened there, between Jack

Jack Hirschman, Yod,
*designed and produced by Pip
Benveniste & Paul Vaughan
London: Trigram Press, 1966*

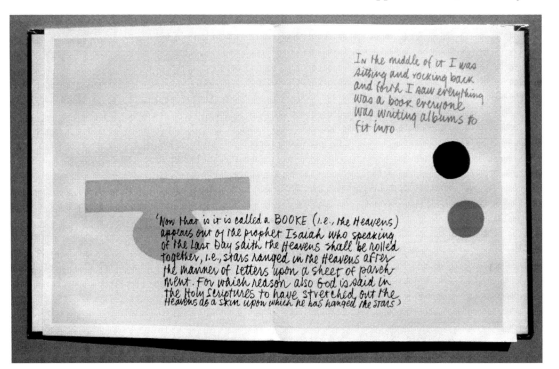

In the middle of it I was
sitting and rocking back
and forth I saw everything
was a book everyone
was writing albums to
fit into

'Now that is it is called a BOOKE (i.e., the Heavens)
appears out of the prophet Isaiah who speaking
of the Last Day saith the Heavens shall be rolled
together, i.e., stars ranged in the Heavens after
the manner of Letters upon a sheet of parch-
ment. For which reason also God is said in
the Holy Scriptures to have stretched out the
Heavens as a skin upon which he has hanged the stars)

and Ruth: it's a typical — you've seen it — whereas the male of the family screws around and then when the female suddenly decides, 'Well if you can do it, I can do it,' and she does it, and then the male says, 'How could you do this to me?' [*laughter*]. This always amazes me. I can cite so many similar stories of people we know. 'How could you do this to me?'

Well, yes, *Yesod*. I had a deep involvement with Jewish mysticism at that time. Curiously mysticism as a contemporary tool of politics — symbolic and actual politics — and of course Asa was very involved with this as well studying Jewish mystical texts: the *Zohar*, texts like that. And of course everyone read Gershom Sholem's books. And Asa's book, *The ATOZ Formula* was filled with that, and even a lot of the signs in that book, a beautiful book. I was very… When I got especially this [hardback] edition, with the tree of life and just the right color, the deep imprint there, that you could feel it. God, you know I miss feeling paper with the indentation of type in it.

AMJ: It's a beautifully made book.

DM: It is, and just the experience of it. So it had been printed. And the Meltzers drove across America. We wanted to show our kids what they were leaving. I read in different places to fund Ramada Inns, and I wound up…all the way through we corresponded. We didn't have e-mail then too. I mean this whole concept to begin with was very Kabbalistic, or hermetic, with correspondence. So to receive mail had so much more of a profound impact, letters would be penned and everyone would read them. So when Asa kept on writing and typing these… What are you going to do when you get here? And Tina was convinced: We just need to get there and it will be just like Bolinas, or something. We will find a place. But no, UK is a whole different set-up.

AMJ: This is London?

DM: London. Camden Town. We parked ourselves in their apartment or house, which was one of those narrow three- or four-stories, but narrow, and they put us up in the top floor, which was incredibly graceful. And of course we were jet-lagged and Pip comes in and she says, 'Well I hope you guys aren't vegetarians, because I've got all of this meat.' Well, we *were* at the time. I could see already little ripples of annoyance. But we endured and you know they were just very generous. And we helped them move then to Stibbard. They had sold the place in Camden Town and were going to a place called Stibbard, the Blue Tile Farm. They lived… We were there

David Meltzer, Yesod,
*London: Trigram Press, 1969
(illustration by the author)*

during the first month or so, but then it became apparent
that the kids, realizing that school was coming up…so…and
I remember in Camden Town, the three daughters were talk-
ing with their peers, in this little island in the middle of the
street. They came in and they were ashen because school was
going to happen in maybe a week or so, and we said, 'What's
wrong?' And they said, 'We can't go — these kids, they speak in
sentences. Paragraphs!' — These are Bolinas-school educated…
everything was "totally" this and that. And these British kids
speaking in this flawless…uninterrupted with "you know"…so
this is when I saw the dream of exile gradually crumbling and
then Tina was finding it harder and harder to find a nest so I
was outvoted. I was having a great time. I was like wandering
through London imagining myself to be sort of in Blakean time.
Hanging out at the British Museum. But, alas!

BOOK I: THE TEN LOST BOOKS OF THE TEN LOST PROPHETS

For Jack Hirschman
For Jack Shoemaker

FRED SMEIJERS

In January 1998 I flew to New York to judge The Type Directors Club's first competition for type design. Another of the judges was Fred Smeijers. I had never met anyone who spoke as lucidly and perceptively about type as Smeijers, so after a long day of judging we set out in search of a real bar to chat.

His typefaces include Quadraat, Quadraat Sans, Renard, Arnhem, and Fresco. He won the Gerrit Noordzij Prize for his type designs in 2000. He is the author of Counterpunch: Making Type in the Sixteenth Century, Designing Typefaces Now *(1996) and* Type Now *(2003), both published by Hyphen Press, London. Smeijers is Professor of Digital Typography at the Hochschule fur Grafik und Buchkunst in Leipzig and at The Royal Academy of Art (The Hague). He is the creative director of OurType, established in 2002 with Rudy Geeraerts.*

AMJ: Would it really matter if there was only Times Roman in the world?

FS: That would certainly make a big difference. It is difficult to imagine a world where Times is the only type design in use. What kind of a world would that be? Probably one where no real people live, where everything is just the same, they all wear the same kind of T-shirt, the same kind of sport shoes, have the same hairstyle. You can tell that they do not drink, let alone smoke. Everything must be 'conveniently' the same and nothing unexpected happens; it must be a kind of McDonald's dictatorship. And in such a world without any real surprises or disappointments, where everything is already there, exactly like the day before and tomorrow, there is no real need to read at all. Consequently, you can do with one typeface.

Human beings not only like little changes, they need them; it keeps us busy, excited and thrilled. In this case it does not matter if you try to improve the design of a bicycle, aeroplanes or serifs. So I would not like to live in that one-type design world, not even if I were a plumber.

AMJ: Well, would you feel the same if there were only, say, Helvetica in the world? As a plumber you might not even notice. You could read maps and street signs, or packages that said, "Open this end."

FS: In general people are aware of letterforms in use. This awareness is not very big of course, but it is definitely there. For example, school kids decorate their notebooks with self-made logos of their own name, the band they like most, etcetera. If the only official typeface were Helvetica, the plumber would certainly notice this, but he probably would not care much about it because Helvetica would work of course. So the plumber would not mind finding Helvetica on his tools, working forms, the packaging of taps and so on. He is comfortable with this typeface as long as it is out there in the world, which has something to say to him. But what happens if the plumber is married (most of them are) and his first daughter is born? Again he would not mind the fact that Helvetica is used when his daughter is registered in the city's population archives. But he would certainly mind when he had to use Helvetica on the card which he wants to send to family and friends to announce the birth of his daughter. This card is something special so then Helvetica is not good enough. It has nothing to do with his private life and all the intense emotions surrounding the birth of his kid. So this has to be something special — at least the name of the baby will be something other than Helvetica. This is just a simple example but maybe it helps explain why I think that everybody is sensitive to the types in use.

AMJ: When did you first become aware of letterforms as something more than everyday symbol-systems?

FS: I am not quite sure. When I went to study at the School of Arts, formal typographers teaching there like Alexander Verberne and Jan Vermeulen were important for our type-awareness. Martin Majoor and I met each other there in the first class. Equally important was that we stimulated each other very much and this grew only stronger when we shared a flat. We shared our experiences, our knowledge and books. We even went to London in search of out-of-print books on type and typography (stuff like Oliver Simon, etcetera). Certainly any training and education in typography took place in our time as art students.

  Before this I was a fanatic draughtsman — not art but commercial illustrations caught my eye: record sleeves and so on. In these, letters were always a part of the job and they were not to be neglected, they too had to be 'cool,' so to speak. Of course the result was something which might be called decorated lettering and there was a lot of difference in this concerning power and quality. You do not need to study graphic design to be aware of that. At the end of the first year at the School of Arts, we started to draw our first italic. Niko Spelbrink, a former BRS partner, made us justify the drawings according to a system divided into units. Now things became really exciting.

  We were familiar with metal type so we understood the basic principles. We soon became aware that we could 'fake' this system with photocopies of our own justified drawings. So we could 'compose' text, reduce it and compare it with, for example, some Garamond Italic.

AMJ: This sounds like a highly innovative way to study letterforms. What other methods did they use to teach typography and lettering?

FS: Looking back, it all seems a lucky coincidence. I myself have been teaching now for some years and only once in a while you have really good pupils. I guess we were just a couple of very enthusiastic students who encouraged each other as well (this is damn important, the best way to educate — at least the basic stuff — is to have a climate where the students take responsibility for each other). Then we had some good, experienced and patient teachers: men who cared about the profession but

*Punk concert poster in stencil
lettering, Groningen, 1986*

who were already old. They had their professional lives, they
did not need to prove themselves or their favorite theories any-
more, thus they were able to take the students as they were,
no matter what. Dealing with youngsters was no problem for
them. I think they were able to get the best out of us in such a
relaxed and natural way that even we did not realize it.

Anyway, we were sure never to miss a lesson and the classes
were always too short. Of course we were fanatic, always occu-
pied with the subject.

Then there was a general rule which allowed the first year stu-
dent to spend some extra free hours a week in a class he or she

especially favoured. Martin and I spent these hours in the class of Alexander Verberne who was at that particular time teaching lettering to the second level. Even that was not enough and we both decided to take this second year programme a few steps further. So we ended up with a nearly finished italic lowercase at the end of the first year.

*Renard type specimen,
Enschedé, 1997 [detail]*

In the second year we had Niko Spelbrink as a guest lecturer. He was only visiting and his purpose was to teach general layout principles. Like I said he was not a member of the staff and had his own practice at BRS. He had a personal interest in the principles of photocomposition. When he saw our italics he took us aside and said, "Don't join the regular programme. I have a better idea: let's justify your italics to a unit system." Frankly, we did not know what he was talking about, but we did not hesitate to agree.

Our activities influenced other students as well and for two or three years there was a little group really interested in type design. This group fell apart when things progressed and became more serious, in fact only the typographically oriented teachers appreciated what we were doing. The others (the failed artists who had spent some time in a studio somewhere before discovering that a full-time teaching job was an even more secure way of paying the rent) thought that what we were doing was old-fashioned and we could not learn anything from this. So there was a strong counterforce and it was always a fight: one side thought it was good to tear pieces of colored paper apart and make something called "compositions" out of it. On the other side if you told them that you were studying contrast and managed to get the right image at twelve point, then this was misunderstood and definitely a waste of time. There was only one thing definite for me then: do not trust your so-called design teachers.

On the other hand, we had to go along or else we simply had to leave school. I worked in illustration for some time and Martin took up photography, but this was just a job on the side. We had to provide the teachers with some stuff to look at and fuss about. The real time was spent in studying and reading about typography, visiting other typographers, and of course we liked to print.

So there was no programme. On the contrary, before we came, hardly anything happened and after us nothing happened. There was only one exception and that was Evert Bloemsma and he too got into trouble because of his studies in type design.

I design type because I believe in it and if I wanted to know something I found out myself or I found the right contacts or places to look at. The same counts for Martin, of course.

AMJ: To what extent do you feel the influence of Dutch design on your work? Your typeface Renard, that you used in *Counterpunch*, has a lot of Van den Keere in it, and some Granjon in the italics (but of course Granjon worked for Plantin). Is this nationalistic pride on your part?

FS: I am Dutch, at least so says my passport, and it is true in terms of my attitude towards certain things. For example, I do not like useless rules simply because they have been there for ages; I do not like hierarchies. We do not have the usual respect for the doctor, professor or the Pope. A three-piece suit or a title are icons, but their weight is far less heavy than in the rest of the world. We have created a certain directness: the Dutch try to avoid unclear situations and say what they think or want, even if this might appear as being blunt. I think this is good.

The Renard is based on a lowercase of Van den Keere, true, but suppose that Van den Keere was an Italian, that would not matter to me very much, I would still like it.

Granjon was French and, according to Mike Parker, possibly the teacher of Van den Keere, but frankly I do not care. For my sake he could be Polish. But the historical material at the Plantin Museum has (in my opinion) not much to do with the term "Dutch Design." For me, at this moment, formal type design has not that much to do with nationalistic peculiarities.

However that could easily be the case if I wanted to. It is possible to give it a twist so that the result looks more French, Spanish or German, but for me formal type design has far more to do with qualities which are considered universal.

AMJ: In designing a digital typeface, you are not only the artist but also the matrix justifier. How much does this technical aspect add to the complexity of the job?

FS: Today we justify our own designs. This is good, because for me, designing the shapes and justifying them is one and the same process. I could not think of giving this work to another and if I did, the other would be simply the executor of my specifications. But even then this would not always work simply because justification can influence the design and the design can influence the justification, even at the point of creation.

To put things more crudely: in onscreen typography, for example, the shape is unimportant (as long as it's legible) but the available space is. In other words the space is the starting point and not a thought like, 'Well, let's design a new roman because I like that kind of serif so much.'

AMJ: It seems that most of the failed digital types are not as bad in terms of design as in terms of execution (though of course there are some hideous ideas about letterforms). Isn't it true that we've lost that sense of the accurate fit of the letters in new type designs? Partly through ignorance of the part of young designers who did not train in punchcutting, but also through the ease with which computers do the work for you?

FS: A proper answer to this question could be another book. It is true in general there is something fishy going on. When we started to work with computers we already had experience and a reference concerning general graphic quality for a lot of things. This experience was shaped in an analog world. In this world, the work itself was clearly defined in separate steps, you simply could not rush through these steps quickly. This was one of the main reasons why, in today's terms, type design took so long in the pre-Mac world. After every step you had to check the result, because it was no use going on if the last step was done badly. When the computer came around, we only had to ask ourselves, 'Do we want to work with this? Yes or no?' My answer was a yes, so the battle began. 'Hey, hey, hey, this machine is a wonderful thing!' — but the result did not match what I was used to. I mistrusted the technology and my non-digital experience became the reference. If things were not right in the way we were used to, we'd work in such a way until it became right, or as good as possible.

Today young designers do not have this experience and a clear standard, and simply take technology for granted. They glaze at a shiny screen which reproduces colors and things which always look nice on that smooth screen.

Then they print it out on a color printer and the trouble starts. The colors are not right. 'Hey, things seem to look different when they are smaller. But that's all the fault of the printer, because in reality,' they say, 'it all looks nice and good.' Their reality is the screen image in the back of their minds which is certainly not my reality or the customers' reality.

Computers can misguide young people. Sometimes they are far away from a number of basics. Most of them want to improve of course, but in my opinion this can be done quickest simply by hand. All this technology means also a lot of distraction from the real problem, it offers you a lot of fancy things and effects. It's also a lot of trouble: you spend a lot of time just to keep the machines going. In the meantime you have to study, improving your visual and graphic *Fingerspitzengefuhl*. This can be done best in the most direct way.

AMJ: By *Fingerspitzengefuhl* you mean instinct or intuition? I find there's not a lot of room for creative accidents using the computer. In fact many designers spend hours with sophisticated programmes like Photoshop and Illustrator trying to degenerate their types and produce effects akin to bad printing from rubber stamps or worn type. But the ingenuity of a typeface like Beowulf impressed me for its very ability to mimic accidents in a non-mechanical way.

FS: Yes, by "*Fingerspitzengefuhl,*" I do mean the designer's instinct or intuition.

Basically what you want with computers is not much more than that which is already there. What you want is the status quo, but you want it easier and faster. A very old thought.

Computers were and are developed not as creative tools or as machines that would change the world, but as a kind of slave instead. Things that can do a lot stupid work easy and fast. Hooray for the computer! (I really mean that.) Does this mean that you cannot use a computer in a creative way? No, of course not. Creative and inventive people use computers in a creative and inventive way but only because they are creative and inventive themselves.

In earlier days there was only a pencil, and if you could not draw, the pencil was of no use to you. The computer however is far more forgiving than the pencil. Other people's type, other people's photos, other people's drawings, others people's maps, a bunch of nice colors, etcetera. It is far easier to believe this way that you are a designer, but in most cases you are just a graphic mixer confirming the status quo or confirming the creativity of others. As is the case with Beowulf. Young designers who liked it a lot a few years ago when this was still new were not creative. They were merely young and confirming the creativity of the inventors, Just [van Rossum] and Erik [van Blokland]. Is this a disaster? Not at all, it is quite normal.

People who put a lot of effort into degenerating other people's type so it looks as if it was stamped or treated with sandpaper need the 'rubberstamp' mood or the 'roughened-up' mood. Somehow this makes sense. These are two useful graphic clichés with a long history. You cannot say goodbye to them just like that. Clichés must be seen as common agreements and that makes them very valuable for those who practice visual communication. Again, only the best can add stuff so new clichés exist, or reuse old clichés in such a way that they look new. What worries me are those spending hours in front of a screen who think that computers will liberate them from the real world.

AMJ: In your book, *Counterpunch,* you talk a lot about intuition and how it relates to both the art of calligraphy and the craft of punchcutting. Do you feel this is a missing element in digital type design, or are there ways that computer users can bring creative dreaming, happy accidents and instinctive responses to their work?

FS: Intuition is of course a human thing, so as long as there are humans there will be a place for intuition. Since humans work with the help of computers there have to be intuitive results with things done on or with the help of a computer. It depends of course on the person whether he or she is open for it and, if that's the case, do you have the gut response to it? This is very common and counts for everything. In *Counterpunch* I talk about certain limitations of punchcutting, which demand an intuitive attitude. In other words, the punchcutter cannot get around not using his intuition — in cutting very small sizes for example, or the way the punchcutter experiments. Today we can enlarge endlessly and the computer saves time and works fast so we can experiment however we like. The punchcutter had to trust his gut in small sizes and as well in his experiments. In the first instance he could not really see it that big in order to rationalize it. In the second he really had to trust his intuition because experimenting in steel takes up a lot of time and effort; it was a very risky thing to do. This counts in a way also for calligraphy and drawing. It is so direct that mistakes cannot be hidden or undone.

These are mediums which simply do not forgive the slightest misstep. If you cannot draw, pencil and paper is not much use to you — a computer is then a better tool. A computer is very forgiving: you can make exact copies, make slight adaptations, decide which one is best, change the color, then 'undo,' etcetera.

Again that does not mean that it is impossible to make good drawings on a computer, you certainly can. But I am also convinced that if you really want to learn to draw, you better take up the pencil and paper and use the computer only after a while when you know what you want and how to draw. Then the computer can become a kind of pencil and paper with pros and cons. This counts in my opinion also for type design.

Learn it the hard way? Yes! You do not have to cut punches in order to become a type designer, I agree with that, but pencils, pens, brushes and paper are needed. There are people who will claim that even this is not true. They are right. You could become a good type designer without touching a pen or piece of paper in your entire life. The trouble is I do not know any. In the end, the computer is just a stupid tool. I always say computers are for the dummies. This sounds rather black and white, but a hundred years ago the globe was covered with poor men and women using a hammer or a spade all day. If you have to use a computer all day, it might be the case that you belong to the same group. Only you are not really poor anymore, so in the end we made some progress.

AMJ: What are you working on now?

FS: A new typeface made from some logos I designed for Philips. They seem to like it very much and they want to continue with it. The logos are used for hair care products, and these kinds of products are released frequently — so for example every new model hair dryer has another name and not a serial number. It was my intent to create logos which are serious, but feminine

*Smeijers' Philishave logo seen
during the Euro 2000 Final
(France vs Italy) on television*

and attractive, but which seem to be composed out of type instead of the usual decorative elements that change things so much that the result becomes a word-thing instead of a word. To generate enough interest with a normal word is only possible if you create letters which have enough character of their own. That is the challenge for me in the shop — the place where the customer decides, and where products are shown next to each other. It is important to make a solid first impression. If product graphics are very different from each other then this will look messy and not very reliable. The typeface I am finishing for them right now will provide the possibility for their designers to create a real family of logos without bothering me too much, resulting in some harmonisation of product graphics. This is an example of how you strengthen the brand's image simply with the help of type. That is something that is very interesting to do.

Plus I always spend some part of my time teaching, just for the fun of it and in order to keep in touch with young designers. Usually this is done in Breda and The Hague. In addition to that there are frequent visits to various places in the Netherlands and abroad for little workshops and lectures.

Then there is the usual productive flow of all kinds of tailored screen fonts. Sometimes interesting, sometimes not, but somehow I keep on doing this simply because I cannot stand bad word images in computer interfaces.

As well as this custom font work and teaching I write little articles. Why? I do not really know, they do not pay, it takes a lot of time but I assume it forces me to make my own thoughts very clear. After all, "we do not write to be understood, we write to understand." as C Day Lewis said. The article I am writing currently is about the differences between commercial lettering and typography for the International Society of Typographic Designers.

Last but not least, there is the design of new typefaces, an activity very important for me personally because I like it so much. But also, a long-term investment, and in a way, a risk. Right now, one of them is a rather big family. The difficulty is it's a serif face, and it has a calligraphic air. I avoided being dusty as much as possible, as I wanted it to be a design of today, so the man on the street would feel that this was could not be created two decades ago.

AMJ: Yes, I see. Would you like another beer?

JACK STAUFFACHER

Jack Stauffacher's career as a "metal man" covers half a century. His typographic peregrinations took him to Pittsburg, where he taught at the Carnegie Institute and established a publishing programme for the Hunt Botanical Library, to Stanford University Press, via Italy where he studied Florentine books on a Fulbright Scholarship, to his present location in San Francisco. The Greenwood Press has remained a model of consistency and the intellectual development of one man in his quest for enlightenment through the constraints of a strict discipline. The "New Typography" has finally arrived through other means than the book, and Stauffacher is revered as a master craftsman.

This interview was conducted on 31 October 1990 at Stauffacher's studio in the Independent Press Room building where the first colour printing on the West Coast was done for Sunset magazine at the turn of the century, in an area that was once the hub of the printing trade in the city but is now represented solely by Greenwood Press (which has been there twenty-four years).

AMJ: One thing that's always impressed me about you is your ability to dream within the realities of making a living as a typographer.

JWS: Do you want to expand on that?

AMJ: To me you're a philosophical typographer, you think a lot about type, you talk a lot about type, you work on book ideas that are unrealised, you've announced four or five books — Heraclitus, Goethe — that you've obviously spent a lot of time on…

JWS: Well, maybe that's caused by the necessity to make a living, to raise a family, and I would take other jobs that pulled me away from that but not enough to make it in a marginal existence, in a sense. I never exploited my so-called talent, and maybe I have this strange vision about typography which is just a means to work out some things about who I am and where I am going. Other people have other ways to keep a certain balance in their working life since there are so many things that cause you to be distracted and lose your way and I think typography for me is a form of meditation on that plane.

AMJ: Right. It's very grounding.

JWS: Very grounding, and even when I walk over to the type case and take some type, it's a form of calming my way of looking at the world, it's a sense of reordering things and putting them back in place again, and recreating something out of it. It's a metaphor for why we're all here, in a sense.

I've always thought of myself as being a craftsman, working on books. With that component there's also this other component of what really excites me is words and thoughts and ideas in readers and writers. This also is an important component and I'm carried away on that particular reason of doing my work. It's a combination of workman-craftsman-artisan trying to survive in a society that supports and yet doesn't support a person like me. In the same way if I was a painter, and happened to have a talent for that, I could have made a different kind of life for myself, but I wasn't. I'd love to be a writer but I've never done it well, I always struggled with it.

AMJ: But you are an artist in your own way.

JWS: I consider myself a craftsman first, but I've always been surrounded by art. The books allow me the privilege of having that right at my fingertips so it's never been outside of my daily life, as something I do on weekends. Every time I walk through that door, I'm thinking and dreaming, doing things that I feel are valuable to me as a searching typographer.

AMJ: Your brother Frank was an artist, and you took a lot of your lead from him.

JWS: He really opened the doors for me, through his world, his sensibilities of art. He was an extension of the whole fabric of where I came from and he prepared the world for me to move out into in a way which, if he hadn't been there, I think would have been more difficult because I was not an academic, I was just lucky to have a brother and also a family that was very supportive.

AMJ: You became a filmmaker later on, and took up some of his pursuits.

JWS: Yes, I did some of those things, and I still have some unfinished films which, before I pass out of this world, I would like to finish. In a couple of years if I can get some time. I did complete a documentary film with my friend Felix Drury in Pittsburgh, *Forbes and Craig*, when I was teaching at Carnegie. I still would like to complete *The Seawall*. I started in 1968, it concerns the oldest building in San Francisco being destroyed. I wish at my age I had the peace of mind to be able to pull back a little bit, but you know you have to worry about the rents…

It's not as bad as I'm saying, it's just that the idea of making books on your terms, absolutely, is the climate I like to work in. Some people come: 'you do the work, you know best, let's work together, you will make the decisions on the typeface, on the format.' I find that a very exciting, creative climate to work in. But you have to work with all these ambiguities about price, or they don't like this type and you have to tell them why. It's like always trying to educate people about the simplest things who can't see, so when they look they have all these subjective opinions and prejudices, it never seems to end, the people become foggier about some basic things. It's just astonishing how the more successful people become the less sensitive they become. Everything needs the proper time and full awareness of the creative possibilities. If you force it, all you do is have a sterile outline without form or content.

One tries to create the ideal where both collaborators on book projects are satisfied, and yet, where you must make final and definitive decisions that hold to your concepts. The compromise can lead to mindless and poor results.

AMJ: Do you think it's a losing battle dealing with, first of all literacy (let alone typography), the fact that we're now reduced to "sound bites" of information, and the avant garde of writing is caught up in deconstruction, making the typographer's job a lot harder. We're no longer reading the way we read from the beginning of literacy up until the 1960s: you had basic ideas about legibility and readability which were consistent, but everything has changed. Now with visual emphasis in our culture, people are becoming less interested in literacy and just the idea of sitting down and reading a book is no longer appealing to a lot of people.

JWS: Absolutely. I find the attention span has deteriorated. There's little attention to reading in the relaxed sense, and for the sheer pleasure of the text: it is almost a bygone luxury. Most people won't do that or they will postpone it, or they will buy the book and read maybe the first couple of pages or chapters and get tired or distracted and they just are not literary enthusiasts. In public spaces you see the topical read that may lead us back to the book but how seldom do I see my fellow San Franciscans carry a real book. We are overwhelmed with books at the stores that can't contain new wisdom for the readers. Fantasies of mine, I guess, but what a pleasure it is when a friend suggests a particular book and likewise you do the same. This sharing is so part of a culture that needs this human exchange. It's not just going into City Lights, which is so big and there's so much I get confused. I mean they have everything and yet nothing really because you can't find it, or the particular book you want they don't have.

As we develop sophisticated tools of communication, there seems to be a reverse in understanding what is going on in the world. We seem more isolated with the media distorting in constant redundancy. Maybe on a university campus you have that exchange, but I'm not talking about that, I'm talking about in a given urban culture, that doesn't happen, only in some artificial way. For me, the pleasure of a book is to sit down and read it and have the calmness to be receptive to it, and be clear in mind and learn from it. The reader has to bring something to a book, the writer doesn't just sit there and entertain you. It has this dynamic which I think is so important, and that's why I feel typography, when it is uniquely done — very quietly done — doesn't assume too much of its presence but there it is: clear. We as technicians look at this, but most people wouldn't see it.

AMJ: Do you find with the increasing use of computers in typography and graphic design it makes the time you spend with books more valuable or that you have to set aside more time to be with the printed page, or the letterpress page, as opposed to the fuzzy glow of characters on the VDT or other kinds of communication that are taking over?

JWS: I don't make that distinction between letterpress and offset. Most of the books I buy are offset. Why is letterpress different from offset, or is there a difference? As people get further away from letterpress they don't know the distinction.

I would like to believe that the knowledge that the "Metal men" — the men who touch metal have a feeling for it — and the module, the way the type sets, the way the designer has fixed for all time the spacing between letters, that is, Monotype Baskerville 169, the setting was like a musical score. I mean there are variations, but it gave you something to rally around.

Now that defined module is somewhat out of kilter because it can be exploited any way at the whim of the computer operator, or he can do things with it that were never possible before, it gives another freedom but it's also another way to create chaos. So on one side it's the same old, time-honored problem that what we're working towards is a clean readable flawless fluid line. Your eyes can't change and we basically read like our forefathers.

AMJ: It's hard to interview you in any provocative way because we are so much in agreement. Let me ask you in this way: Is the reader's respect for the materials of the book changing in a disposable culture?

JWS: It's a big question. I can't put my pulse on how people read these days. I can imagine. I can see living in this society today in 1990 with television as an absolute overpowering medium. It's all-pervading, touches everybody. How the book, a little slim volume, can continue to exist as we have known it… people get facts and information from books and they can put those on computer: encyclopedias that will give you all the information on disk, you can even press a button and they play the music, get the whole history of Beethoven's life. You buy disks for information, but they're just facts and information.

I just read Gibbon's *Decline and Fall*. They could make a short documentary, a TV film forum of that information, quoting the author. I bought the abridged version, and started to read it, and what attracted me, the more I read it, was the magical use of words and how he brought you into history in a way which no film could ever do. He allowed you to enter doors which were so subtle. You would go on from there but they were all building, they were like a large piece of an object he was creating, that was so magnificent, but you had to read it: there were no shortcuts, and I think we're being deprived of that magic and mystery if we don't read books in the deeper sense, or if we don't have the curiosity and interest. I think that in this country especially, we're becoming illiterate, we can read but we can't understand what we read. We have no sense of the thrust of the power of that language, or the magnificent grasp of a great writer. One sentence can change your whole life if you really understand.

AMJ: You're increasingly going back to the classics.

JWS: Well, I read modern writers and I think any good modern writer also has the echo of the past in him, in his language, he pulls you back somehow not just in a figurative way, but he resonates some sense of the past, in the way he uses words. Not in the manner of the past but as a contemporary man he feels the pulse of life. If you talked to him he would maybe love Plato's *Phaedrus*.

A well-educated man has all the resources around him, that's why he collects books, they surround him waiting to be read and then at some inspired moment he goes to his bookshelves and there's that book waiting for him. That to me is better than any goddamn computer. You can maybe pull it up out of the computer but it's not the same thing as this old worn dog-eared book that you loved ten years ago. You still have it, with all kinds of memories, the physical thing starts to bring you together. That has value too. It's not always the fine editions.

I like to perfect my craft, but I also play around. I'm privileged to do it. My friend Michael Taylor translated this new edition of Book One of Horace's *Odes*; it becomes not just the publishing of a book, it's the opening of new doors of knowledge, you learn so much, I never knew Horace before Michael's introduction — I had an edition of the book and read it when I was young and never dealt with it with any seriousness. What a privilege. I can handset this new translation, it becomes a ritual for me. It's necessary. I guess that's the dreaming aspect of Greenwood Press.

AMJ: Do you think you can get too fanatical in your perfecting of your craft, to the point where it's impractical, where it's no longer going to pay off in terms of the final product? I mean obviously you're never going to realise your costs in your labour. There's a story that when you were at Stanford and went into the pressroom, the pressmen would stop all the presses and refuse to work till you left the pressroom!

JWS: Where did you hear that?

AMJ: Because you would stop them to put in a one point lead in the gutter and then say "ok take it out again." [*laughter*]

JWS: Well, that's exaggerated — where did you hear that? — I used to go back in the pressroom, especially to tell them to cut down on the ink, they used to flood it.

AMJ: Typical.

JWS: It's hard for me to sum up what I am, what I'm trying to do. I've been so long with it. I'm reaching a certain age now that I've been in harness a long time. Doing my thing, trying to find my way, enjoying myself. The Horace has been a great pleasure for me. I've read a lot, thought a lot. It's extended my knowledge, coupled with all kinds of other crazy things.

AMJ: For Horace, as for Plato, the book was a scroll, a long continuous roll. Have you thought of that in terms of the way the book is now cut and folded paper? Are you trying to get that panoramic vista in your edition?

JWS: There's an opening in my talk on Horace where I discuss this. It's by Maurice Blanchot, and it answers that very well: "The book rolls up time, unrolls time, and contains this unrolling as a continuity of a presence in which present, past and future become actual."

Isn't that a beautiful thing? When you think about it in that context, the scroll book, what happened each time I tackle some of these ancient writers and I try to discover where it all started from, I start to gain real respect, one step at a time, I reach out there and finally come to these fragments, it's not a complete roll at all, just scraps.

It turned out that Horace was more fragmented than Plato. We at least have some evidence of a papyrus of Plato. With Horace it took a thousand years before we had any evidence — 900 AD — and he died before 8 BC. For a hundred years after his death, Horace was read. After that, he lost popularity. We have to remember what popularity meant in those times.

When the Christian era started about 400 — the breakdown of the Roman Empire — by that time Horace was not read. The only person that was continually read was Virgil, and when the Christian Church took power, Virgil seemed more in keeping with the symbols of Christianity. The evidence of Horace was totally locked in eventually by a few monasteries. In the fourteenth century Petrarch revived him. He began to be studied, manuscripts started to be copied, but by the time printing came there were only about two hundred manuscripts known.

AMJ: How did they compare textually? Were they from one source?

JWS: Three sources I believe, and they began to compare one to the other and leave out or add words and scholars would make marginal notes. It was a very unique experience for me. I went to the Bodleian Library and handled the first printed Horace from 1471.

AMJ: In terms of your printing interests, you started out on the Kis-Janson trail which led you to Florence where Updike had noted the types, and you looked at Cecchi's work which led you to the later Florentine work of Torrentino.

JWS: No, Torrentino was earlier. I started to work backwards from Cecchi to find out where he came from.

AMJ: Now you're getting into the very early Renaissance.

JWS: In a sense I never went beyond print, my interest was printing, and manuscripts were something I did not think about in that context.

AMJ: So now you've made the leap back into the handwritten papyrus codex. So that's opened up the whole other world of paleography, a different world from typography.

JWS: Typography wouldn't have any meaning without that whole past history, in terms of the written forms, the literature of those times. In Florence of the late fifteenth century there was a huge upwelling of printing: printers were printing all these manuscripts from the great libraries, and that was basically Torrentino's mission.

So you know it's been a very haphazard scholarly endeavor on my part but that's the way I fashion my interests between study and involvement with the press. It's not just theory. I read Horace and was enlightened and feel I am somewhat of a conduit between all these other things I've seen, like the 1471 edition.

AMJ: Now you just need your own Maecenas.

JWS: Yes.

AMJ: You mention your need of non-interfering patronage. What about your involvement with Lapis Press. Hasn't that been a creative effort?

JWS: That's another story.

AMJ: When North Point Press started, Bill Turnbull brought you in and then somehow or other you got put in the revolving door, but they took over your typographical style.

JWS: I helped them with an aesthetic quality, a shape; it's so simple, nothing mindboggling. I just put them on the right track, that's all I did. I mean, anyone could do that. There's no secret.

AMJ: But it's certainly taken a long time for the West Coast to catch up with European modernism, after all *Asymmetric Typography* and *The New Typography* were written in the twenties. Is it because like the wagon train it has to come slowly all the way across America, that we're still reluctant to deal with these issues?

JWS: I've always lived in California, it's where I was born and shaped my love for typography and books. The influences are many, and yet my first introduction to the aesthetics of the typographic art came through the William Morris Arts & Crafts movement. It was only later when I was exposed to the modernism of say Tschichold and others, that I started to explore other concepts in the architecture of typography.

Actually it was an intellectual reaction, a need to question and find answers that started me to move away from the earlier influences. But each phase was a step towards greater clarity between content and form. These elements have been the ongoing dynamics of every creative process. You may ask where do content and form separate? Each mirrors the other if finally realized. Also, I was a child of the Second World War: this profound experience gave birth to a new consciousness. The split between before and after, from innocence to maturity was integral to my typographic growth. ·

There were so many unanswered questions from the aftermath of the war — the whole thrust of the modern movement

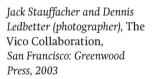

Jack Stauffacher and Dennis Ledbetter (photographer), The Vico Collaboration, *San Francisco: Greenwood Press, 2003*

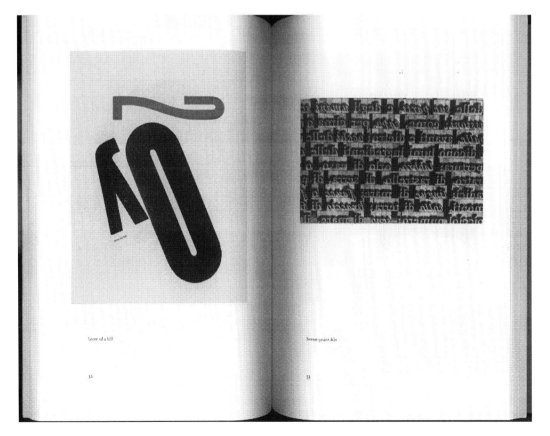

lorem of a hill

Seven-point Kis

32

33

in painting, writing, and experimental filmmaking was still to be discovered.

I should say, both Edwin Grabhorn and Edward Taylor held a strong presence in San Francisco's pre-War era in book design. And for the young novice, I was enamoured by their beautiful books. Cubism now is almost one hundred years old, and I'm surprised that that momentous movement in modern art did not have any direct influence on our books. Maybe the analogy does not hold, but this revolutionary phase in plastic arts — Braque — did redefine the way of seeing, to rearrange our perspective in space.

There was another component which had nothing to do with books, and that was people here were on the western edge looking into the Oriental world. There was always a lot of Oriental studies and ashrams on the California coast: it's been there since the twenties, especially in the south. You have [Aldous] Huxley, [Alan] Watts, [Friedrich] Spiegelberg, who came as refugees, and that was very stimulating. But all of that stimulation in the arts, writing and poetry never filtered into the body of what we call the California book: we're still tied down by the Arts & Crafts movement. I think it took literature and poets to be more radical and they would do their own books in a clumsy way which are very vital and interesting. They don't have any connection with the so-called Philistines of the book.

AMJ: Do you mean people like Bern Porter?

JWS: Bern Porter was part of that so-called American avant garde of poetry, New Directions, and all those people like Rexroth, Varda, Henry Miller, Patchen (a difficult man), Lamantia, Broughton and George Leite. That colored and shaped me. You do not just have one door that opened. That was a very important period just after the war when I settled into my life.

AMJ: What was *The Soul of Plants*?

JWS: That was a book by a German named Francé. I had it translated and had Gordon Cook do the illustrations, he did some nice etchings and I set a few sample pages, but the translator, a fellow from Cornell, was so outraged by the illustrations he didn't want me to proceed. Then somehow I lost interest.

AMJ: It became an impasse. It reminds me of one of Horace's maxims, which I don't mean to use in a pejorative sense, he says, "He has the air of one who promises many things."

JWS: I'm still working on this Persian poet.

AMJ: Arifi?

JWS: Arifi, yes. I've had some problems with that. I had a translator, expert in Persian language. Literally it's all there, but it's all so dull and pedantic — it needs a poet's touch.

AMJ: Set it in Legenda type and then it'll be unreadable and look Arabic!

When you did the Camus book, *Neither Victims Nor Executioners*, it was turned down by the various award committees and contests, and you got irritated. For me it was one of your great works, a far-seeing design with Xerox-degenerated illustrations and type-high Linotype slugs and mixed typefaces. Didn't you feel that the fact that they wouldn't put it in their shows or give it an award was a clear indication that it was ahead of its time?

JWS: Knowing who the Western Book people are — they are fuddy-duddy in most cases — I thought it was a good book and worthy to be judged and I think they passed it up because it was not the genre that they were used to. I was very happy with that book. I was going through a period of exploration.

You've seen my Vico? It was a real typographic experiment.

AMJ: Are we in a "Ricorso" right now?

JWS: I think so.

AMJ: Tschichold says, "Typography is not meant to function as an allegory of its time. It must be itself." Do you think that's true?

JWS: I have a little problem with that. I think it does reflect its time, I mean it can't be isolated from it, I think it's very reflective, also of architecture. I think of Corbu in a period in which there was that wonderful relationship, an analogy to some of the great works he did and some of his contemporaries did in that marvellous twenties modern architecture, but as we look back it was heroic.

AMJ: You see that in Bayer whose typography was architectonic.

JWS: I think Tschichold's wrong there. At that time he was fighting a rear-battle.

AMJ: He was trying to justify symmetry by attacking his previous stance which had been carefully thought-out and elaborated.

JWS: Now I think in the full span of time, as we come into the nineties, it doesn't really make any difference, you can do anything you want — asymmetry, symmetry — and it will not put you in one group or the other. I think now we're much more eclectic.

Asymmetry is just as hard as symmetry. Sometimes asymmetry is the solution for a particular text. I tend towards asymmetry not because I reject symmetry, it just works better for the immediate solution. Symmetry looks sometimes too static and clumsy and doesn't really tie together very well. Othertimes symmetry works. I'm going to look at symmetry a little more again. I've been basically into asymmetry because a lot of times when I'm doing art catalogues, I can solve solutions quickly; it clarifies the spatial problems. It sets up the right echoes that aren't dull visually.

But I know there are symmetries that can be very subtle and beautiful if you do it after you've done a lot of asymmetries too. If you've never done asymmetry but only symmetry you're a dead duck because you just can't refine that position. Whereas if you use asymmetry well you can do symmetry too, you can do both. You can spin interesting symmetries off asymmetry.

*Poster advertising ITC
Bodoni, 1994, designed by Jack
Stauffacher*

SUMNER STONE

After teaching a semester of typography at UC Berkeley Extension, I pulled a deus ex machina by bringing Sumner Stone to class. At the time, he had just left Adobe to start his own firm and was working on the now-successful ITC Bodoni. Among his types are a proprietary typeface for Print *magazine, the Stone family (which included an "Informal" set), Silica, Cycles, Basalt and Magma. A former student of Lloyd Reynolds, he is also well-regarded as a calligrapher. Interview at UC Berkeley Extension Annex, San Francisco, 20 April 1994.*

AMJ: First of all, is that your real name?

SS: [*laughing*] It's actually an English name. There's a Summoner in Chaucer…

AMJ: He's the guy who comes round to give the bad news you've been summonsed. The bailiff…

Stone is a great name for a type designer.

SS: There must have been stone masons back there somewhere.

AMJ: Have you ever tried stone cutting?

SS: A little bit. I did a workshop with David Kindersley.

AMJ: The remarkable thing about Stone Print, when you compare it with Times and Century is that the other two don't look condensed at all, so it's a wonder they were ever considered at all as good typefaces for tight text setting, they have very wide *o*'s and *n*'s. But the amazing thing is, Stone Print still retains legibility with what looks like a large x-height, but it has big ascenders and very big descenders, so I figure there must be witchcraft involved. I can't see how you did that. Does the size of the x-height have something to do with how condensed it is? They all look like they have pretty much the same x-height.

SS: Century is bigger, and actually Print is a little bit smaller than Times. I really thought it was important to have adequate ascenders and descenders and I figured that would make it more legible. The theory about this is that what we read is the shapes of the words, and to make something like this where you're stressing the legibility of the type anyway then you should at least have that, because it doesn't hurt.

AMJ: Then *Print* magazine's typesetters go out of their way to letterspace the lowercase when they have a loose line.

SS: Well we had a dispute about this.

AMJ: About ragged right instead of justified?

SS: Well that was the first thing. They were completely opposed to that.

AMJ: It's interesting that they were excited about having their own typeface yet they won't use it in a way that shows it off to its best.

SS: Yeah, well, they're very… The Art Director Andrew Kner is very conservative. I think their general attitude towards the design of the magazine is they want it to be unchangeable. They definitely do not want to set it ragged right. Then we went through a long little dance about the H&J settings in Quark and it's still going on, the struggle. The struggle for wordspace! *Print* is run by editorial people, not designers, people who come from a background of writing. Their feeling was the worst thing that could happen with text was to have rivers. White spaces that floated down because the wordspaces got large. They thought that that would be the worst possible outcome of any kind of setting, so when we set the type without letterspace allowed, of course you got more rivers, so that was the conclusive bottom line of this experience. So then they just went back over to the other extreme which was to allow letterspace between letters. They have backed off a little bit, there's a smaller area of space so it's a little bit better. I think this typeface looks worse when that happens than other typefaces because it's so condensed that it falls apart very quickly. I have become very sensitized to this issue because of what happened in the magazine.

Almost everyone who sets short columns in trade publishing now does this. It's very rare, only the book review section of *The New York Times* doesn't do it, and a few other people. They have a slightly larger column, but in almost every magazine they allow space between letters...

AMJ: Do you think a solution might be to use a wider version of the face and substitute it in those lines where there would otherwise be letterspacing?

SS: I have seen some experiments with this where people have made software that does H&J by substituting wider characters in lines that need that. I'm not sure that it's very much better. It looks very odd.

AMJ: Ingenious though...

SS: It's very clever but it looks very strange. Gutenberg did this, he used ligatures and all those clever things, but you know the texture of the lines is rich whereas the texture of these lines, it's almost as bad as allowing the letterspacing.

AMJ: When Apple came out with the LaserWriter, it had a very weird group of fonts. Were you part of that decision-making process and how did you make those decisions?

SS: Yeah, it was a typical corporate process, in my opinion. We called in all sorts of experts from other corporations to tell us what to do. Like Linotype and ITC. There was a lot of interaction from Apple because it was an Apple product. The Times and Helvetica were decided before I got involved. Times was the most popular serif typeface, Helvetica was the most popular sans serif typeface: done.

AMJ: Plus Monotype and Linotype had a stake in getting their types in there.

SS: In this case it was Linotype. But I think independently of that, before that, the people who made the software decided they had to be there because they were the most popular type-faces and that was not a difficult decision. And Courier was the same way, they needed a mono-space typeface and that was the most popular one. So that was it. There was a symbol font and that was it for the original faces.

But then what was next? We tried to make some rational framework; you should have some sort of variety. I think that Palatino was a very obvious choice. It was a modern design and not like Times Roman, and it also was extremely popular. Lots of people who were involved in the process liked it, including myself. That one was pretty easy. Century Schoolbook was also pretty easy: it was well-known, sturdy, distinct from the other serif faces, very American. Part of the problem was that nobody knew what the LaserWriter was going to be used for. The people who were making it, Apple, and the people at Adobe thought the primary market for the LaserWriter would be people who were going to do sales presentations and corporate presenta-tions. But that turned out to be wrong. It got used for everything you can possibly think of that comes on paper.

What were some of the other typefaces? Avant Garde was of course another sans serif, and the Zapf Chancery was something

*First showing of Stone Print,
in* PRINT *magazine,
September 1991*

informal, something that was fun, useful for invitations and informal documents. At one point there was a certain faction that wanted ITC Gorilla.

Bookman was really the strangest one. It was the afterthought; there was another slot, and Bookman was sort of the compromise, not something everyone really wanted. Helvetica Narrow and Oblique were free because it was just an algorithm: they came with the others; they cost nothing. The amount of space was important.

AMJ: Did you have to redesign these typefaces?

SS: The original Times and Helvetica were done before I arrived, by computer scientists. They were pretty awful. They got redone several times. Courier was also redone at least twice. In retrospect they seem pretty strange and random.

AMJ: But they had a huge impact on printed culture for ten years. Do you regret any of it?

SS: All of it was done by committee. The whole thing was done for industry needs. It was not a choice that was based on clear typographic reasoning, other than, "We need one of those." And certainly nobody thought the LaserWriter would be used for serious typographic publishing, or real text. So there was Times and there was Palatino: those were the serious text types. If we had known, we could have had other roman types and other sans serifs typefaces in there also. But some of the typefaces got used a lot more than others. I think Century Schoolbook and Bookman did not get used much. It was mostly Palatino.

AMJ: And Courier because of the default.

SS: And Courier…

AMJ: How did you get started on the Bodoni project?

SS: We worked from his books. We also took photographs of the punches. My feeling about it was we really wanted it to look like a contemporary printed page. But that's impossible, because the printed page of Bodoni's time depends on squeezing the pieces of metal onto the paper, which is why this [digital] stuff intrinsically doesn't look like it.

I think that it really helped to look at the punches because it gave more of a feeling: you could really get a direct sense of how the type was made — the shapes made by scraping of the metal — and I think that was really valuable. Looking at the punches in terms of actually drawing the type turned out to be useful for the large sizes. Mostly, though, we were looking at the printed work and trying to capture that.

This is an issue to do with any historical revival of metal type.

People have tried a lot of different approaches to this, from the photographic versions to very much abstracted, kind of looking more at the punches. It's one way of thinking about all of that. I think that good results can be obtained by immersing yourself in, working with the typeface, not by trying to figure out some specific set of strategies. That analytic approach tends to not be very useful. It's more useful to absorb yourself in it.

AMJ: There's some seemingly very erratic drawing in the small sizes of the Bodoni, like the crossbar of the "e". Was that intentional to keep the spirit and color of the characters when you enlarge it, rather than doing it mechanically?

SS: Absolutely.

AMJ: Was this something you found in the small sizes?

SS: At some point we will publish them, perhaps in *Upper & Lower Case*. I sent them off all of this material last week. It is very interesting to look at the photographic enlargements, to look at the drawings. You can see where these kinds of things come from. The woman who did the drawings for the small size, Holly Goldsmith, did a fantastic job of it. It is simplified yet still maintains some of what I think makes it legible when it's that small.

AMJ: That's the importance of keeping the different sizes, as you've done, rather than having one. It's like, if you take twenty-seven recordings of "Mood Indigo" by Duke Ellington, and you say "what's the optimum one?", you end up splicing a little bit of Barney Bigard here, a little Cootie Williams there, you'll end up with something weird. It may sound overall like "Mood Indigo" but it's not a particularly good version, and this is something that has ruined a lot of type revivals: the committee approach where you say we'll second-guess William Caslon and assume if Caslon had access to modern technology, with coated stock and laser printing, this is what he would have done, but it is not necessarily so.

SS: Or you assume something was a mistake. That's the way it generally comes out when people do redrawings: "We'll just fix it!" Because it doesn't look regular. Whereas in fact what gives it character is all the "mistakes."

AMJ: I was really glad to get in the mail yesterday from Matthew Carter his new type, Big Caslon, because maybe to a certain extent he was dissatisfied, as I was, with Adobe's Caslon which ended up being a gutless old style lacking the real wild characteristics which I see in your large sizes of Bodoni.

SS: If you look at the display sizes, they are different types.

They work well, and no one has yet made one, so why not do it? They're fantastic, wonderful.

AMJ: Like Bodoni, Caslon cut many sizes of type, and over a period of years. In fact among the types we call Caslon, the earliest are by Moxon, and the later types, in Bodoni's style, were cut by Isaac Drury for Caslon's grandson's widow decades after he was dead.

SS: I think display type is fundamentally different from text type. And all of the problems of making and using it are completely different. "Display type" does not necessarily have to mean that you make bizarre typefaces, it could be the same contrast you make for text but if you are going to make something for use at large sizes, and only a few words, you see a completely different thing.

One of the really fun things to do, if you are a person who makes letters, is to make these big letters, they really have more personality. When you're making a text, you want it to be legible, you want it to be easy to read. That's the primary thing you want. And whether it's cute or funny or sexy, that is irrelevant. In fact, if it looks like that you need to get back to work on it. You want it to be anonymous, and want it to disappear. You want to be able to just have the text come through and not have things get in the way. But with display type it is completely different, there the personality of type is very important: that's what's talking to you. But somehow that's fallen by the wayside in all of this technology.

AMJ: Partly I think the arrival of GX fonts — maybe even more so than Multiple Masters — will make the bigger font repository possible. I've been unable to run Multiple Masters on my Mac, I just get blank space. I've tried. The breakthrough of GX with a larger group of characters will make more possible. The laziness or fiscal meanness of people who didn't buy all the characters in the days of the Linoterm will be obviated, because you'll get the stuff handed to you. You won't have to be "expert," you'll just have to know where it is, which door to open to get the ligatures.

SS: Right.

AMJ: On the subject of revivals, at the Stanford ATypI conference in 1983 — which you did the poster for — Hermann Zapf made a statement to the effect that we don't need more historical revivals: it's time for newer and better modern types. Do you agree? Or are there areas of history that need to be investigated?

SS: I fundamentally agree with Zapf. My experience is, as I said earlier, I always like the original better than the copy — even the ones I have worked on myself. I think that there's a lesson in that, which is that making a thing that is of today and made in the current world in which we live has great value. I'm totally in sympathy with Hermann on this issue. On the other hand, the commercial reality is that people love to use the traditional typefaces, and a big part of the revenue of type foundries comes from selling those types. They're very popular, and for some reason people get all excited about them, like this Bodoni. The number of Bodoni fans is astounding! Everyone I've shown it to says "Oh! I've always loved Bodoni!" Really! Even people I'm really surprised by. It's amazing.

  I myself like to make my own typefaces, I'd much rather make my own letters than copy someone else's. On the other hand, from the point of view of my own education, since I'm still doing the assignment, I do learn an incredible amount every time I do one of these revival projects. A very good way to learn about letterforms is to try to copy someone who made good ones. This is the way you learn how to do Chinese calligraphy, and to be a student of Chinese calligraphy you copy one of the masters, and what you learn is it's really hard. And when you think that you've done it that's when you learn that you haven't done it.

AMJ: Any speculation about the direction of contemporary type design?

SS: Right now we seem to be reliving the nineteenth century. It's remarkable, the entire nineteenth century seems to be speeding towards us on the Macintosh, again. At an incredible rate: sped up, in fast forward. Maybe we'll get done with it, and then we can go on to doing something else.

AMJ: Is that because of the democratization of type design, with Fontographer, etc?

SS: It's easy to make a typeface.

AMJ: Those programmes have a lot of built-in shortcuts, like making everything bolder or oblique, that ultimately destroy any worth the type could have.

SS: Well you can do a bad job but you can also do a good job. Some people are doing a good job with remaking those old types, a pretty good job. I don't know, it's really difficult to say. It seems there's more energy focused on it of late. The more energy part applies all across the spectrum, so not only are you gonna get the "Beavis and Butthead" font, but you also get Matthew Carter making Big Caslon.

The range has gotten greater, more people are doing it. There was an exhibition at the Seybold Conference in Boston a few weeks ago of so-called new type designers. There were ninety people who called themselves type designers who exhibited at this show. Five years ago there were not ninety people in the world who called themselves type designers. So that's been a huge change. We'll just have to see where it's going.

AMJ: Do you think philosophically it's possible to create a new alphabet?

SS: Obviously we have to make typefaces that people can read. The more thought-up they become, the less useful they are. The more constructed and bizarre the typefaces become... they're interesting objects in themselves but they're not very useful as typefaces. They're wonderful objects to look at, but what do you do with them? One of the interesting things about making type is that it's very constrained, very restraining. You can't do something very odd or otherwise people are not going to put up with reading it.

So why make a new typeface at all? It's a question I have been asked since the beginning of doing the Adobe business. We have so many already, why do I do that? And I think the real answer to that for me is that... recently I read something about the ability to simulate three-dimensional models of actors on video and you could make somebody's image say things they never said in real life, through a simulated image of the person. There was speculation at the end of this article that maybe actors would disappear altogether, and there would only be these images of the past actors. But that seems equally absurd to me in that the life that is in the actor, or in the letterforms, comes from a continual process of doing it over and over, and having people engaged in doing it, and that seems to me the value in doing it. It is the same kind of feeling that we've already figured out enough ways to prepare food so we'll just make all of the same recipes that we already have and we won't try any new ones. That's how absurd it seems to me to think like that. I mean food is pretty constraining too. It's interesting that just the reverse has happened because of the technology. It's not that people have stopped doing things and decided we have enough: just the opposite has happened, and people are making new types like crazy.

AMJ: Having left Adobe and set up on your own as a small foundry, do you feel the impact of piracy?

SS: Well I obviously can't afford it. It's not an easy way to make a living. But I feel that it's built into the situation really. It's just outrageously easy to make a copy of this thing: it takes a few seconds. Typefaces, of course, are not the only thing. Software is pirated as much as fonts, but the thing about fonts that distinguishes them from other software is the fact that they do not, so far, go through the same upgrading process as other software. Software, when you buy it the first time, is not finished. In fact, it's never finished, it turns out. You have to keep buying it over and over again, every year or so, every eighteen months. 'Oh, it turns out it wasn't done: You have to buy it again.' It's a great racket, and this is how software companies make a lot of their profit, through upgrading. Another benefit is, if you ripped it off the first time, then pretty soon your ripped-off copy is going to be obsolete, so maybe you'll buy it eventually. Fonts have not changed since they were first made. A few of them have been remade. I'm really seriously trying to figure out a good way to keep upgrading the fonts.

AMJ: Or some kind of degeneration virus that goes into successive copies.

SS: Peter Fraterdeus was trying to figure out a way to come up with exploding fonts!

AMJ: There recently has been some friction between Zapf and ATypI over the misappropriation of his fonts. He's a prominent figure yet was apparently burned by some of the biggest corporations.

SS: Font piracy exists on many levels. The type business has gotten more cut-throat. The one you're talking about is not people copying diskettes, it's companies. It's a different issue. This has been going on a long time, but it's now more visible because type has become more public and more visible. It used to be if you were a designer, you never saw a "font"; typesetting was something you bought from a typesetter.

There are some cases where it's clear what happened. Take Zapf and his faces, and it's quite clear they took Palatino and called it something else. It has gone on for the last thirty years with his typefaces. I worked for companies that did that.

AMJ: Have you seen the Stone Sans clone called Granite?

SS: Right, they ripped me off too.

AMJ: It's a copyright issue.

SS: Well, the legal part is unfortunately very unclear and difficult, especially protection. In the US it's bad; it's better in Europe since they enacted legislation. In England they have very strong copyright laws; in Germany and in France typefaces are protected. None of these things apply to typefaces that were designed before they passed the laws. I'm glad Hermann is out there screaming and yelling.

AMJ: I suppose one of the attractions of historic types is they're public domain. There are several foundries that market identical versions of Imre Reiner or Rudolf Koch types; you look in *Font & Function* or the FontHaus catalogue and there are types that are completely indistinguishable from one another: Metropolis, Skyline, Corvinus Condensed. One's a European version at $149, one is from San Rafael at $39, so you know which one will be sold.

SS: The early twentieth century is popular now.

AMJ: Suddenly it's the era of Bernhard, Weiss, Koch all over again; they're the popular types. We're reliving the German 1930s in design. Perhaps we're on the verge of the Nazi resurgence.

  I wanted to ask you about this Silica specimen, which is interesting, first of all, because it's letterpress. But what were you thinking of when you kerned the display at the top?

SS: I liked it actually. I think that the rules for display type are very different from the rules for text type. We have a funny legacy from metal type, not having letters touch each other, which people started doing in phototype, I think probably Herb Lubalin was most responsible for this...

AMJ: Abomination is what we call it!

SS: Getting letters to be closer together. The real problem with that is that people started doing it for text setting. Then it's a disaster. But if you look at letters before metal type, people had letters touching all the time, it's very common. Of course they didn't tend to make letters so bold, except in the blackletter tradition, where they touch also. So anyway, when I was playing around with the bold version of the type and trying to stick it together I liked it very much, the way it looked, and I think you can read it. It's not meant to be used small.

AMJ: The light weights are very legible. What really impresses me about it, is that it has the overall feeling of a slab serif like Rockwell or Stymie but when you look at it it has more of the Eric Gill Humanistic cursive quality to it, so it's a remarkable sort of industrial strength outline but with the calligraphic feel of the Renaissance.

SS: That was exactly the idea: to make a slab serif type that was not typical. I thought a slab serif type that has Humanistic proportions might be a useful type, because slab serifs get used an enormous amount. They are very useful because you have many of the advantages of the sans serif type: it's a monoweight, as you say, industrial-strength letterform. But I think even for short passages of text having the serifs is an advantage — that was the idea. The very bold versions get quite odd, which I like.

AMJ: You could certainly use the lighter weights as text. The very light weight reminds me of Gill's Joanna, which is almost a monoline type. It has an elegant quality.

SS: There was a very clear kind of hole in the typographic libraries of almost everybody in the early days [of digital type]. There aren't very many slab serifs, and a lot of them have funny, quirky qualities to them. Serifa and Glypha, for example, which are very nice typefaces, really look like Univers with serifs on them. They're very regular and in that tradition of mechanical…

AMJ: Most of the thirties ones, like Scarab and Rockwell, are like sans with slab serifs added.

SS: So the idea to do a slab serif came up very early on: Everyone said "more slab serifs." I then heard James Mosley give a lecture at this event in New York in '87 where he was talking about the history of sans serif types, and apparently the generally accepted notion was that sans serif types were really slab serif types with the serifs taken off. He said that is not the way that it happened; if you look at the sequence of how they got made, the slab serif types were really sans serif types with the serifs put back on them. A light went on, and I thought, yes, they look like that, and that's probably why I don't like them very much. It would be a good idea to start out with the idea in the beginning that you were going to make a slab serif and have the whole thing come out of that.

AMJ: Some of the earliest slab serifs by Thorowgood and Figgins are remarkable because when they did the caps it was fine but when they did the lowercase everything went out the window. The only one digitally I can think of that retains that quality is Egiziano, which has some very unusual characters like the lowercase *a*, *f* and *r*. Dennis Ortiz-Lopez cloned it from the Nebiolo foundry version.

Do you look back fondly on your days at Adobe?

SS: Absolutely. It was fun. The part I liked best was designing typefaces and working with other people on the typefaces, but the longer I was there the less I got to do that, so I escaped.

HOLBROOK TETER

Holbrook Teter (1930–1999) attended Stanford in 1948 graduating summa cum laude in International Relations. This was the first of six degrees he earned, and he spoke five languages including Arabic and Urdu. He was a mental health counselor and social worker, working with refugees and trauma survivors. He visited Chernobyl and Guatemala, and as a member of California Prison Focus, corresponded with prisoners while working for penal reform. He also ran Zephyrus Image Press in San Francisco and Healdsburg in the 1970s.

On Wednesday 9 July 1997, I interviewed him (before a standing-room only crowd) at the San Francisco Center for the Book, about his printing work with Michael Myers. This was the first time Teter had spoken publicly about his work at Zephyrus Image. I transcribed some of his comments for a special issue of the Ampersand (vol 16 no 3) called "The Fall of Love" (A pun on the "Summer of Love," and also his relationship with Michael). This was also the last time Teter spoke about his work. He died of a heart attack on New Year's Day 1999. At that point I decided I should begin writing Zephyrus Image: A Bibliography (Poltroon Press, 2003).

AMJ: I am the default historian of printing and publishing in the Bay Area. I don't know how that happened, but that appears to be my lot. I came here in 1974 and worked as a letterpress printer and was astounded when I came across the work of Zephyrus Image. The first time I met them was at The Pub on Geary Boulevard in Spring 1974, and over the drinks I couldn't stop looking at Michael, he was so unusual looking. First of all he was the only white person I had ever seen with dreadlocks, a kind of wasted Shirley Temple do; he also had a Girl Scouts of America shirt on which I thought was extremely hip and bizarre at the same time. Right next door to The Pub was their shop which was a hive of activity: poets were arriving, local publishers were having work done. But the thing was they weren't doing this to get rich: they were giving it away. You'd go over there and they'd say, "Have you seen this?" and you'd kind of wait for them to say, "Would you like to buy a copy?" But, no: "Here's our new book." They gave everything away. If you happened to be there you got whatever they were doing. They were very influential on a lot of the presses in the Bay Area at the time, and subsequently. What has become known as the Artists Book movement can be traced to the concepts they had about books, their lighthearted attitude towards the materials and presentation. They are definitely one of the formative influences on this movement.

Holbrook, at what point did you get interested in printing? I believe it was when you came back from Pakistan.

HT: Well, we had decided that we were gonna open up some kind of cultural center when we got back from Pakistan. We were going to have an alternative school and a press and a library and a place for music and theater: any kind of cultural activity like that. And so when we got back we did open up an alternative school in Petaluma first and then came down here to San Francisco and helped organize the Huckleberry alternative school at Huckleberry House. Then since I'd decided we were going to have some printing and newspapers and stuff I decided I would find out about that. I found out about Clifford Burke and went over to his place and asked if I could hang out and learn about printing. And about that time Jim Brooke was there and he wanted to get rid of his equipment: he had a Linotype machine and a whole bunch of hand-set type. When you work for the American Friends Service Committee you get money at the end of your time, so I had a little bit of money and so I bought Jim Brooke out, and that's how I started. And then Michael showed up one day — he'd hitch-hiked over from Berkeley and he had the block "Ford" — he had this linoleum block wrapped up, he didn't have bus fare to come over from Berkeley. He had this block wrapped up in newspaper. When I saw that Ford block I said I was going to work with Michael, and we did for the next twelve years.

Terry Horrigan [*from audience*]: Why did Michael come to you?

HT: He had heard from Adrian Wilson that maybe he could print some of his blocks over at our place. So he came.

AMJ: He came out from Wisconsin, having studied with Walter Hamady, and he came out here intending to start a press?

Ford block, the first work of Zephyrous Image (note spelling). Opposite: Richter ® Household Seismometer (repro proof of the first state, 1971).

HT: Yes.

AMJ: Since so much of the work is fragile and ephemeral we are just going to show slides of most of it, so this will also help prod Holbrook's memory. If you've ever cut linoleum, and have ten fingers left, you'll know it's impossible to get these kinds of lines without slicing through them. But this was Michael's forte, to cut these linoleum blocks that look like .00 Rapidograph line drawings. They must have taken hours to cut.

SHAKE WITH KMPX
AT 106.9 FM IN SAN FRANCISCO

Richter

The Original Household Seismometer

Copyright 1971 by Zephyrus Image Graphics, 241 Collins Street, San Francisco

HT: Certainly something like this took a couple of weeks. This we did and took it to the Berkeley dump to put up.

AMJ: You also used his blocks over and over. So the "Liberate Berkeley" block also read "Detonate Sutro Towers."

HT: That was the time when Berkeley was liberating the world, so we thought we'd work on Berkeley too.

This is the International Harvester block. The inside linoleum block was done for a pirated edition of Allen Ginsberg's *Indian Journals*. We gave a lot of these to NORML, the campaign for the legalization of marijuana.

AMJ: This is about the time Michael got arrested for having drug paraphernalia. He suffered from diabetes and was picked up in a raid, and was put away for a while.

HT: Right, but you don't always use a spoon though with diabetes. [*laughter*]

AMJ: So then after he came out of Santa Rita he moved in with you and Joan, is that right?

HT: Yeah. He had no place to go, no money, no nothing.

AMJ: "The Declaration of Independence for Timothy Leary" from 1971 is signed by a lot of local writer and poets. Did you put this together?

HT: No, I think Ginsberg put it together, and brought it to us.

AMJ: Here's "Get back, Sheriff Matt!"

HT: When [Richard] Hongisto was running against [Matthew] Carberry for Sheriff, there was an article that ran in the *Chronicle* that we printed up. Michael did the blocks and we put the stars in. And then I put on my Sunday suit — my wedding suit — and took it to St Mary's Cathedral before Sunday Mass and welcomed everybody and handed it out to people going to Mass.

AMJ: This was about how the Sheriff would go down and sing songs to the ladies in the jail to help them sleep.

HT: Right.

AMJ: So what was the reaction when you handed this to people, outside the cathedral?

HT: They thanked me and took it into the church.

AMJ: Another of your publications, or *public actions*, from this time was a list of things that make the President a criminal, "yes" or "no" questions about what Nixon was doing. How did you distribute this one?

HT: The return address was the *Press Democrat* in Santa Rosa and the *San Francisco Chronicle*. We'd open up the newspaper boxes and stuff each paper with one of these personal opinion polls. We did a lot, just the two of us. Sometimes we got our family to help out.

AMJ: The IRS Tax Coupon book contains $60,000 worth of official-looking IRS tax coupons. They look very convincing. "Can be loosely inserted in loophole."

HT: We wanted to bring relief to people. I refused to pay my taxes one time during the Vietnam War and the FBI came right down to the press and interviewed us.

AMJ: Now the Hermes Free Press: Did you have specific things in mind when you used that imprint as opposed to Zephyrus Image?

HT: It was meant to be clearly free work and often with a political aspect.

AMJ: Flying on the wings of the moment. I remember when you gave me the Household Seismometer, I was thrilled. Once during an earthquake I watched it swing back and forth to see if it was working and try to guess the magnitude.

HT: We did several of them for each year for the earthquake. This one has Kissinger, you're supposed to pin the bead through his forehead. We sent one to Richter. He didn't reply.

AMJ: The Clang Association block fascinates me. With this very bizarre picture of a man eating cress, is it?

HT: We referred to it as nails. We used to buy, well, not buy but pick up boxes of cuts when newspapers would throw them away. We found this block and there was a Chinese print shop going out of business so Michael arranged the type according to beauty.

AMJ: … some of it is upside down …

HT: And we put them up, for example, on the mailbox next to The Pub, you mentioned, on Geary and Masonic. We did see an Asian couple stop to mail something and they saw that and went away and came back and looked at it again and tried to read it.

AMJ: These found zincs were really a source of inspiration I think, like this label for Wong Yee's Herb Preparation. You've added "Opiates and Tincture of Hashish" as the particular herb that's in there. So out of these found zincs came this early book, *Spirit Photography: The Fireside Book of Gurus.*

HT: In the explanation it talked about this swami who would not allow his image to reach the negative.

AMJ: So these are all gurus refusing to be photographed. It's really, I think, a transcendent work!

You followed that with *Accordion to St Luke*, with an introduction by Theodore Mack. It has a beautiful little two-colour initial. And a perfect use for an accordion structure! These are also found zincs?

HT: Yes. All of them accordions. We had lots of zincs. It was a Christmas card done by Michael. Ted Mack has a golden halo.

AMJ: …which has slipped.

About this time Ed Dorn showed up and was greatly impressed with your work and wanted to collaborate and you began to collaborate with Ed on *Bean News*. And *Bean News* was a semi-annual?

HT: Well this is the main *Bean News* right here. Everything else was minor stuff. It's eight pages.

AMJ: It's on newsprint, some are on cigarette paper.

HT: India paper, yeah.

AMJ: A massive amount of typesetting: I guess you did all that on the Linotype?

HT: Right.

AMJ: All sorts of stuff going on in here. The page numbers are cuneiform, right?

HT: Yes, cuneiform and lino blocks.

AMJ: This was one of your interests?

HT: Yes, I was studying it at that particular time, so we figured it out and Michael did the blocks.

AMJ: Now you were hoping that if you did three, you could get an NEA grant, right?

HT: Right.

AMJ: I mean the NEA was giving money to anyone who did three of anything! Now, Ed did a lot of the writing? And Raworth?

HT: Raworth, people across the country.

AMJ: This broadside, "Mrs Shapely Takes a Stroll," was by F Eugene Warren.

HT: We were going to do a book, but never got it done.

AMJ: Here's another, "Mr Never Laugh Drops His Load." How many of these were there?

HT: Six or seven. He was a guy from Missouri, we never met him actually. He was a friend of a friend — Rob Rusk.

AMJ: You worked with Oyez!, [Bob] Callahan's Turtle Island; you also worked with Frontier Press? Weren't they around?

The Dick & Pat Fly-Swatter printed on newsprint with linocut title by Michael Myers. Opposite: Snack-time Ranch-Raised Gourmet Earwigs, linocut by Michael Myers (the last work of the press).

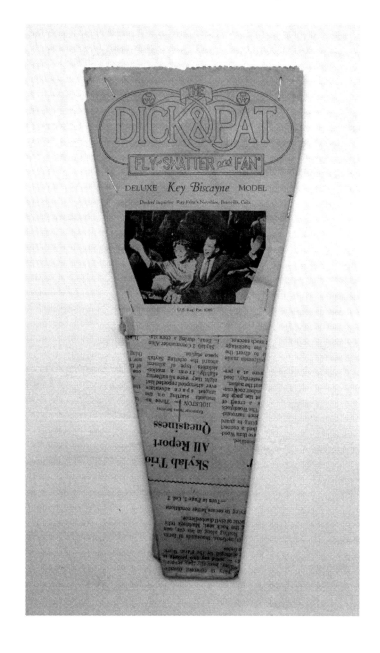

HT: Well, we have all of Frontier Press' books in the barn. We tried to help them out a little bit.

AMJ: Did you do actual printing work for them, typesetting, or was it just...

HT: No, I don't think we ever did.

AMJ: Some broadsides maybe?

HT: We did some broadsides, yes. Then they gave us Herbert Huncke's book. We got that typeset, but we never actually published it.

Steve Lavoie [*from audience*]: Whose press was Frontier Press?

HT: Harvey Brown. He set it up in order to publish the books suggested by Charles Olson. A whole series of books that were out of print that were of great value according to Olson's point of view. So he published a lot of stuff that Olson had recommended. One of my favorites is *Prison Memoirs of an Anarchist* by Alexander Berkman.

AMJ: This is *Seen*, an essay by Stan Brakhage.

HT: Stan Brakhage showed a movie of light refracted in a glass ashtray. You couldn't tell it was an ashtray. The whole movie was just the shifting of light, rainbow light, in the ashtray for a very lengthy time. After he showed the movie he talked about his own life and development as an artist and what he had to say was so turned on, so accurate and beautiful. Somebody had taped it so we transcribed it and put out this book. The cover has a linoleum block on the mylar.

AMJ: Nice choice of materials, and then the inside has a smoky film over the title-page. This is "Snack-time Ranch-Raised Gourmet Earwigs," 1982. Linocut on wood veneer. The last work of the press.

HT: It took a long time to get this out because I only used earwigs I found dead on the property.

ARNE WOLF

Arne Wolf is a painter and calligrapher. His works in response to the poetry of Paul Celan were on display at the Goethe Institute Gallery in San Francisco at the time of the interview. A native of Germany, where he studied Design, he taught in Atlanta, at UC Berkeley and at York University in Ontario before settling in the Bay Area. He is Professor Emeritus of Art at California State University in Hayward. Having done some original letterpress work with wood and metal type, as well as large-scale woodcuts, his vision finally outstripped the capabilities of his 18 x 24" Hacker Proof Press. His wife Anna is a paper marbler and book artist also. Walter Hamady and I conducted this interview at the Wolfs' Berkeley home overlooking the foggy Golden Gate on Saturday morning, 5 November 1988.

AMJ: I loved your Paul Celan work.

AW: Thank you.

AMJ: I was sorry I didn't get a chance to take Walter. It's a series of paintings that incorporate poems by Paul Celan and they're really amazing.

WSH: Where are they?

AMJ: In the Goethe Institute Gallery in downtown San Francisco on Bush Street.

AW: It worked out very nicely.

AMJ: The fabric is great.

AW: I did several three-dimensional ones, with layers of gauze, and bedsheets and pillowcases and epoxy…

AMJ: Calligraphy on ribbons…

AW: …calligraphy on ribbons, press-on type…

AMJ: They become more like broadsides, because of the textual content, although it's hard to read, but the text is otherwise available.

AW: Celan was a Romanian; he was born in 1920. He lived first in Vienna where he started writing, then went to Germany. He didn't like Germany very much though he wrote in German all the time. Then he went to France, married a French woman. In 1973 he committed suicide; he was barely fifty. His poetry is very difficult to understand, or to penetrate, I should say. But I find it very easy to get along with somehow, in terms of what the sense of it is, but to explain it is something else. As a symbiotic kind of experience, I really respond to it. So I think the legibility…

AMJ: …becomes an expressive component?

AW: I got really enthralled with it.

AMJ: Did it create some kind of mystical position that you were being driven to, or that you were seeking in the painting, that was something not necessarily connected with the words, but a feeling of some other kind of expression?

AW: Well, I think the closest is the white cloth; also the big white sheet with the lines going across it, where he talks about being set down or expelled into and left there:

Driven into the
terrain
with the unmistakable track:

grass, written asunder…

It's one of his longest poems, and I really felt like getting into a physical area where I was like an ant. I could really see the original part "grass like tree-trunks" or like a jungle. You were in there, and every little rock is a mountain, and that got to me really very emotionally. Whereas the *Todesfuge* I've been working with a long time, and that's in a way more of a design project than a direct emotional response. The white one really worked very well. So the paintings are a little different I guess but, yes, I really felt that it was a process of self-elucidation, if that's a reasonable word to use, rather than the illustrative "this means this and this means that." Of course, like most of the pieces which I feel with, it has a lot of visual imagery and that's always obviously such a challenge, you know a poet uses words to make a visual picture, but you can't reproduce it because immediately it's corny — it's not language that you use. So the grass which is "written asunder," I think it's a terrific image, but to start drawing leaves of grass has nothing to do with what he is really saying. I mean the idea behind it is different from what that image strictly says. I think it's that kind of metamorphosis in language which is interesting.

Arne Wolf, Paul Celan series, 1988. Mixed media: paint and ink (calligraphy & press type) on ribbon, paper, gauze, canvas etc
Detail opposite

AMJ: I want to read you something I found in a book by the founder of the Japanese Shingon sect, Kōbō Daishi, whose pen name was Kūkai: "Although words may be used in transmitting truth, people can be made to feel truth only by means of colour and form. Esoteric teachings hold that profound truths are difficult to express in written or spoken words. For those who find enlightenment on subtle points difficult, it is essential to resort to art to inspire a sense of hidden meanings." Would you go along with that?

AW: I would, yes. But poetry, of course, has already the power to transform. With the symbiosis of visual art and poetry, there's a very close relationship, that they're seen much more as one than actually two. What I understand about it — which isn't much at all — I think such poetry (I'm thinking of haiku for instance) is much more straightforward than our poetry. It sort of encapsulates and shortens something into one very pregnant statement which describes the situation very directly and in a very powerful way. I think of our poetry as less philosophical, or less mystical maybe.

AMJ: We had the Imagist movement which Ezra Pound started around 1917 or so, and that was the same thing — to encapsulate a visual moment in a way that transcended the moment. Something would go *ping* in your brain and people would realize that it referred to the larger framework, but that was essentially a poetry of describing, which haiku is as well, sort of like a mental photograph, you just say, "clouds obscure the moon/the pine tree creaks in the wind/Ah, the night is long."

AW: Bly is very good at that.

AMJ: He translates a lot of haiku, and borrows a lot.

AW: He's good at that descriptive kind of thing which demands a discerning eye to start with, to see a little more than what we usually see. But I think the way Celan writes is a much more existential kind of statement than simply a visual description of something, and I think in all of his poetry this really dark side which he had, and all this experience which came to him as a child and a young man, are manifest and his suicide seems almost predictable in retrospect throughout the whole thing. What struck me, is he got very much involved, rather late I take

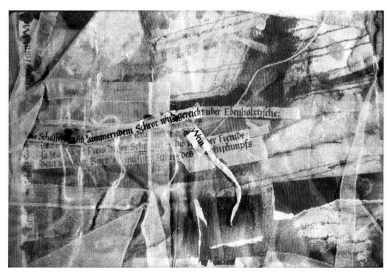

it, in the Kabbalah, and he started reading about Jewish philosophy and religion. But he was a total agnostic, and that one poem which I used which starts out:

What did I do?

Seminated the night, as though
there could be others, more noctural
than this one.

This opening line, "What did I do?" and that end phrase, "where my pulse dared the counter-beat," really reminds me of that Job I did. I think Job asks the same question. "Lord have mercy upon my soul," he says, but basically he says, "Lord what have I done?" and he means "What have I done to deserve all this?" But he always has that refuge of saying "It's the Lord's doing." In the end he is restituted to the state he was in before, because he had faith. Celan, you see, had to jump into the Seine, because there is no Lord and no faith. He asked the same question, "What have I done?" and in the end there is no salvation. I think you feel that throughout his poetry, there's an enormous sense of being thrown onto your own resources, and I think that's the area of the grass which is "written asunder" and that "unmistakable track" which I think is his own fate as he sees it. It's very tragic from the beginning, and he wrote it out all the time. I guess it's presumptuous to try to do something with it, like I have, but on the other hand, what can you do? You hope there's some sort of balance to it.

Arne Wolf, excerpt from
Genesis (wood type)

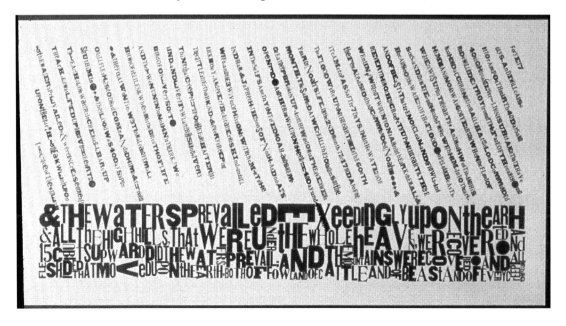

AMJ: Right. Well your response, it seems to me, and certainly in the other calligraphy I've seen you do, is closer to a pictographic kind of writing. If there was a Western pictographic syllabary, then that would be what you are doing. You are taking letter-forms and making them or using them to suit your own ends: you're using blackletter and changing color; you're taking the letters and using them as pattern and abstraction.

AW: I think when I started — you remember those big wood-cuts I did, the Lorca ones — I did those with a house-painter's brush. They were six feet by three feet. I took words, sometimes phrases, from Lorca poems, like "black horses," which I thought was a central motif of "The Ballad of the Spanish Civil Guard," and I think the impetus for it really was the Chinese or Japanese pictographic calligraphy, saying that the letters directly should express what they are about. Well I tried to do it. Of course I do it differently now, but the idea, in an enlarged sense, is the same certainly: the image and the word. I call it fused visual/verbal imagery.

AMJ: But you seem to have progressed a lot. I'm not saying that the Lorca stuff is not a developed idea. But you've evolved so that now it's more in the realm of painting than calligraphy.

AW: Calligraphy doesn't really become any part of this. I would use calligraphy if it seems indicated. But I used a lot of press-type in the Celan, for instance, because, in the first place, I thought calligraphy was almost too personal already and I wanted neutrality. And with press-type I can go across a corrugated surface, up and down, and literally press it in there. With calligraphy I would have to write it before, integrating it into the surface, gluing it down, and then I don't know what goes under or over it. But I'm more interested in verbal content rather than calligraphy per se, so I want to work with the words, yes, but I don't want to work with the words calligraphically necessarily. And that is something that's very difficult to explain to calligraphers because they think that's heresy.

AMJ: One of the calligraphers who was at the opening came up to me and said, "I want to know where Arne gets this pen that changes color mid-stroke."

AW: It's so simple. I mean that's the first thing you learn when you make a mistake by picking up the wrong ink and putting it in the pen. Where you have black ink you put red and out comes this color change. I think a lot of calligraphers are drawn to that. They ask — and you sort of raise the same question — they ask technical questions, "How did you do this?" which really has very little to do with what you really did. I mean, the technical knowledge or facility is really a given at that point. If you don't have it, you have to acquire it or you don't do what you're doing. So you don't talk about it really. What you do with it is something else. If all you can think about is the technique, then you're going to do it that way all the time, and you won't get to anything else. But if you can start thinking about the concepts behind it, then you use the technique to do whatever, and if you say well, this is a beautiful sheet of paper but I like it better if it's crumpled up, you'll buy a five or ten dollar sheet of paper and crumple it up. Somebody else can't get beyond picking it up just so, so there isn't a dent in it. Well, I like paper too and I pick it up just like that but I'll slash through it too. I have a bunch of them scratched through in the show so that the ink would run when it gets into the scratch.

Arne Wolf, García Lorca: Voces de Muerte, 1963 (woodcut 36 x 72"). Opposite: unused cover for Tom Raworth's Nicht Wahr Rosie? *(Poltroon Press, 1979).*

AMJ: So you actually preplan some of the things that are happening that look like accidents?

AW: I wrote all of those at least four times. But I always do them as if I'm doing the real thing on the real sheet of paper. From that point of view, I plan it as I go, but, if the last word works out not to be just right I do the whole thing over. And if something goes wrong someplace else — the color doesn't quite go where I want it, or whatever, or a better idea turns up — then I do it over again. And so I have several versions sitting down there in my studio, some of them not quite completed, some of them completed but I didn't like them, so I did them over. It's not really planning: it's more working to where you want to go, and if I have to do it over, I do it over.

WH: What do you do with the near-misses?

AW: I use the backside, or I cut them up, so they don't really go to waste. But it's not like ceramics where you have slightly damaged seconds you can sell a little bit cheaper. It's this or nothing. I use them over or I experiment with them, write over them again. It's really against design philosophy and practice. I was trained as a designer, and you really don't want anything unexpected to happen — that's bad, that's anti-design, and of course I grew up with that kind of thing, that you really can predict what you do, and if somebody says I want a sign that says "No Smoking," and if you come up with a beautiful one which says, "No Milk Sold Here," he'll say, "What the hell are you thinking about?" and he doesn't give you anything for it, so you have to come out with what you promised. I think the process of working on these visual/verbal things is exactly that they have a life of their own, and they start taking over and then you react to that, you adjust to it. They direct themselves to a certain degree, and you have to let that happen. And that process is much more exciting than being able to plan something from the beginning to the end and saying this is what it's going to look like. You see the trouble with printmaking: I love starting the prints and I love printing the first few, then I only make editions of fifteen. Then one after another: it's always the same thing.

AMJ: And the idea is to make them as uniform as possible.

AW: Of course. That's only work. I mean you have to be careful and you have to know what you're doing and all that, and you have to watch and you have to be attentive all the time, and that maybe the worst thing, that you have to be attentive for really not very much, for just another print.

AMJ: But you can change the colour and start reducing the block as you're going and have it evolve. But there's no going back to the good one that was three ago which was okay.

AW: And what is the gallery going to say?

WSH: That's why this whole business of monoprints are so popular. It doesn't take any skill in editioning, which has always been held in high regard by printmakers.

AW: It's a separate, a very real skill. And I think it's why a lot of people are going to professional printmaking places where they run the edition. Like Dali signing blank sheets.

AMJ: Well, that was conceptually one of the greatest artworks of the century. Half a ton of blank Rives BFK signed by Dali has got to be a Surrealist masterpiece.

WSH: I don't know about that.

AMJ: The French customs stopped this truck at the border from Spain and opened it; it was full of blank BFK paper, all signed by Dali, and they said, This paper is worth a lot of money, because it's by Dali. The driver said no, it's just worth the value of the paper. They ended up impounding it. But Dali of course has an autograph machine which does his signature for him because he's too infirm to write.

AW: It's terrific, and of course they were quite right, because you could sell it as works of art for almost anything you care to name.

WSH: What does that say about our culture?

AW: Being famous is better than being good. I think in the end it's the fame that sells.

WSH: Not the substance or the intent.

AMJ: It's the nature of our society to consume personalities.

AW: One of the things I do regard with some glee, is that all these people like Rauschenberg and Jasper Johns and Beuys and Kiefer have been making all these things which have a very restricted lifetime, and the curators are pulling out their hair trying to conserve them. In five years it may be gone. Either the glue is gone, or whatever they used is eating through the whole business, it's falling apart like a computer program with a worm in it, and there they sit, out of the money — and that's why they bought it in the first place. But I can't commiserate with those guys.

NOEL YOUNG

Noel Young (1923–2002) was a small press publisher in Santa Barbara, California who produced over 300 titles, many of them chapbooks, by authors including Henry Miller, Anaïs Nin, Raymond Carver, Ross Macdonald, James D Houston, Charles Bukowski, Lawrence Clark Powell, Diane Di Prima and Lawrence Durrell. In 1969 he took Graham Mackintosh into partnership and changed the name of his press from Capricorn to Capra. At the time they had a C&P in a small storefront studio on Anacapa Street, but once they acquired a cylinder press they moved to State Street to larger premises close to the editorial offices of Black Sparrow Press. Young, who always had a twinkle in his eye, had a great success with a series of books called Western Man in Water. *I interviewed Noel Young in 1974; the interview has not previously been published.*

AMJ: One of the first small presses in Santa Barbara was Unicorn Press of Alan Brilliant and Teo Savory. I met them last year [in 1973] when they were about to move to the University of North Carolina at Greensboro; their pressman, Rudy Villaneuva, was jailed for avoiding the draft and they offered me the job, but I didn't want to relocate there.

NY: Alan didn't know a thing about printing. He had his own ideas about book design from looking at books but he didn't know how to set type until he came here. Often he'd bring in his hand-setting and I'd print it for him.

   He and Teo Savory were both active in the peace movement to the extent that when there weren't demonstrations and petitions to be signed, a lot of these people would come in and set type to help the cause. So that made it possible for him to have work done that would have been very costly otherwise.

AMJ: Before they became a foundation they were bankrolled by Ken Maytag, the washing-machine heir, weren't they?

NY: When Maytag withdrew his $35,000 per year support — to buy a helicopter or a submarine — Brilliant was in a desperate situation; after only three years he wasn't firmly established. He had no one to back him up but the sale of books. He turned to me, hoping to form a partnership but I didn't need an opinionated editor, and Capricorn Press was barely subsisting at that time too.

AMJ: Didn't Brilliant bring you the Black Sparrow connection?

NY: John Martin was an office furniture salesman and collector who had hired Saul Marks to print five broadsides by Charles Bukowski. Graham [Mackintosh] was working there at the time, late 1969. Saul was the prince of the traditional small press printers. The atmosphere was just too precious for Graham though; he's too rambunctious a fellow to work in the almost mediaeval confines of Saul Mark's shop, as much as he appreciated Saul's work. But it was pretty tight work and Graham is more conceptual. He referred to Saul's meticulous craftsmanship as "needlepoint." So Graham came up to Santa Barbara and joined me. By then John Martin turned over the books that would have gone to Graham in San Francisco to me. It wasn't a contractual arrangement; we just went from book to book and for a while he was having Saul Marks do about one out of every four books because he wanted the special Saul Marks touch — Saul had Monotype and certain faces that we just don't have. Saul soon priced himself out of reach for John who saw that Graham and I together were producing some books that were quite satisfactory — in fact a lot of them were stunning in a way. So we began doing all of John's books which began to accelerate. We began doing a book a month then three books every two months and now we're going along fairly steadily at a book every two weeks.

Our own catalog is accelerating too. We just became completely book oriented: we bought a bigger cylinder press; Graham brought in the Linotype and Compugraphic. So between the two of us plus the pressman and the people in the bindery we were able to do a book a week.

One thing that made it possible from an economic standpoint was Bookpeople, the Berkeley distribution company, making the "Whole Earth" organisation work for a conglomerate of small presses. This encouraged a lot of the small press poetry books that were coming out.

AMJ: So you are able to make it as a letterpress shop?

NY: The world is full of very capable, productive offset printers and the editing, designing and marketing of books is the publisher's big job, and as long as I'm doing small editions of literary work I don't have to worry about offset at all. As soon as I get into anything that's full of photographs or should hit big editions like 20, or 50,000 or more, as some small press books have done, I'll consider offset. *The Tassajara Bread Book* and some of the Shambhala books from Berkeley are now reaching a half-million copies and so on.

AMJ: Your two best-sellers, *Hot Tubs,* which you wrote pseud-onymously, and *The Grandmother Conspiracy Exposed*, were taken over by larger houses for mass market editions.

NY: There's a lot of interest in West Coast publishing where some publishers are eking by on editions of less than a thousand, making little money. The Eastern publishers are feeling some-what limited, going on as they have all these generations. They're looking for a fresh outlook and approach to living and the ideas that are germinating out here. The *Hot Tub* book is a very atypical book of ours but it was being a little exploitive of one of the more obvious lifestyle traditions that were started here. From the rev-enue from that we can be even more ambitious with our literary publishing which is or main purpose.

Our capacity is so limited we can only do six or eight poetry books a year and then we have to do some prose books — fiction or essays — as long as it's in the literary market, like our books from Henry Miller, Lawrence Durrell and Anaïs Nin. Those are more or less the lead names. Hopefully to help carry the unknowns or first books, because it's quite an adventure to find someone like Faye Kicknossway whom I personally am very excited about.

Of course, in the case of Miller and Durrell, I'm not getting their mainstream writing and I don't hope to because that's where they make their living. But there is still a great market for all the incidentals that come along. So I am in a position where I'm a small printer doing the best scraps I can find, although often they can be keys to something bigger.

We hope to think that our books are like a handmade pot as opposed to something coming out of a factory that produces "chinaware" that's pumped through mechanically, if in any way it's a display of sensitivity towards typography or the making of a book. So these are handmade books in a sense, yet they are not as preciously "handmade," for there's a dividing line: you can get to the other extreme where you grind your own inks, you make your own paper and you print fifty copies of a book and it takes you a year to do it. The way Bill Everson, then Brother Antoninus, did, printing one page at a time, hand-braying each forme and so on. I'm not patient enough for that kind of a world either. Nor do I want the Detroit-production world.

Noel
Young

The Dance of the Minotaur
by Leighton Steele (Santa
Barbara: Capricorn Press,
1970)
 Typography by Noel Young
in Caslon, with a linocut by
Graham Mackintosh

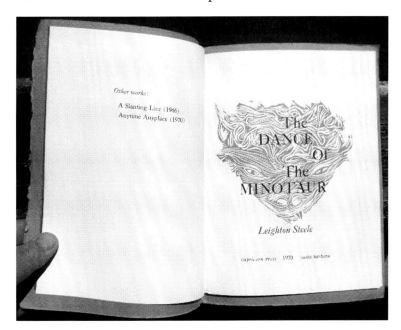

AMJ: What about the other small presses coming up in Santa Barbara, which Teo Savory refers to as the "Minicorns"?
NY: Christopher's Press was started a few years ago. Before they acquired Monotype machines we would set most of their books on the Linotype and give them the galleys. Gary Albers

has become a very good pressman and a good designer as well in his own way. Missy had the Unicorn bookstore out in Goleta while she was Ken Maytag's wife. When she got together with Gary, whose first attempts were issued under the Water Table imprint, he was looking for a job and came here and pitched in a lot. We loaned him type, gave him tips. Now they're putting out a very nice series of books; they have their own authors for the most part. After the books are printed they bring them down and we do the perfectbinding and trimming for them. So we still work together. We took them under our wing in the beginning but now they handle themselves very well. They only have a small Heidelberg platen up there so they're printing their pages two-up which means a hell of a lot of collating, but they're doing it. They don't have any employees and don't rent a shop. It's really a very pleasant, less-pressured way of living than we've got here. We have twentyfive people directly and indirectly dependant on this shop for sustenance, with the girls that live between Foodstamps and the bindery.

In fact, talking of expansion — taking in offset equipment and so on — if anything I'd like to shrink it. I still want the contact with each book that comes out of this shop, otherwise I'd just

Tree by Tolkien by Colin Wilson, Capra Press, 1974 Typography by Graham Mackintosh in Trump Medieval with illustrations by his daughter, Caitlin

somehow revolting. (When I mentioned to a widely read friend—who is also an excellent critic—that I intended to write an essay on Tolkien, he said: 'Good, it's time somebody really exploded that bubble', taking it completely for granted that it would be an attack.) Angus Wilson told me in 1956 that he thought *The Lord of the Rings* was 'don's whimsy' (although he may have changed his mind since then).

I first tried to read the book in about 1954, when only two volumes were out. I already knew a number of people who raved about Tolkien, but who seemed unable to explain precisely why they thought him so significant. I tried the first twenty pages of Volume One, decided this was too much like Enid Blyton, and gave it up for another ten years. In the early sixties, I started to work on a book about imaginative literature, triggered by the discovery of H.P. Lovecraft; John Comley, a psychologist friend (who had himself published a couple of good novels) asked me if I didn't intend to include Tolkien in the book. I said: 'I thought he was pretty dreadful.' 'He's *very* good.' So I bought the three volume edition of *Lord of the Rings*, and started to read it in bed one morning. The absurd result was that I stayed in bed for three days, and read straight through it. What so impressed me on that first reading was the self-containedness of Tolkien's world. I suppose there *are* a few novelists who have created worlds that are uniquely their own—Faulkner, for example, or Dickens. But since

their world is fairly close to the actual world, it cannot really be called a unique *creation*. The only parallel that occurs to me is the Wagner Ring cycle, that one can only enter as if taking a holiday on a strange planet.

I have read the book through a couple of times since— once aloud to my children. On re-reading, one notices the sentimentality. I could really do with less of Tom Bombadil, and Gimli's endless talk about the Lady of Lothlorien; but it hardly detracts from the total achievement. But on the second reading, I also noticed how Tolkien achieves the basic effect of the book—by slipping in, rather quietly, passages of 'fine writing'. Not really 'purple passages' in the manner of some of the Victorians (the 'Penny Whistle' chapter of Meredith's *Richard Feverel* is the obvious example). They are too unobtrusive for that.

'Almost at once the sun seemed to sink into the trees behind them. They thought of the slanting light of evening glittering on the Brandywine River, and the windows of Bucklebury beginning to gleam with hundreds of lights. Great shadows fell across them; trunks and branches of trees hung dark and threatening over the path. White mists began to rise and curl on the surface of the river and stray about the roots of the trees upon its borders. Out of the very ground at their feet a shadowy steam arose and mingled with the swiftly falling dusk.'

This is from 'The Old Forest' chapter, and in a sense it is functional. There is nothing here as

8

9

be a production manager and I just don't have the tolerance to be any more than I am. If I spend an hour or two a day doing book-keeping or cost-analysis, that's more than enough for me. The rest of the time I'm reading, designing, typesetting, writing letters.

When you're working with everything within reach, with just a couple of people, everyone's doing everything. Graham and I lean over each other's shoulder. There's nothing most of us can't do in the shop, though some things we do better than others. We've got a family personality going: Graham and I are like the two fathers. As far as the taste in things we do, the kind of paper we use, the amount of ink we like to see carried on the press, it's instilled through everyone working here. So if Graham and I aren't here one of the others will do the job in much the same way we would do it, although the particular idea for a book usually originated with Graham or me. But beyond that certain things are a matter of course.

The Grabhorn brothers as traditionalists that made such a name in San Francisco were the two brothers who'd spend a whole week on a title-page. Now they were being picky and were working with typographic refinements, but the overall conceptual thing, of the impact of a page, didn't come through spontaneously. There's no reason to spend that long on anything. It's not that a page doesn't deserve it, but you've got to sing with it fairly quickly — not because time is short, but because there's a spirit in doing something — like a dance, you jump and it gets done.

INDEX

267
Index

Legibility–
National
Endowment for
the Arts